HILARY PUTNAM

Continuum Contemporary American Thinkers:
Saul Kripke, Arif Ahmed

Forthcoming:
John Searle, Joshua Rust

HILARY PUTNAM

Lance P. Hickey

continuum

Continuum International Publishing Group
The Tower Building　　　80 Maiden Lane
11 York Road　　　　　　Suite 704
London SE1 7NX　　　　　New York NY 10038

www.continuumbooks.com

© Lance P. Hickey 2009

All rights reserved. No part of this publication may be reproduced or transmitted in any form or by any means, electronic or mechanical, including photocopying, recording, or any information storage or retrieval system, without prior permission in writing from the publishers.

British Library Cataloguing-in-Publication Data
A catalogue record for this book is available from the British Library.

ISBN: HB: 1-8470-6076-5
978-1-8470-6076-1
PB: 1-8470-6077-3
978-1-8470-6077-8

Library of Congress Cataloging-in-Publication Data
Hickey, Lance P.
Hilary Putnam / Lance P. Hickey.
p. cm.
"Select writings of Hilary Putnam"—P.
Includes bibliographical references (p.) and index.
ISBN: 978-1-84706-076-1
978-1-84706-077-8
1. Putnam, Hilary. I. Title.
B945.P874H53 2009
191—dc22

2008028882

Typeset by Newgen Imaging Systems Pvt Ltd, Chennai, India

CONTENTS

Introduction	1
1. The Road to Semantic Externalism	7
1.1. The Legacy of Logical Positivism	7
1.2. A New Theory of Natural-Kind Terms	13
1.3. Early Putnam and Scientific Naturalism	15
1.4. The Meaning of "Meaning"	18
1.5. The Scope of Putnam's Externalism	37
1.6. Conclusion	46
2. Externalism, Realism, and Skepticism	49
2.1. Renegade Putnam?	49
2.2. Scientific Realism and Metaphysical Realism	51
2.3. The Problem of Truth	54
2.4. The Model-Theoretic Argument	61
2.5. Verificationist Semantics?	66
2.6. Internal Realism	70
2.7. The Brains in a Vat Argument	79
2.8. Conceptual Relativity	90
2.9. Conclusion	94
3. Mind, Body, and World	97
3.1. The Rise of Functionalism	97
3.2. The Fall of Computational Functionalism	106
3.3. Problems with Perception	116
3.4. Pragmatic Realism and Intentionality	125
3.5. Conclusion	133

4. Neo-pragmatism and the Revitalization of Philosophy   135

    4.1. The Turn to Pragmatism   135
    4.2. The Primacy of Practice   138
    4.3. The Fact/Value Dichotomy   146
    4.4. Antiskepticism and Fallibilism   154
    4.5. Neo-pragmatism: Putnam versus Rorty and Brandom   159
    4.6. Conclusion   166

Notes   169
Select Writings of Hilary Putnam   181
Select Bibliography   183
Index   189

INTRODUCTION

Hilary Putnam has been without question one of the most influential American philosophers of the late twentieth and early twenty-first centuries. His original contributions include one of the first attempts to model the mind on that of a computer, the development of quantum logic, a theory of meaning for natural language, arguments for and against various kinds of realism, and (more recently) a thoroughgoing critique of the scientistic/materialistic outlook characteristic of most Anglo-American philosophy during the latter half of the twentieth century. Richard Rorty, another major philosopher of the same generation, has aptly compared him to Bertrand Russell, "not just in intellectual curiosity and willingness to change his mind, but in the breadth of his interests and in the extent of his social and moral concerns."[1]

Despite Putnam's undeniable importance, there have been few full-length studies of his philosophy as a whole.[2] This is not surprising, since it is a daunting task to try to provide a synthetic overview of his many contributions; indeed, one historian of philosophy, John Passmore, has remarked that trying to catch Putnam's philosophy is like trying to "capture the wind with a fishing net."[3] This is true to some extent, not only because of the range of his writings, but because he has shifted his position several times on some key philosophical issues. Nevertheless, one of the central themes of this book is that there is far more unity to Putnam's thought than has been seen so far by the philosophical community. This is so not only in terms of content—Putnam's shifts are best seen as changes of emphasis rather than wholesale rejection of former views—but also in terms of methodology. I propose that Putnam has always employed a pragmatic methodology, according to which the main purpose of philosophical inquiry consists in clarifying philosophical concepts through a critical analysis of our actual sociolinguistic practices. There is a normative element built into the fabric of our language use which militates against various "isms" propounded by philosophers, whether it be metaphysical realism, the anti-realist views advanced by positivists and their descendents (such as Michael Dummett), or the scientific naturalism shared by most philosophers of mind.[4] Most traditional and contemporary philosophy, Putnam argues, errs by conducting philosophical inquiry independently of these norms, in the process creating philosophical concepts and problems that upon analysis are shown "not to be fully intelligible."[5]

While I shall begin my assessment of Putnam with his early critique of logical positivism, my approach will be mainly thematic. I begin by focusing on his work in the philosophy of language, in particular the semantic externalism propounded in the justly famous paper "The Meaning of 'Meaning'." This theory can serve as a lynchpin for understanding Putnam's thought as a whole, for it has crucial implications for other areas in the philosophy of science, mind, epistemology, and metaphysics. I believe that Putnam's externalism can be defended from many undeserved criticisms, so long as it is interpreted as a sociolinguistic proposal and divested of some problematic metaphysical commitments. In particular, I shall argue that externalism is inherently antithetical to both metaphysical realism and attempts to naturalize intentionality. Drawing these implications will go a long way toward explicating Putnam's recent thought which centers on arguing against his earlier functionalism and formulating a more pragmatic response to questions of truth, meaning and content.

Putnam's thought can roughly be divided into three stages, each characterized by a different brand of realism: (1) early *scientific realist* period (1957–1975), (2) second *internal realist* period (1976–1988), and (3) recent *pragmatic realist* period (1988–present). In the early period, Putnam explores the breakdown of logical positivism, arguing against conventionalism in both science and mathematics, and against verificationism in all of its guises. Along with Quine, he attacks the analytic/synthetic distinction and the intensionalist semantics that goes with it; unlike Quine, he does not succumb to a skepticism concerning the concept of meaning but rather tries to develop a theory of meaning that respects the crucial role of the

INTRODUCTION

social and physical environment. The three positions that characterize Putnam's early work best are: (1) scientific realism, which holds that truth can play an explanatory role in science and which countenances the existence of theoretical entities, (2) semantic externalism, which holds that meaning is, *inter alia*, to be determined by the nature of the social and physical environment, and (3) functionalism, the view that mental states are to be identified with computationally defined states causally responsible for producing behavior. Putnam has always retained theses (1) and (2), but he will come to argue that they actually militate against thesis (3), his own functionalism, and metaphysical realism (or any view that insists that truth is a radically nonepistemic notion).

In his second period, Putnam turns epistemological, paying more attention to the nature of the "theory-independent" entities posited in his earlier view. He now argues that scientific realism can be accounted for on either a realist or an anti-realist concept of truth. These considerations, coupled with the influence of Michael Dummett, lead him to reject metaphysical realism and its correspondence theory of truth, in favor of "internal realism," which links truth with rational acceptability. Two of Putnam's most famous arguments—the Model-Theoretic argument and the Brains in a Vat (BIVs)—are offered as a two-pronged attack on metaphysical realism. Despite their ingenuity, they fail to fully convince, mainly because they are attempts to produce *a priori* transcendental arguments against the skeptic. Such arguments are motivated by the same metaphysical urge to account for the truth or meaning of our statements independently of our common practices. Indeed, Putnam has since come to repudiate his earlier internal realism, seeing as it was a misguided attempt to replace the unintelligible picture of metaphysical realism with a rival picture. What we do not need is a negation of the absolute perspective, for that is itself just a mirror image, a rival metaphysics. Rather, we should question the full intelligibility of both sides of the debate and opt rather for a commonsense or "pragmatic" realism, which would (in Wittgenstein's famous phrase), "brings words back from their metaphysical to their everyday use."[6]

Putnam's recent work turns back to issues in the philosophy of mind and perception. His major concern is to argue against any view, such as his own earlier functionalism, which seeks to place a barrier or *interface* between the intentional agent and her environment. Again we see Putnam straining to put the mind and the world together, this time by arguing against any form of representationalism. Putnam's work in this area has been greatly influenced by John McDowell (as well as by classical pragmatists like William James), and I parcel out what I see as the good and bad elements of Putnam's appropriation of these thinkers. I argue that Putnam's critique of functionalism and other naturalist theories of the mind is mainly on target, though he still leaves us with some unresolved issues, such as how to account for the explanatory nature of our beliefs and desires. Utilizing the insights of his own pragmatic pluralism, I argue that there are different notions of content that are needed in order to account for the complexity and contextuality of our mental lives. For normal purposes of translation and interpretation, the standard externalist picture of content is indispensable, but in order to explain an individual's behavior, we will often need to appeal to a more fine-grained notion of content (which is nevertheless an *intentional* notion of content that reflects the agent's point of view).

As can be gleaned from this brief sketch of Putnam's corpus, one theme predominates throughout: the relation between language, mind, and world. Indeed, at the beginning of his article "After Empiricism" (1990), Putnam writes "if any problem has emerged as *the* problem for modern philosophy in the twentieth century, it is the problem of how words 'hook' onto the world." From Wittgenstein's early-picture theory to Quine's aptly titled *Word and Object* analytic philosophers have grappled with this question, in this way establishing a clear line with the tradition of philosophy going back to Plato's *Cratylus*. More than any other philosopher of the late twentieth century, Putnam has struggled with this issue: hence his forays into the philosophy of science, his work on the theory of reference, and his writings on the realism question, which Michael Dummett has called "the greatest question of metaphysics." And yet Putnam's recent work now suggests a different response to this question: we cannot step outside language and mind in order to determine the relations between language, mind, and reality, as though we could adopt some absolute perspective on these relations. In this sense, the attempt to reduce reality to mental constructions or situate reality outside of our conceptual schemes both rest on the same faulty picture. Along with Rorty and other so-called post-analytical philosophers, Putnam does not think that we should engage in the traditional philosophical game of trying to offer definitive solutions to the canonical philosophical problems.[7] Putnam arrives at this perspective only at the end of a long journey and many misguided attempts of his own to solve the traditional problems (e.g., to solve the language/world problem through a causal theory of reference, or the mind/body problem via his functionalist theory of mind). Unlike Rorty, however, Putnam does not think that our philosophical questions are simply "optional." Once we dismiss the absolute conception of the world we defuse a host of philosophical problems, but these are replaced by the "ultimate issue," which is "the position of man in the world."[8] Philosophy remains as a deeply important human activity, aiming at articulating a coherent perspective on the world whereby our various projects take on a deeper meaning as a result of our sustained reflection upon them. This humanistic orientation allows Putnam to affirm the classical pragmatist insight that philosophy is "the attempt to achieve the good,"[9] where "the good" is seen not in absolute terms but in pluralistic terms as the goals or ends of our various inquiries and activities. As we move into the twenty-first century, this issue of articulating a philosophy that brings ethics and science together, affirming a core of rationality while allowing for the plurality of our norm-governed discourses, will become increasingly important. Thus, unlike most other commentators I view Putnam's recent work to be ultimately his most important and enduring contribution to philosophy.[10] The Neo-pragmatist movement which he helped to initiate is gathering in momentum, and I shall conclude this study with a critical look at this new approach and its potential for revitalizing contemporary philosophy.

CHAPTER 1

THE ROAD TO SEMANTIC EXTERNALISM

1.1. THE LEGACY OF LOGICAL POSITIVISM

Putnam's early work devoted itself to a critique of verificationism in the philosophy of language and behaviorism in the philosophy of mind. Both of these theses were inextricably linked together: if the meaning of a statement consists in the publicly verifiable circumstances that make it true, then the meaning of a mental statement must be the publicly observable behavior that is evidence for *its* truth. The backdrop to these views was Logical Positivism, for verificationism was one of the hallmarks of the Positivist theory of meaning. Putnam viewed verificationism as a form of idealism and thus his defense of realism (more accurately, *scientific* realism) was of a piece with the critique of Positivist and conventionalist views of language. Putnam's relationship to Positivism was more complicated than this suggests, however: he regarded his teachers Hans Reichenbach and Rudolph Carnap as "sophisticated verificationists" whose views were not easily dislodged by the standard criticisms, including his own. To take just one example, against the standard Positivist view that we could test the meaning of an empirical statement one-to-one against experience, Reichenbach held that the meaning of such a statement is a probabilistic inference made within a body of theory.[1] Furthermore, Reichenbach was not a phenomenalist: he upheld the commonsense view that we perceive objects in the world and that sensory impressions are inferred from our perceptions of things (rather than the other way around).[2]

Putnam's criticisms, then, were mostly directed to the more naïve verificationism and phenomenalism that was widely taught to be the Positivist view (just as his critique of Quine was often directed to the "popular" misreading of Quine rather than Quine himself).

Despite the limited scope of this critique, then, it resulted in his own positive views that were to have such an impact on analytic philosophy in the second half of the twentieth century: scientific realism in the philosophy of science, functionalism in the philosophy of mind, and semantic externalism in the philosophy of language.

There is another problem with situating Putnam's early philosophy as a critique of Positivism: while he ostensibly disagreed with Positivist arguments and conclusions, he seemed to be in agreement with at least one aspect of their underlying methodology. The Positivists of course prided themselves on being the philosophical heirs of the Scientific Revolution: the goal of philosophy should be to articulate theories that were in tune with the concepts of modern science. Closely connected to this overarching goal was the ideal of coming to a rational consensus on the solution of traditional philosophical problems. One of the major motivations for the Positivist elimination of metaphysics stemmed from the conviction that metaphysical disputes rendered rational agreement on philosophical issues impossible. Agreement presupposes that there are shared criteria for evaluating the correctness of a given claim, but metaphysical viewpoints do not offer criteria that are acceptable to all rational agents. Given the conditions for rational inquiry and debate, then, metaphysical questions are irresolvable and in this sense "meaningless." The method of verification was adopted in order to preclude idle metaphysical speculation and establish a common ground upon which philosophers could rationally adjudicate the issues and come to agreement.

This is a rather commonsense or even "pragmatic" starting point and it is one which Putnam adheres to as well.[3] However, the Positivist vision was accompanied by a rather rigid theory of meaning which ultimately proved to be untenable. The motivations were clear enough: to combine the insights of traditional empiricism with the logicism of Frege, Russell, and Wittgenstein. This could be accomplished in one fell swoop by demarcating those statements that are analytic and *a priori* from those that are synthetic and known only by experience. Contrary to Kant, mathematics is not synthetic *a priori* and there is no need to resort to the quasi-mysticism of pure intuition in order to justify it. Rather, it can be reduced to logic, which delimits the most general conditions of rational thinking. In Carnap's conception, we can build other analytic truths from logic by substituting synonyms for synonyms.[4] So, to take the time-honored example, "all bachelors are unmarried" can be rendered logically true by virtue of substituting "unmarried male" for "bachelor" to get "all unmarried males are unmarried." The resulting conception of analyticity then became any statement that is logically true or true by virtue of its "meaning." Carnap in particular was unabashed in his view that the analytic/synthetic distinction was the key to the resolution of philosophical problems. As he writes:

> [we need] an explication for the distinction between logical and descriptive signs and between logical and factual truth, because it seems to me that without these distinctions a satisfactory and methodological analysis of science is not possible.[5]

Carnap's conception differed significantly from Frege and Wittgenstein, however, insofar as he abandoned the concept of absolute analyticity and introduced instead his "Principle of Tolerance." For Carnap, there is no single conception of logic that can be said to govern all thinking; rather we are free to adopt various logical frameworks, and to define analyticity as relative to those frameworks. Carnap believed this delivered the concept of analyticity from technical objections such as Godel's Incompleteness result, but it could not immunize him to the critique that Quine was to provide in his "Two Dogmas of Empiricism" (1952).

Quine famously argued that the crucial terms of the analytic/synthetic distinction such as "analyticity," "synonymy," and indeed "meaning" itself have no objective basis in fact, and the idea that we can test the meaning of each empirical sentence individually against experience was part of a "museum myth" that needed to be supplanted by a more holistic conception according to which the meaning of each statement was rather "the whole unit of empirical science." Quine's criticism was motivated by his own naturalistic viewpoint—a naturalism that carried with it certain affinities with the verificationism and behaviorism of the Positivists. If, as Quine writes, "there are no meanings, nor likenesses nor distinctions of meaning beyond what are implicit in people's dispositions to overt behavior"[6] then it is unlikely that we will ever come up with a criterion for "sameness of meaning," since peoples' behavior radically underdetermines what they mean or refer to.

Putnam's own viewpoint differed remarkably from Quine's. Rather than criticizing positivists from the standpoint of naturalism or behaviorism, he criticized them on the grounds that they were not in fact adhering to features of actual scientific and linguistic practice—data for a theory of meaning. Putnam agreed with the basic thrust of Quine's argument that the analytic/synthetic distinction has no weight, but his own critique appealed to specific examples involving scientific theory change. For example, with the adoption of Einstein's Theory of Relativity, the concept of "kinetic energy" underwent a radical change: as in classical mechanics, if a force is applied to an object in the direction of motion, the object gains energy because the force is doing work, but an object cannot be accelerated to the speed of light, regardless of how much energy it absorbs. Its kinetic energy continues to increase without bounds, whereas its speed approaches the (finite) speed of light. This means that in relativity the kinetic energy is not given by $1/2\ mv^2$ as it is in classical mechanics. According to Carnap, with the adoption of Relativity there was a change in linguistic frameworks: basic meanings of fundamental concepts like "energy" and "straight line" changed, and new definitions were given that served as axioms guiding further scientific investigation. But this has the very counterintuitive result that "kinetic energy" in pre-Einsteinian theory and "kinetic energy" in Einstein's theory has completely different meanings. We cannot even say that they are about the same quantities, for that would suppose that we had some framework-independent way to make such an evaluation. But the Carnapian model misdescribes scientific practice: scientists engaged in assessing the explanatory value of the two theories *do* take themselves to be talking about the same thing; if not, there would be nothing for them to agree or disagree *about*. The new definition of "kinetic energy" surely resulted not from a change in the "rules of language" but rather from a physical discovery about the world.

Putnam is actually deploying a typical Positivist argument against the Positivists themselves. Reichenbach in particular had insisted that the development of non-Euclidean geometries, Relativity, and Quantum theory had demonstrated without a doubt that there are no empirical judgments that are *a priori* valid for all time. But Putnam takes this one step further: the very same revisability argument can be directed not only against the synthetic *a priori* but also the analytic *a priori*. Except in trivial cases (to be discussed below), the absolute distinction between questions of meaning and questions of fact is just not sustainable.

One way of putting Putnam's point is to say that there is a norm embedded in scientific practice stating that one ought to construe the meanings of such terms as "kinetic energy," "electron," and "straight line" as remaining the same even through theory change. Niels Bohr was guided by this norm when he treated the reference of "electron" as the same in both his 1904 Bohr-Rutherford model and his 1934 theory, despite the radically different descriptions of electrons in those theories. What underlies this norm is the fact that terms like "kinetic energy" enter into many physical laws, and many of these laws remain unaltered through theory change.[7] Any one of these laws (such as e = $1/2\ mv^2$) can be given up without changing the identity of the law-cluster concept. What we cannot say is that any *particular* description involving these terms is analytic, just as we should not say that "all men are featherless bipeds" is analytic, given that we would still call someone a man even if (to our astonishment) he was born with feathers.

Characteristic of his tendency not to swing to extremes, Putnam *does* hold (against Quine) that there is an analytic/synthetic distinction. He basically agrees with the Strawson-Grice contention that a distinction which is so commonly made must have some basis to it.[8] A statement like "all bachelors are unmarried males" *is* analytic, for it is what Putnam calls a "one-criterion term": we cannot revise this statement without changing the meanings of its terms. Using the law-cluster terminology, we can say that there is only one law involving bachelors, namely, that bachelors are unmarried males. Given that there is no other cluster of laws to provide for its identity, if this law is given up, the meaning of "bachelor" would go along with it.

Some of Putnam's own examples, however, tend to show that even such statements as "all bachelors are unmarried males" could be given up if we imagine the right circumstances. In "It Ain't Necessarily So" (1962b), for example, Putnam considers the statement "All cats are animals." For Positivists like Carnap (and linguists like Katz), such a statement is analytically true, given that "cat" is synonymous with "feline animal." However, Putnam asks us to imagine the possibility that we discover that cats are actually robots being programmed from Mars. If we found only a few cats that were robots, we would say that they were not cats but robots. Or if we found out that cats had been replaced by robots several years ago, we would say that there are no longer any cats around.

But if we discovered that all cats have always been robots, we would say that cats are in fact not animals. "All cats are animals" is not necessarily true, and since analyticity implies necessity, it is not analytic either.

As this example shows, there seems to be an important similarity between theoretical terms like "electron," "kinetic energy," and vernacular natural-kind terms like "cat," "water." Like "kinetic energy," "cat" occurs in a lot of true statements that would not suddenly become false if we discovered that cats were in fact robots. Cats would still display the behavior they always had: they would meow, scratch, chase mice, and ignore humans when they so deemed it appropriate. Although no particular description is synonymous with the kind term, the collateral information associated with the term ensures that "cat" would continue to have the same meaning through theory change.

But if we are allowed to imagine such scenarios, we could construct a parallel argument to show that "all bachelors are unmarried males" is not analytic.[9] Suppose (to keep the extraterrestrial theme going) that Martians came down to Earth, but they were all one sex (they reproduced by cloning). Nevertheless, same-sex marriage is legal on that planet and some Martians are unmarried. It would seem to make sense if one of the earthlings found an unmarried Martian attractive and asked "Is that one a bachelor?" But if so, then it would be rational to suppose that there can be a bachelor who is not male. Thus, "all bachelors are unmarried males" is not necessarily true—and not analytic either.

There is of course a difference between statements like "all cats are animals" and "all bachelors are unmarried males," but it does not seem to turn on the issue of revisability or analyticity. We want to say that the meaning of "cat" is determined by natural facts in the world whereas "bachelor" is *more* a matter of convention. The stereotypical effects we associate with cats are caused by something with an underlying structure, DNA if cats are animals or computational structure if cats are robots. Putnam writes that this "something" is an *essence*, and that the essence is the important thing to consider when determining what a natural-kind term refers to. In "Is Semantics Possible?" (1970) Putnam develops this into a new theory of natural-kind terms, one that would have significant consequences for core issues in the philosophy of language and mind. Indeed it was this theory that would provide the background for

Putnam's groundbreaking semantic externalism as articulated in his landmark paper "The Meaning of 'Meaning'" (1975).

1.2. A NEW THEORY OF NATURAL-KIND TERMS

Putnam's theory (and he does emphasize that it is an *empirical* theory based on the actual use of these terms in the linguistic community) is that the meaning of a natural-kind term like "water" or "lemon" is vectored to the following components:

(1) syntactic indicators—for example, "concrete noun," "sortal"
(2) semantic indicators—for example, "natural kind," "liquid"
(3) stereotypical description—for example, "yellow," "fruit," "tart taste"
(4) reference/extension—for example, object individuated by DNA structure.

Such a meaning vector provides the conditions for the correct usage of a natural-kind term and makes it possible to determine whether a speaker attributes the appropriate meaning to that expression or whether its usage has changed enough to cause a difference in meaning. Putnam points out that while the stereotype is what a speaker normally has in mind when they use a natural-kind term (and what ensures linguistic competence), there are no analytic truths of the kind "every lemon has a P." "All lemons are yellow" is not analytic, for example, since there can be fully ripe green lemons that are still lemons. A better characterization (which is still not analytic!) is to say that "this X is a lemon" means that "X belongs to a natural kind whose *normal* members have property P1, P2, ... PN." When we say "belongs to a natural kind" we mean that there are certain *essential* characteristics that all lemons share, regardless of accidental features such as color. Further, "what the essential nature is is not a matter of language analysis, but of scientific theory construction: today we would say that it was chromosome structure in the case of lemons, and being a proton-donor in the case of acids." Putnam takes care to note that even the chromosomal description of lemons is not analytic, given that our current science might be wrong to think that those are the essential features.

Putnam sounds an anti-Fregean note when he observes that one upshot of this theory is that "meaning does not determine extension," inasmuch as no list of descriptions or concepts provides necessary or sufficient conditions to determine the reference of a natural-kind term. Obviously "meaning" here is taken to be akin to "Fregean sense," and Putnam offers the following argument to show that Fregean sense does not determine reference. In characteristic Putnamesque fashion, it proceeds by way of thought experiment: suppose that a colony of Earthlings space-travel to another planet. Over time, they forget the chemical structure of aluminum (if they ever knew it), and cannot distinguish it from the metal molybdenum. They end up incorrectly applying the term "aluminum" to molybdenum and "molybdenum" to aluminum. Putnam writes that "it is clear that 'aluminum' has a different meaning in this community than it does in ours: in fact it means *molybdenum*" (p. 151). "Aluminum" expresses the same concept (Fregean sense) on Earth as it does on the colony, but on Earth it refers to aluminum and on the colony it refers to molybdenum. Hence, Fregean sense does not determine extension. Putnam actually concludes though that we can still preserve the idea that meaning *does* determine extension *if* we construe the extension as part of the meaning.[10] Thus, because "aluminum" has a different reference on the colony than it does on Earth, it would have a different meaning as well.[11]

Published in 1970, this is historically the first explicit argument for semantic externalism to be presented in the literature. Putnam muddies the waters a bit at the end of the article, however, when he considers a species of fruit that is biologically unrelated to lemons but indistinguishable in appearance (Siberian oranges, perhaps?). He says that in such a case there are two possible things to say: (1) we could still call them lemons, indicating that "lemon" is a word for a number of natural kinds though not a natural-kind term itself, or (2) say that they are not lemons at all, as the biologists no doubt would. The former would be a Fregean response, since now (to go back to the aluminum example) "aluminum" on Earth and on its colony would have the same extension after all (*aluminum or molybdenum*). Putnam himself opts for (2) but he gives no argument for it. This crucial hole in the case for externalism will be filled in "The Meaning of 'Meaning'" (1975) where Putnam will appeal to indexicality (and Kripke's related views on rigid designation). Just as importantly, Putnam has not yet told us how the reference of natural-kind terms gets fixed—he has only told us that no description serves to fix it. As we shall see, here he will appeal to Kripke's causal chains and to his own idea of the division of linguistic labor. Finally, Putnam did not yet draw any of the radical conclusions concerning concept possession or content individuation that would later become the real "hot issue" regarding externalism.

One consequence that early Putnam *did* draw from this new theory of meaning is that it pointed to a broadly realistic view as opposed to the idealism he saw endemic to Positivism. If "electron" refers to the same entity through theory change, then there are certain facts that obtain in the world independently of our current descriptions or theories. And if the meaning of natural-kind terms is determined at least in part by their essences, and these essences might be undetectable by scientists, then perhaps there are truths about the world that may never become part of our knowledge. However, we should pause before attributing this kind of metaphysical realism to early Putnam, for the following obvious reason: to say that "electron" refers to electrons independently of any particular theory is not to say that it could refer independently of *all* theorizing. To use Kantian terminology, Putnam's theory of meaning is clearly committed to an empirical realism but for all that it could be rendered consistent with some kind of transcendental idealism. And indeed we will see that Putnam himself will later utilize his own theory of reference to argue *against* metaphysical realism. In hindsight it appears that early Putnam was not really interested in the subtleties of the realism debate and was not committed to any particular metaphysical viewpoint. Rather, the methodology is to construct an empirical theory based on data culled from our actual linguistic and scientific practices. These practices do suggest a certain realistic picture, but it remains to be determined precisely what kind.

1.3. EARLY PUTNAM AND SCIENTIFIC NATURALISM

There is no doubt however that there is a tension between the norm-based approach and a scientific naturalism in Putnam's early philosophy. According to scientific naturalism, philosophy should proceed by assuming, *prior to an investigation of our linguistic practices*, that only science "limns the ultimate nature of reality" (to use Quine's words).[12] On this conception, we should *assume* an ontological commitment to the entities proposed by the hard sciences and only construct philosophical theories that adhere to this commitment. Clearly this metaphysical assumption is not something that is made within scientific practice itself, since it makes an extrascientific claim about other domains of inquiry (viz., that if they are not specifiable or reducible to hard science then they are not genuinely real). We find Putnam explicitly espousing such a view in two areas: the philosophy of mathematics, and the philosophy of mind.

In the philosophy of mathematics, Putnam famously argued for mathematical realism by giving the following argument (what has since come to be known as the Putnam-Quine Indispensability Argument):

(1) One must be ontologically committed to all and only those entities that are indispensable to the best scientific theories
(2) Mathematical entities are indispensable to the best scientific theories, THUS
(3) One must be ontologically committed to mathematical entities.[13]

The "only entities" referenced in the first premise is a blatant appeal to scientific naturalism. The "all entities" is justified by confirmation holism (also called the Duhem-Quine thesis): empirical statements are not confirmed in a piecemeal fashion but only as a whole, thus there is no basis for excluding any of the entities referred to in a well-confirmed theory. This poses a problem for the nominalist who wishes to exclude the existence of sets and non-Euclidean geometries but to include the existence of electrons and other unobservable entities in physics. A mathematical realism is affirmed, but one that does not appeal to Platonic intuition or even the *a priority* of mathematics. For early Putnam, mathematics belongs essentially to the domain of the natural sciences and thus is not *a priori* but rather "quasi-empirical."

It is important to see, however, that Putnam's argument still works if we drop the "only" and with it the dogmatic appeal to scientific naturalism. It is enough to say that *within* scientific practice scientists do in fact use mathematics as an indispensable element of their theorizing. Because of confirmation holism, there is no good reason to accept the existence of theoretical entities while discounting the existence of abstract entities. Putnam's indispensability argument, then, is better seen when viewed as ontological commitment *within science* rather than as a sweeping claim about ontological commitment in all areas of inquiry. There may be, for example, good reasons for countenancing the existence of moral values, even if these values cannot be formulable within physical science. He argues now, however, that a consistent modal logic can be worked out that can express mathematical truth without positing any set-theoretic objects.[14] And he has derided the whole contemporary debate concerning "moral realism," arguing that moral objectivity can be safeguarded without our ethical judgments referring to any moral objects or "facts" (this will be taken up at length in Section 4.3, "The Fact Value Dichotomy").

The idea that mathematics is "quasi-empirical" has certainly been hotly contested, but even more controversial is Putnam's argument (against Positivism but in keeping with naturalism) that logic itself is empirical.[15] Putnam once again steals a page from Quine's playbook, in particular his comment in "Two Dogmas of Empiricism" that no statement is immune to revision—even the sacrosanct laws of logic could be given up, if we made compensatory adjustments elsewhere in our total theory of the world. Yet again, Putnam takes a Quinean idea and concretizes it by applying it to a specific example, in this case quantum mechanics. First, Putnam makes an analogy between the laws of logic and laws of geometry: just as Euclid's postulates had to be given up in order to accommodate the non-Euclidean geometry of Relativity theory, so we might have to give up the laws of classical logic in order to accommodate quantum physics. In particular, if we are realists about the physical world, then we must understand objects as having the properties of momentum and position. But Heisenberg's Uncertainty Principle holds that for quantum objects, either momentum or position can be determined but not both at the same time. Putnam saw the only possible resolution of this paradox to be the adoption of a quantum logic, which gives up classical laws of logic like the principle of bivalence and the law of the excluded middle. Putnam's argument for quantum logic was obviously motivated by scientific naturalism and its method of taking science at face value and then forcing philosophical revisions in order to accommodate the latest science. Putnam has since come to reject quantum logic for technical reasons, but he would also balk at the naturalist motivation underlying such a radical revisioning of our mathematical and logical practices.

The other area where early Putnam was committed to scientific naturalism was in the philosophy of mind, where he famously proposed a new solution to the mind/body problem, computational functionalism. The details of this theory will not be discussed until Chapter 3; for now, it is enough to point out that Putnam proposed a theory which would characterize all mental states (intentional and qualitative) as computationally defined program states. He applied the notion of a probabilistic Turing machine to the human mind in order to provide a completely mechanistic account of mentality. Obviously this program to explain the intentional in terms of the nonintentional was motivated by a desire to give a reductive scientific account of intentionality (even though functionalism of course was *not* committed to materialistic or neurobiological versions of such a scientific account). Putnam has since come to completely disavow computational functionalism, though I will argue that some kind of functionalism can remain when divested of its original naturalist motivations.

It is evident that Putnam had not yet come to terms with the clash between his pragmatic methodology and his commitment to scientific naturalism. Beginning in the mid-1970s, however, he will begin to become more aware of the epistemological issues underlying his theory of meaning, and as a result will begin to veer steadily away from naturalism. As we shall see in the next section, one of the major conclusions to be drawn from the semantic externalism presented in "The Meaning of 'Meaning'" is that intentionality *cannot* be naturalized. Contrary to Fodor and others, this conclusion would not mark "the greatest intellectual catastrophe in the history of our species,"[16] but simply a principled antireductionism which could serve as an antidote to the rather dogmatic scientism dominant within analytic philosophy in the latter half of the twentieth century.

1.4. THE MEANING OF "MEANING"

Putnam begins the article[17] by proclaiming in rather dramatic fashion that there are two main assumptions of traditional theory of meaning that cannot be jointly true:

(1) Knowing the meaning of a term is just a matter of being in a certain psychological state

(2) The meaning of a term (its Fregean sense or intension) determines its reference or extension

If both of these assumptions were true, then we could deduce:

(3) Being in a certain psychological state determines extension

But Putnam will argue that (3) is clearly false; hence by *reductio ad absurdum*, either (1) or (2) must be false. Putnam himself urges that we give up (1), thus ironically pressing a more radical antipsychologism against Frege himself, the presumed father of antipsychologism in logic and semantics.

It is important to see that from the very beginning Putnam uses "psychological state" based on what he calls the assumption of "methodological solipsism," according to which a psychological state is to be defined completely internally, as something "in the head" and which could retain its identity independently of there being anything in the external world. No doubt it is because Putnam has this sense of "psychological state" in mind when framing premise (1) that he will conclude that we should reject it rather than premise (2)—and thus with it the assumption of methodological solipsism. Since Putnam's article, these states have come to be known as "narrow psychological states," as opposed to the "wide psychological states" that *do* bring in essential reference to the external world. Whether or not this distinction between narrow and wide states is intelligible is, as we shall see, one of the main issues in the debate that Putnam's argument started.

Given methodological solipsism, the states *of knowing the meaning (intension) of A* and *knowing the meaning of B* are internal psychological states. Putnam argues that all traditional theorists made this assumption: even Frege and Carnap, who believed that concepts are public and shared by more than one person, believed that grasping these concepts was an individual mental act. Now given assumption (2), the extensions of A and B should follow from the intensions of A and B. Thus, if the extensions of A and B are different, the intensions of A and B are different. And if the intensions of A and B are different, then the narrow psychological states *knowing the meaning of A* and *knowing the meaning of B* would also differ. But Putnam will argue that this consequence is false: speakers in possible worlds can be in the exact same psychological state with respect to term A while A has distinct extensions in those worlds. Thus the extension is *not* determined by psychological state.

Putnam considers three examples to show that psychological state does not determine extension: the meaning of "water" on Earth and Twin Earth, the switching of the terms "aluminum" and "molybdenum" on Twin Earth, and Putnam's own use of "elm" and "beech" on Earth. The last example shows that Putnam's argument does not rely on imaginary possible worlds or counterfactual communities to get the desired externalist conclusion (though as we shall see, some commentators believe this to be the weakest argument and hence that Putnam *has* to resort to the other examples).

Let us set the scene for the basis of the first two arguments. Putnam asks us to imagine that somewhere in the galaxy there is a planet, Twin Earth, identical to Earth in all respects except that the substance called "water" on Twin Earth (similar to our water in all ostensible characteristics—it is a thirst-quenching, transparent, odorless liquid that falls from the skies and fills the rivers and lakes) has a different chemical composition, abbreviated by the formula XYZ. Putnam further supposes that this world is peopled with *doppelgangers*, or identical twins of those of us on Earth, type identical "down to the last atom." Now consider the use of "water" by Oscar and his Twin in the year 1750, before the chemical composition of water became known by Dalton. Putnam declares that when Oscar uses "water," he refers to H_2O, and when Twin-Oscar uses "water," it refers to a different substance, XYZ. The extensions of their terms are different, but by hypothesis they are in the exact same psychological state. Hence psychological state does not determine extension. In keeping with his previous views, Putnam chooses to accept the Fregean slogan that "meaning determines extension," insofar as we make the extension itself part of the meaning. The conclusion, then, is that the meaning of "water" is different on Earth than it is on Twin Earth. Or, as Putnam famously puts it, "cut the pie anyway you like, meanings just ain't in the head" (p. 227).

Putnam's second example is a slight variation from the one given in "Is Semantics Possible?" Suppose that the terms "molybdenum" and "aluminum" are switched on Twin Earth, and laymen like Oscar and his twin cannot distinguish the two metals. In such a case, while Oscar uses "aluminum" to refer to aluminum on Earth, his twin uses "aluminum" to refer to molybdenum on Twin Earth. Once again, we see that although they are in the exact same inner psychological state, the extensions of their terms differ. Putnam's third example does not make use of science fiction. Putnam blushingly confesses that he does not know the difference between an elm and a beech tree. He does know that they are both common deciduous trees, and that is enough for him to use those terms successfully, despite his incomplete understanding. But when he says "elm" he is referring to elm trees, and when he says "beech" he is referring to beech trees, despite the fact that his "concept" of an elm and a beech are qualitatively identical. Once again we have the case where nothing internal to the mind is sufficient to distinguish between the two uses, but nevertheless there is a difference in the reference.

Putnam's argument so far relies on two assumptions: (1) that someone can be credited with knowing the meaning of a word despite having an incomplete or even mistaken understanding of what it refers to, and (2) that the extensions of a term like "water" would in fact differ in the counterfactual situations he describes. As to (1), Putnam will introduce a hypothesis which "seems, surprisingly, never to have been pointed out," the division of linguistic labor. Typically, speakers of a linguistic community will have an incomplete understanding of the meanings of natural-kind terms. They may understand some of the stereotypical information associated with the term—for example, that elms are common deciduous trees, but they may not be able to distinguish elms from beeches or other kinds of trees. There may not be any description in their minds that uniquely picks out the referent, and yet we can understand them perfectly well when they use such terms in a conversation. This is puzzling on a descriptivist view, for it is hard to see how we can credit someone with speaking about *elms* when the description in the mind applies to several different kinds of trees. Putnam surmises that meaning is a collective rather than an individualistic affair: when a speaker uses a natural-kind term, there is a tacit understanding that the reference will be determined, not by what is in that speaker's mind, but by experts in the community who have a more fine-grained knowledge of the reference. Putnam's limited understanding of the term "elm" allows us to credit him with "knowing its meaning" insofar as he knows the stereotype and would be credited with using the term successfully;[18] but the referential component of the meaning is determined by the experts (in this case botanists). Every time a speaker uses a natural-kind term successfully, its reference (and hence meaning) will get vectored to that substance which is picked out by experts: this insures that Putnam's use of "elm" refers to elm trees and not beeches. As Putnam concludes, while individual psychological state does not fix extension, "the sociolinguistic state of the collective linguistic body to which the speaker belongs *does* fix the extension" (p. 229).

The division of linguistic labor might be able to explain Putnam's elm and beech case, but there are other cases where Putnam concedes that even the greater sociolinguistic community cannot fix the extensions of natural-kind terms. This leads us to assumption (2), whether or not we should take "water" to have different extensions on Earth and Twin Earth. Putnam asks us to consider the use of these terms in 1750, before any expert knew the chemical composition of "water." At that point, Putnam claims, the division of linguistic labor would be of no help to individuate the reference of "water" on Earth from Twin Earth. Yet he argues that even then "water" would have different extensions and thus different meanings on the two planets. What accounts for the difference, Putnam writes, is the fact that natural-kind terms have an indexical component. A natural-kind term like "water" is typically introduced into the language by way of causal contact with local samples of the substance. From then on, something is to count as water if and only if it bears the relation *same liquid* to those local samples. The relation *same liquid* is to be determined by scientific research: we now know that it is the chemical microstructure that determines the behavior of water, thus it is chemical microstructure which identifies the essential nature of water. On this view, "water" has an indexical component just like "I." When two people say "I am cold" they could be in the exact same psychological state (qualitatively), but their different contexts will pick out different referents. Similarly "water is wet" can be used to pick out different referents, depending on context. On Earth "water" refers to that substance which has the same microstructure as the local samples (which was H_2O even back in 1750). On Twin Earth "water" refers to that substance which has the same microstructure as local samples (which was XYZ even back in 1750). Thus, even in 1750 "water" had different extensions on the two planets—it was just that no one was yet able to realize this fact. Here we see that extension is determined not by the sociolinguistic community but by the nature of the world itself. This has sometimes been called "physical" or even "metaphysical externalism" to distinguish it from the social externalism derived from a mere appeal to the division of linguistic labor.

It isn't hard to see a similarity between this appeal to indexicality and Saul Kripke's concept of rigid designation, and Putnam himself appeals to Kripke's modal apparatus as a more technical way of making the same point. According to Kripke (1980), a term is rigid when it refers to the same thing in *all possible worlds* in which it exists and does not refer to anything else in those possible worlds in which it does not exist. Kripke introduced this concept in the context of challenging the traditional descriptivist view of proper names. He pointed out, for example, that a name like "Otto Van Bismarck" could not mean the same thing as "the first Chancellor of the German Empire," given that Bismarck might have died in infancy and thus never have become the first chancellor. That is, there is a possible world where Bismarck was not the chancellor of Germany, but there is no possible world where Bismarck was not Bismarck. Now suppose we actually did discover that the man referred to as "Bismarck" was not the first chancellor—that some impostor took his place, and suppose further that the only thing a German schoolgirl knows is that Bismarck was the first chancellor of Germany. How can she use "Bismarck" to refer to Bismarck, given that the only description in her mind actually picks out a different person? Kripke answers that she can use the term to refer to Bismarck through a causal chain: so long as she intends to use the term to refer to the same person as her teacher does, and we can trace this chain all the way back to the initial baptism of "Otto Van Bismarck" when he was first born.

Putnam (and Kripke) claim that this theory can apply to natural-kind terms as well: we first baptize a term like "water" by saying that it refers to whatever substance is the same as the ostended sample in the local environment. Given that we have discovered that water is identical to H_2O something will count as water only if it is also H_2O. Thus, if there was a world where something was qualitatively like water but had a different chemical composition, then that would not be water. Of course our knowledge of the fact that water is H_2O resulted from a physical discovery about the world and thus it is known *a posteriori*. The rather surprising conclusion to this is that there can be statements that are necessary but not known *a priori*. This idea has itself spawned a huge controversy, with much debate directed at some of the modal concepts that Kripke assumes in his argument. In what follows we will only be interested in the argument insofar as it relates to Putnam's externalism.

If Kripke's causal-historical account were correct for natural-kind terms, Putnam would definitely be able to justify assumption (2), that the extensions of "water" on Earth and Twin Earth are different, for the term "water" would be used rigidly on each planet to pick out different substances. However, while the account has some plausibility when applied to names, it runs into difficulty when applied to natural-kind terms. First, it is unclear whether or not the concept of an "initial baptism" makes sense when applied to a term like "water."[19] At what point did someone declare that "water" would be used to refer to any substance that bears the relation *same liquid* to that ostended sample? And how are we to know exactly what ostended sample was picked out? It may have been the water from a stream or the ocean, but with equal plausibility it could have been urine or beer. If in fact "water" had been used rigidly to refer to beer, then it would follow that every time we now mention "water" we are in fact referring to beer, which is absurd. Furthermore, there is an inconsistency in holding that "water" serves as an indexical *and* that it is rigid. If "water" were truly an indexical, then its meaning would remain the same even if its reference differed with context; but if "water" were rigid, its meaning would *be* its reference, and hence its meaning would change with each context of use.[20] In fact, given Putnam's vector theory of meaning, a natural-kind term cannot be *either* indexical *or* rigid. It cannot be indexical, since part of the meaning of a natural-kind term is its extension. And it cannot be rigid either, since part of the meaning of a natural-kind term is its stereotype. Putnam himself admits that natural-kind terms are *not* like proper names. Kripke claims that one can refer to "tigers" even if one knows absolutely nothing about tigers, whereas Putnam writes "one cannot use the word 'tiger' correctly, without knowing a good deal about tigers . . . in this connection, it is instructive to observe that nouns like 'tiger' or 'water' are very different from proper names" (p. 247). Clearly it is Putnam here and not Kripke who is taking a more plausible line: if someone had no true beliefs at all about tigers, we would not credit her with using "tiger" to refer to tigers at all. But if so, Putnam should not appeal to Kripke's concept of rigid designation to support his case.

More recently Putnam has made it clear that while he still maintains his externalism, he completely disavows any appeal to Kripke's metaphysical essentialism.[21] Kripke in effect assumes that there is some fact of the matter as to what our terms refer to, a metaphysical essence "out there" prior to any theory construction or conceptualization on our part. For Kripke, even a demonstrative like "this table" implies an intuitive knowledge of what is essential to that table, that is, an "intuitive grasp of the limits of possibilities in which the hypothetical object would bear the primitive logical relation '=' to the table I am pointing to." On this view, criteria of table-identity are not up to us. Rather, facts about identity depend on facts of nature that may remain wholly independent of our knowledge. Putnam now rejects this appeal to essences; any such view is committed to the myth of a "ready-made world," a world which has certain built-in properties independently of being described or conceptualized. For Putnam, there is of course an independent world, but the criteria for identity and therefore for what counts as a property or an object depend in part on decisions we make given various interests and purposes relative to different sorts of inquiry. If a wooden table changes slowly over time, for example, by having a splinter removed from it every minute, it does not make any sense to say there is some "fact of the matter" as to when it ceases to be that very same table. The same applies to natural kinds: there is no fact of the matter as to whether a given substance is water or not: the reference of "water" depends on norms that guide our linguistic and scientific practices. According to our current practices, there is a norm that stipulates that the reference of the term will be determined by chemical structure, since our current science teaches us that chemical structure is responsible for water's publicly observable behavior. But this norm is based on empirical and revisable truths about the world, not on intuitions concerning metaphysical essences or possible worlds. On Putnam's current view then, not only is a natural-kind term not rigid, but the whole concept of rigidity is metaphysically problematic.

In any case, I believe it can be argued that Putnam does not need to appeal to indexicality or rigidity to justify his externalism, and that the division of linguistic labor itself can do the job. The crucial idea behind the division of linguistic labor is that laypeople are willing to defer to experts when it comes to determining the reference and meaning of natural-kind terms.[22] When one uses such terms, one implicitly acknowledges that the meaning of the term is "unsaturated" and that it is to be filled in by the greater sociolinguistic community. Given this feature of linguistic deference, when one uses "water" one will defer to the experts to determine what it actually applies to—and given that the experts *would* conclude that "water" applies to H_2O on Earth and XYZ on Twin Earth, the term will get different reference assignments on the two planets. Now recall the situation in 1750, where it was argued that at this point no expert knew the chemical composition of water, and hence the division of linguistic labor could not individuate the reference. I think this can be handled simply by appealing to "retroactive" meaning assignments. We today can assign different meanings to "water" on the two planets in 1750, given what we know now. From our vantage point, we can look back and judge that there was indeed a meaning difference since we now know that the terms have always referred to different substances. Furthermore, speakers in 1750 *would have* made such a meaning differentiation had they known of the chemical difference. Deciding the individuating conditions for meaning does not depend solely on the inferences people in fact make, but rather on the inferences they *would* make under various (counterfactual) conditions. To say this is simply to say that there is a norm governing our use of natural-kind terms, according to which we would *judge* that if the underlying chemical compositions of the substances differ, then the meanings of the terms referring to those substances should differ as well.

This norm that guides our actual linguistic practice is similar in some ways to the speech act which Putnam takes to point to the indexical nature of natural-kind terms. We do take a natural-kind term to refer to entities that have a certain underlying structure causally responsible for their manifest behaviors—indeed; it is part of the fourth grade curriculum to learn that water has certain properties only explicable in terms of its chemical composition, such as boiling at 100 degrees Celsius, and freezing at 32 degrees Celsius. This is why there is an important difference between the usage of these terms and other terms, such as "chair," about which any competent user of the term can be said to be an expert. But this norm does not require there to be any original speech act requiring a term like "water" to behave a certain kind of way—rather, most likely, the usage of "water" evolved as culture and science evolved. There is no *a priori* guarantee that "water" would have been or will continue to be used as a natural-kind term, and there are circumstances we can imagine where its usage would in fact change (as we shall see below with the first Fregean objection to the Twin Earth argument). The important thing is that the term is pretty well settled at the present time and thus the norm mandating linguistic deference to experts concerning its reference is pretty well entrenched.

With these observations in place, we can proceed to consider some of the commonly held objections to the externalist conclusion Putnam draws from the Twin Earth (and related) arguments. We shall see that some of these objections may have weight against a metaphysical-based externalism, but they have no force against the social externalism espoused above.

1.4.1. Fregean Response I: The Disjunction Objection

Perhaps the most common Fregean response is to challenge assumption (2) above, namely, that "water" has a different extension on Earth and Twin Earth. First of all, it is pointed out that intuitions may vary: some people might think that "water" has a different reference on Twin Earth, but others might not. Perhaps we *would* continue to call the substance on Twin Earth "water," and go on to say that we have discovered that there are in fact two different kinds of water. I will label this the "disjunction objection," insofar as it is claimed that the extension of "water" on Earth and Twin Earth is actually the same, namely, the set of all things that are either composed of XYZ *or* H_2O.

Putnam himself anticipates this objection in the "The Meaning of 'Meaning'" when he discusses the case of "jade," which can apply to two different minerals, jadeite or nephrite. Although these gemstones have different microstructures, they have the same superficial characteristics: a translucent, green, glassy stone. In China, the stone became prized as an ornament on many ceremonial objects. Obviously, it was this usage that came to determine the meaning of "jade" and the difference in underlying microstructures was deemed irrelevant. Here we have a case where two stones were both plentiful in the same region, and a single term came to be used to apply to either of them insofar as they had the required ornamental features. This is clearly a contrast with the Twin Earth case: here we are to imagine two separate worlds with different causal histories. Furthermore, on each of these worlds, the use of "water" has come to apply to a particular kind of substance with a microstructure responsible for its observable behavior—in short, on both planets "water" is used as a natural-kind term. The disjunction objection would have us suddenly—simply because of stubborn resistance to an externalist conclusion—stop treating "water" as a natural-kind term! Now it is true that we can imagine circumstances where "water" would no longer be used as a natural-kind term—if, for example, there was enough interaction between Earth and Twin Earth such that "water" came to be applied only to the superficial characteristics.[23] We could also imagine scenarios in which it turns out that what we call "water" would no longer exist at all, which would surely change its reference. Such possibilities do not affect Putnam's thought experiments, which are based on our actual linguistic practice and not some hypothetical alteration of it.

1.4.2. Fregean Response II: Searle's Self-Referentiality Argument

Unlike the disjunction objection, which holds that the extension of "water" would be the same on the two planets, John Searle concedes (for the sake of argument) that the extension of "water" would in fact differ—only he argues that this is consistent with a broadly Fregean view of indexicals. The main idea behind "intension determines extension" is that the intension sets certain conditions which anything has to meet in order to fall into a term's extension. But if "water" is used as an indexical to refer to "that stuff which is the same as our local ostended samples" then that indexical description will itself make up the intension of the term. On earth, this intension will uniquely pick out H_2O and on Twin Earth it will uniquely pick out XYZ. In either case there is an intentional content "in the head" that picks out the extension.

Searle's position here is very unusual, since it depends on his unorthodox view on the self-referentiality of perception. Suppose that there are two identical twins looking at two distinct yellow station wagons that are nevertheless indistinguishable in appearance (perhaps they have just been released from the assembly line). As a first approximation, their perceptual experiences can be described by the same that-clause: "I have a visual experience that there is a yellow station wagon there." But it would then seem that both perceptual experiences have the exact same content: how then could their perceptions be of distinct station wagons? Searle claims that the satisfaction conditions for perceptual beliefs must include the condition that the visual experience "must itself be caused by the rest of the conditions of satisfaction of that visual experience." Thus the appropriate content of the visual experience would be rather: I have a visual experience *that there is a yellow station wagon and that there is a yellow station wagon there is causing me to have this visual experience.* Searle labels this the "causal self-referentiality of perception." On this view, causal relations to objects external to us *do* play a role in determining meaning and content, but this is no argument for externalism, since the causal element is part of the agent's intentional content "in his head." As applied to the Twin Earth case, even if Oscar and his twin have phenomenologically identical experiences, the indexical nature of "water" will determine their contents to have different conditions of satisfaction, and we can say this without requiring there to actually be anything external at all.

Even if one rejects the indexical nature of "water" and appeals solely to the division of linguistic labor, Searle argues that there still is an intentional content in the head that determines the extension. For now the intensional description for "water" would be something like "the liquid called 'water' by experts whom I defer to in my linguistic community." Since the experts in my community identify water with H_2O, and the experts in the Twin Earth community identify water with XYZ, "water" will have distinct references. Once again we see that there is an intensional description in the head that successfully sets the conditions required for something to fall into the extension.

There have been many objections to Searle's self-referentiality of perception and I will not rehearse them here.[24] Rather I will focus on Putnam's own response to Searle which I believe is more than sufficient to show the untenability of Searle's account.[25] Let us take the division of linguistic labor first: suppose that some community, say Nova Scotia, has "elm" and "beech" switched such that what are beeches are called "elms" and what are elms are called "beeches." On Searle's account, since the meaning of "elm" is "whatever my community's experts call 'elms'" it would turn out that "elm" has the same meaning in Nova Scotia as it does in Massachusetts, which is absurd, since "elm" in Nova Scotia means *beech*. Searle's view as to the indexical nature of "water" initially seems more promising, since here at least he does make a distinction in meaning based on a causal relation to the environment. The oddity, however, is that Searle locates this causal relation in the intensional description itself, rather than as a relation between the intension and the object in the world. That is, Searle can preserve his Fregean internalism while conceding that the extension of "water" is different on Earth and Twin Earth only by *stipulating* that the causal relation to the object is part of the intensional description itself. Not only is this *ad hoc*, it violates how we ordinarily assess sameness and difference in meaning by completely ignoring whether or not our terms *actually* refer to an object or not. Putnam can simply enlist all of the examples of his previous articles—whether it be the meaning of "kinetic energy," "electron," or "cat"—as counterexamples to Searle's theory.

1.4.3. Naturalist Response I: Fodor's Critique

While a full discussion of the implications of Putnam's semantic externalism for issues in the philosophy of mind will await the third chapter, some mention here has to be made of one of the most popular naturalistic responses to Putnam's argument. One of the major research programs in the philosophy of psychology has been to legitimize commonsense belief/desire explanations by integrating them into a more general scientific theory. We typically explain behavior by citing peoples' beliefs and desires: thus I went to the store because I desired some milk, and I believed that the store had some milk. But beliefs and desires are intentional states, and it is notoriously hard to provide identity conditions for such states, or show how they could play a causal role in producing behavior. For many years Putnam's functionalism seemed to be the best candidate for giving a naturalistic account of intentionality: we identify beliefs and desires with the causal role of physical states to produce behavior given inputs, outputs, and other states of the system. But Putnam's Twin Earth argument raises an immediate *prima facie* problem for functionalism: the twins by hypothesis are physically and functionally type identical, so according to functionalism they should have the same beliefs and desires. But when Oscar says "water is wet" he means and believes *that water is wet*, and when Twin-Oscar says "water is wet" he means and believes *that twin-water is wet*. At least on a common view that concepts are word meanings, we would ascribe different concepts and hence beliefs to the two twins, even though there is nothing in their heads that could distinguish them. This appears to have the curious consequence that mental states as well as meanings are not in the head![26] In any case, philosophers pursuing the project of naturalizing intentionality would be immediately threatened by the *prima facie* result of the Twin Earth argument, and there has been no shortage of attempts to block its conclusions, most notably by their ringleader, Jerry Fodor.

Fodor's strategy is to basically accept Putnam's conclusions concerning the meaning of "water" in the public language, and also the externalist consequences concerning our ordinary ascriptions of propositional attitudes.[27] However, the idea is to accept these conclusions while arguing that nothing serious follows regarding a naturalistic treatment of intentionality. All that is needed is to cook up another notion of the "content" of intentional states that meets two conditions: (1) it is sufficiently similar to, or related to, our ordinary belief/desire ascriptions, such that we can preserve the idea that our actions are caused by our beliefs and desires as ordinarily described; and (2) it is construed individualistically, such that no reference needs to be made to anything outside the head, as externalism seems to require. Fodor believes he meets both of these conditions by appealing to a notion of "narrow content." Narrow content is that aspect of the twins' intentional states that is the same: it is, say, the sentence in the head both share when they say "water is wet." By itself, it is not semantically evaluable, but only becomes so when relativized to context. That is, when Oscar says "water is wet" his narrow content, in that linguistic community, will be mapped onto the broad content *that water is wet*, while the same narrow content expressed by Oscar will be mapped onto the different broad content *that twin-water is wet*. For scientific purposes, we can ignore the broad contents and focus solely on the narrow ones, since those are the ones that are really doing the work in causally explaining the twins' behaviors.

There are indications that Putnam himself, in "The Meaning of 'Meaning'" favored a similar kind of position, which makes sense since he had not yet abandoned his earlier functionalism, and thus wanted to preserve some sense of "intentional state" that would be amenable to a functionalist analysis.[28] However, by his 1988 *Representation and Reality* Putnam explicitly states that he "has come to bury the narrow/wide distinction, not to praise it," and he has become increasingly critical of any attempt to naturalize intentionality. The notion of narrow content that Fodor hankers after faces many difficulties: (1) it effectively divides content into two parts when it is more economical to have one unified notion of content; (2) it is notoriously hard to provide identity conditions for narrow contents or say exactly what they are, since they are not semantically evaluable: Fodor himself writes,

> Indeed, if you mean by content what can be semantically evaluated, then what my water-thoughts share with Twin "water" thoughts isn't content. Narrow content is radically inexpressible, because it is only content potentially; it's what gets to be content when and only when it's anchored.

It's pretty hard to see how psychologists are going to go along with the proposal that one of the most crucial concepts in psychology is "radically inexpressible";[29] (3) Sometimes Fodor suggests that narrow contents as sentences in an internal language of thought. The problem here is that this syntactic specification may be too fine-grained to be the notion of content needed for purposes of psychological explanation. Indeed, insofar as we need a notion of content to play a role in psychological explanation, it is plausible to look for one that reflects the agent's point of view, but narrow content does not seem to fulfill this role;[30] (4) It may turn out, as Burge, Jackson, and others have argued, that functional states, particularly perceptual states, will need to be characterized in terms of the objects an agent is intentionally related to. If so, the notion of narrow content is not going to be the one we need to explain what the functional states of a system are; (5) recent Putnam has several arguments—inspired by his new pragmatic perspective—against any view of the mind that seeks to put a Cartesian barrier between the intentional agent and the world. Narrow content or any "common factor view" which doesn't immediately relate the agent to the world will fall prey to these criticisms. They will be discussed in more detail when we come to Putnam's natural realist theory of perception, in Section 3.3.

1.4.4. Naturalist Response II: Noam Chomsky

Putnam and Noam Chomsky have had a curious relationship: while they were colleagues at MIT and allies in the university protests against the Vietnam War, Putnam became a trenchant critic of some of the more metaphysical aspects of Noam Chomsky's revolutionary new linguistics. In his paper "The Innateness Hypothesis and Explanatory Models in Linguistics" (1967a) Putnam specifically argued against Chomsky's idea that we are born with an innate Language Acquisition Device. Chomsky had argued that this hypothesis was the best explanation for a range of phenomena associated with learning language, including the relative ease with which a child learns its original language, with little or no reinforcement. Putnam responded that Chomsky underestimated how much time is dedicated to language instruction, and he also pointed out that a lot of learning which Chomsky would not claim innateness for does not seem to require reinforcement to any significant degree. The Putnam-Chomsky debate on this issue has continued to this day with no real definitive victor, though Terrence Deacon's groundbreaking book *The Symbolic Species* (1998) appears to give Putnam the advantage. In any case, several years later in his article "Explaining Language Use" (1992) Chomsky would repay Putnam's compliment by initiating his own attack against Putnam's views, specifically the externalist conclusions reached in "The Meaning of 'Meaning.'"

Like Fodor, Chomsky is a scientific naturalist: he would accept only those philosophical categories that can help us to understand the mind and the world from a strictly scientific perspective. Unlike Fodor, however, Chomsky does not believe that any notion of content that is related to our commonsense attributions of propositional attitudes can be naturalized. This view is derived from a skepticism regarding our ordinary concepts expressed by "water," "energy," "human being," etc. These are terms that are used in a variety of ways in our common practices, and they reflect particular human interests and perspectives. As such, it is highly unlikely that we are going to get a general, theoretical account of what we mean when we use such terms. When we do chemistry, we might focus on the chemical properties of water and judge that "water" simply means H_2O; whereas if we are thirsty, we might hold that "water" is whatever liquid quenches my thirst. Externalists ignore these multiple uses of language by insisting, implausibly, on a univocal sense of reference and meaning.[31]

It is this mistake, Chomsky says, that carries over to the issue of mental content attribution. For externalists typically reason that since "water" means different things on Earth and Twin Earth, we can simply map these different meanings onto their beliefs to get different belief ascriptions. A "startling" conclusion is reached—that beliefs vary with regard to the environment and not by what is in the head—but only if one insists on the univocal sense of meaning, which is arbitrary in some cases and unreasonable in others. Chomsky adds that insofar as a naturalistic analysis is pursued, it will concentrate on what people *do* when they use such terms, which will shift the discussion to a study of mental representations in the brain and their various computational properties. A naturalistic analysis will *not* conjure imaginary worlds like Twin Earth or counterfactual sociolinguistic communities, nor will it truck with normative considerations. Insofar as we remain sober-minded naturalists guided by scientific method, we are going to look inside the head to explain what a person is doing or thinking. And insofar as we attempt to do justice to our commonsense judgments, it is unclear what we would say about Twin Earth and similar thought experiments. What is the substantive issue behind our decision to say that Oscar and his twin have different meanings and beliefs? There is none, Chomsky assures us.

Now up to a certain point, Putnam agrees with Chomsky. Putnam agrees that concepts like *water, energy, human being* reflect human interests and perspectives, and that for this reason they are resistant to naturalistic analysis. He agrees that "meaning" as ordinarily construed will not be captured by cognitive science, even if it ever became a fully realized science. As I have put it throughout this chapter, the attribution of meaning is normative, based on our actual social and linguistic practices, and hence cannot be carried out independently of those norms that guide these practices. But Chomsky infers that since judgments of meaning depend on "commonsense understanding," nothing "general" or "useful" can be said about them. At one point, Chomsky goes so far to say that they are only of "literary interest." Here we can see Chomsky's dogmatic naturalism at work: he infers that since a naturalistic account cannot be given, *no* account can be given (or at least none that is "general" or "useful"). But I think we have shown that Putnam's theory of meaning is both general and useful: it is general in the sense that it captures how speakers typically use words like "water," "lemon," etc., and it is useful insofar as it provides an account of how we communicate and understand one another when we use such terms. The concepts of *understanding* and *communication* are themselves based on human interests and perspectives, and so by Chomsky's standards, will not be captured by a naturalistic analysis. Does that mean that we cannot say anything general or useful about such concepts? No, it just means that we will need a different account of these concepts, one which is not naturalistic but not merely "literary" either. A clarificatory analysis of the norms that guide our everyday linguistic practices can provide such an account.

Chomsky concludes that "reference" is of no explanatory value in the study of language; he goes so far as to say that it is meaningless to even say that a person refers to London when she says "London is polluted." Chomsky is led to such extreme measures only because he insists on a naturalistic account of reference. Putnam, by contrast, has no problem with saying that a person refers to London when she makes such an utterance; this is in fact what we do say, in order to make sense of the speaker. I may be led, upon hearing that statement, not to take a trip to London. If it were merely her own private conception of London that she was talking about, I would not take such an action. What this shows is that there is a clearly understood sense of "reference" employed in ordinary discourse which has explanatory value, even if this kind of account is not one that fits under tight naturalistic laws of the kind that Chomsky hankers after. According to Putnam's externalism, and in full consonance with his new pragmatism, we should not be led to recoil from the failure of naturalist theories of reference to the conclusion that reference does not exist at all.[32]

1.4.5. Neo-descriptivist 2-Dimensional Semantics

Despite its "neo-descriptivist" title, the 2-dimensional semantics proposed by Frank Jackson and David Chalmers is really an attempt to reconcile classical descriptivism with the insights of a Kripke-Putnam externalism.[33] One way of seeing neo-descriptivism is as extending Kaplan's distinction between character and content beyond demonstratives to the linguistic meaning of any meaningful expression in natural language. While the proposal may have merit for certain terms, I believe that it fails for natural-kind terms— and this for all of the reasons Putnam adduced when developing his own theory of natural-kind terms in the early 1960s and 1970s.

The leading idea behind 2-dimensional semantics is that there are two intensions associated with any meaningful term—a primary intension which captures an expression's conceptual content, and a secondary intension which captures an expression's metaphysical content. The primary intension is similar to Kaplan's character—it is a context-independent sense that is said to be grasped *a priori* by any competent speaker of the language. In the case of a natural-kind term like "water" the primary intension would be tantamount to Putnam's stereotype—it would be a description like "that transparent, thirst-quenching, odorless liquid which falls from the sky and fills the oceans and lakes." The secondary intension is similar to Kaplan's content, which is determined by the primary intension and the actual context. In the case of water, it would be its essential nature, H_2O, a necessary but *a posteriori* fact that may lie outside the epistemic ken of the speaker. On this view, so long as we make a distinction between the conceptual and metaphysical aspects of meaning, it turns out that traditional descriptivism and externalism are both correct. Traditional descriptivism is correct about the conceptual dimension of meaning, since that can be completely captured by conceptual information known *a priori* by the speaker. But externalism is correct about the metaphysical dimension of meaning, since that can be captured by word-world causal relations outside of the speaker's head.

The 2-dimensional semantics can be immediately suspected of trying to resurrect an analytic-synthetic distinction with its distinction between conceptual and metaphysical aspects of meaning. And in fact, all of the arguments Putnam originally gave against the analyticity of statements like "all lemons have property P" can with equal justice apply to the notion of a primary intension. According to 2-dimensional semantics, there is a single set of conceptual information associated with a natural-kind term that any competent speaker of the language has to grasp in order to know its primary intension. But Putnam convincingly showed that we should not expect there to be any such list of concepts that a speaker *must* grasp in order to use natural-kind terms successfully. Someone could still refer to lemons even if they think that all lemons are green (perhaps because in that region all the lemons *are* abnormally green). And we can imagine a world which contains all the normal characteristics of water except that the liquid is not transparent but the color red—and we would still be speaking about water. True enough, Putnam did argue (against Kripke) that one did need to have *some* true beliefs about the natural kind to count as successfully using the term—but this is a matter of interpretation and contains a certain vagueness when applied to actual cases. Insisting that there is a precise set of conditions that a kind *must* meet to make up its primary intension is exactly what Putnam originally argued against, and Chalmers and Jackson present no reason to think that their account scores any better than traditional descriptivist theories on this front.

1.5. THE SCOPE OF PUTNAM'S EXTERNALISM

So far we have focused almost exclusively on natural-kind terms in presenting Putnam's externalism, but Putnam himself claims in the "The Meaning of 'Meaning'" that his conclusions "apply to the great majority of nouns, and to other parts of speech as well" (p. 160). He even argues that externalism applies to artifact terms, terms whose meaning seem to depend on convention and not on any causal factors external to the speaker. In this section, I will examine this claim and will argue that Putnam's externalism is more limited in scope than he believes—it does not, for example (except in rather exceptional cases), extend to artifact terms. Then I will consider Tyler Burge's argument on behalf of extending externalism to other general terms. We shall see that while the social aspect of Burge's externalism is laudatory, his arguments rely on an implicit appeal to the analytic/synthetic distinction which poses serious problems for his account.

In "The Meaning of 'Meaning'" Putnam argues that other terms besides natural-kind terms have an "unnoticed indexical component" and hence that the externalist conclusion that "meanings ain't in the head" applies to them as well. While he does not give us a detailed analysis, he does spend some time on the meaning of artifact terms like "pencil." He writes, "When we use a word like 'pencil' we intend to refer to whatever has the same nature as the normal examples of the local pencils in the actual world. 'Pencil' is just as indexical as 'water' or 'gold'" (p. 243). This claim should immediately strike us as rather odd: do we really intend to use words like "pencil" to refer to a substance that has an underlying nature, or are we more interested in what can satisfy the normal function of a pencil (thus, for example, including mechanical pencils in the extension of "pencil")? But Putnam argues that we can run a Twin Earth argument on "pencil" just as we can for "water." Imagine, for example, a Twin Earth where everything is just as it is on Earth except for one difference: on it, what is called a "pencil" is (unbeknownst to anyone) actually a living organism. When the two twins say "pencils are fun to write with," they can be in the same psychological state and yet their terms will have different extensions—for clearly what is called "pencil" on Twin Earth is a very different type of thing from what is called "pencil" on Earth.

Putnam arrives at this conclusion because he thinks "pencil" has an indexical component, and we have already seen that there are problems with this appeal to indexicality. One might argue, however, that Putnam can arrive at his conclusion simply by an appeal to the division of linguistic labor. For if speakers would defer to experts when determining the extensions of artifact terms as well as natural-kind terms, then the extension of "pencil" would presumably differ, since the experts would distinguish between an organism and a nonorganism. I think that the question rides on how the scenario is described. Given our actual linguistic practice, it is highly doubtful that there *are* any experts with respect to artifact terms like "pencil," "chair," etc. Or better: *we are all experts* insofar as we know how to use these terms, and there isn't a parallel case of there being a distinction between superficial and hidden/explanatory properties, as in the case of natural-kind terms. If we imagine a situation where "pencil" actually refers to living organisms, most likely we are imagining a situation where the meaning of "pencil" would change: "pencil" would in fact become a natural-kind term. In such a case, the average speaker would be committed to defer to the latest science in order to determine the true nature of these curious specimens. If, however, we imagine a case where "pencil" simply refers to a different molecular structure on Twin Earth (or imagine mechanical pencils on Earth), I do not think we would be committed to a difference in extension. For what a pencil *is* does not depend on internal structure in the same way a natural kind does. As long as it carries out its function as a utensil for writing and preserves the stereotypical characteristics of pencil-writing (as opposed to, say, ink-writing), it is a pencil regardless of its different physical constitution.[34]

Putnam is probably correct however when he states that the majority of our general terms are like natural-kind terms insofar as the average speaker would not be able to individuate their meanings fully, thus allowing Twin Earth arguments to be constructed for them. Economic terms like "arbitrage" and mathematical terms like "set," for example, would fall into this category. Other terms may be harder to determine, but likely fall on a continuum between artifact terms and natural-kind terms. Consider the word "shaman," for example. A typical speaker might only know that a shaman is someone who is supposed to possess magical powers or influence the spirit world in some way. Perhaps this would be enough for the speaker to acquire the word, but it would not suffice to individuate shamans from sorcerers. In order to tell if the extensions of "shaman" and "sorcerer" are the same, one must defer to experts, who in this case might be religious scholars or those engaged in such practices. Someone who says "Don Juan was an amazing shaman," intending to refer to the protagonist of Carlos Castaneda's novels, would be saying something false and stand to be corrected, since "shaman" is used to refer to someone who influences the spirit world for purposes of healing and bringing good to the community. Don Juan, however, says that his major purpose in using magic is to "obtain mastery," and he himself is careful to always refer to himself as a sorcerer and never as a shaman.

1.5.1. Putnam's Externalism versus Burge's Social Externalism

These comments may provide a useful segway to the views of Tyler Burge, for more than anyone else he has sought to elaborate on Putnam's social externalism and to apply it to other general terms besides natural-kind terms.[35] Burge's own original example appeals to the meaning of "arthritis," which he claims is *not* a natural-kind term but has come to be used by our linguistic community to refer to "any inflammation of the joints." Burge asks us to consider a patient Bert who goes to see his doctor, and tells his doctor that he has arthritis in his thigh. Importantly, the patient has many true beliefs about arthritis: he knows that it can occur in the joints, that it is a painful swelling, that older people usually contract it, and that his Uncle also suffered from it. According to our ordinary attribution of belief, we would say that Bert believes *that he has arthritis in his thigh*, but he is mistaken since one cannot have arthritis in the thigh (by definition). Next we are asked to consider the same patient in a world in which the only difference is the conventional meaning of the word "arthritis." Here, "arthritis" designates arthritis *and* other rheumatoid ailments, including the patient's thigh ailment. Burge claims that in this scenario, we would not say that Bert believes he has arthritis in the thigh—while he would be phenomenally and physically in the same state as actual-Bert, his utterance

"I have arthritis in my thigh" would be *true*, not false. Accordingly, if we are to report the patient's belief, we would need to coin a word that reflects this usage of "arthritis" and say rather that he believes *that he has tharthritis in his thigh*. The beliefs that Bert has in the two cases are different, but the only difference between them is the conventional meaning of the word "arthritis." Here we see that the different uses of the word (and nothing "in the head") determine Bert and his twin to have different beliefs. Burge explicitly draws out the anti-individualistic consequences of this analysis, arguing that it shows that commonsense belief/desire attributions do not supervene on anything in the head, much to the dismay of functionalists like Fodor who need supervenience in order to provide a naturalistic account of intentionality.

Central to Burge's reasoning is the claim that Bert is not making an ordinary empirical mistake when he says "I have arthritis in my thigh" but rather a conceptual (or linguistic) one. Bert has misunderstood the concept of arthritis, yet he has beliefs (importantly, *de dicto* beliefs) containing the concept. As Burge writes, if the thought experiment is to work, "one must at some stage find the subject believing (or having some attitude characterized by) a content, despite incomplete understanding or misapplication. An ordinary empirical error appears not to be sufficient" (p. 83). If Bert's error were simply empirical (and "arthritis is an inflammation of the joints only" were an empirical rather than conceptual truth), then the disagreement between Bert's community and the counterfactual community would be one of theory, not meaning. Thus, it would be open to say that the counterfactual community simply has a slightly different theory about the same disease, *arthritis*, not that it has a completely different concept, to be coined by the word *tharthritis*. Thus, Burge believes that it needs to be a conceptual truth, or "true by definition" that in Bert's community, "arthritis is an inflammation of the joints," in order to derive the externalist conclusions that Bert and his counterfactual twin have different beliefs.

The problem with this should be evident in light of the criticisms of Quine and Putnam himself against the analytic-synthetic distinction. Burge's distinction between empirical and conceptual mistakes is a not-so-veiled rehabilitation of the distinction between questions of meaning and questions of fact.[36] As Putnam pointed out, "kinetic energy" could continue to have the same meaning even if its definition came to differ widely through theory change. This ensures that scientists are communicating with each other and agreeing or disagreeing about the same quantity as they formulate their successive theories. But similar remarks could also apply to words like "arthritis" which are embedded in complex medical theories—descriptions or hypotheses about the true nature of the disease can vary while the meaning remains constant. Now Burge has since claimed that his distinction between conceptual and empirical is *not* tantamount to the analytic/synthetic distinction, and that the notion of a "conceptual truth" is no more than a "weakly analytic statement" that can be determined by an ordinary dictionary definition.[37] Be that as it may, Burge still needs a distinction in the meaning of "arthritis" in the two communities based on the conceptual information as contained in the dictionary definition. And this would still be subject to the criticism that "arthritis" could mean the same thing in the two communities *despite* the different dictionary definitions.

From our vantage point here, while Burge's specific argument may be problematic, his thought experiment and the social externalist conclusion he draws from it are essentially correct. That is to say, we *would* attribute different beliefs to Bert and his twin, and this largely because, as Burge correctly emphasizes, "the subject's willingness to submit his statement and belief to the arbitration of an authority suggests willingness to have his words taken in the normal way—regardless of mistaken associations with the word" (p. 101). But this is because of Putnam's division of linguistic labor—laypeople are willing (and committed) to defer to experts when determining the *extensions* (and therefore meanings) of their terms. Since Bert's medical community and the counterfactual medical community apply the term "arthritis" to different diseases, the terms have different extensions and therefore meanings.[38] This difference is reflected in our ordinary belief ascriptions: if the two twins mean different things by "arthritis" they should be attributed different concepts and beliefs. But none of this requires us to view a definition like "arthritis is an inflammation of the joints only" as an analytic or a conceptual truth. That is an empirical identification as determined by current medical theory which may change as theory changes. It may even turn out that our current theory is wrong and "arthritis" is in fact a disease that can also cause inflammation of the thigh. In that case, we would say that "arthritis" in fact picks out the same disease in both communities. But if we are to take the norms of our current practices seriously, the term "arthritis" would indeed pick out different diseases and the externalist conclusion can be seen to apply to medical terms as well as natural-kind terms.

1.5.2. Naturalistic Brands of Externalism

While Burge seeks to elaborate and defend externalism in a social, anti-individualistic direction, other philosophers have sought to appropriate externalism for a naturalistic semantics, whereby the notion of reference is rendered scientifically respectable by being characterized in wholly causal or nomic terms. This in turn would have the promise of legitimating the concept of intentionality, insofar as we characterize intentional states in terms of their referential component. What has emerged is an "informational theoretic semantics" first proposed by Fred Dretske in terms of the causal-historical relations between a speaker's terms and the environment.[39] More recently Jerry Fodor has converted to a nomic form of informational semantics: as opposed to the "narrow content" theorist described in Section 1.4.1, Fodor has now conceded that we need an externalistic account of content that figures in psychological explanation. The goal of preserving a scientific account of intentionality can still be attained, since this externalistic content (now construed along information-theoretic lines) can be given a completely naturalistic treatment.

Putnam's externalism, as we have seen, originated as a sociolinguistic proposal rather than an attempt to naturalize semantics or intentionality. Even if we focus solely on Putnam's views on indexicality and rigidity, the reference of a natural-kind term depends in part on the intentions of the agents (viz., to intend "water" to refer to whatever liquid bears the same relation to *that stuff* in the local environment). And if we attend to the division of the linguistic labor, as we have stressed in the social externalist interpretation, the reference of "water" is mediated by the greater sociolinguistic community. Since reference depends on intentional and social factors, Putnam's externalism is strongly antithetical to these naturalistic forms of externalism, however they are redressed. As Putnam happily puts it now, the attribution of reference to a speaker's terms depends on *normative* considerations endemic to our practices of translation and interpretation.[40] For example, we interpret a Thai's use of "meew" to refer to *cat* even though he may have many different beliefs about what he calls "meew" (he may think, for example, that they are divine creatures), for doing so best enables us to make sense of the speaker and to converse with him. The idea that we could give scientifically precise identity conditions for when two people refer to the same thing independently of these norms is a "utopian project" that not only will never succeed, but is poorly motivated to begin with (since it assumes reference and content *must* be naturalized *else* they do not exist). Putnam doesn't stop there, however. He has also brought many specific arguments to bear against naturalistically motivated theories of reference, in particular Fodor's version of information-theoretic semantics.

On Dretske's causal-theoretic view of reference, a tokening of "cat" comes to carry information (and hence possess meaning) by virtue of an actual causal relationship with cats in the world: "cat" refers to cat because cats cause "cat" tokenings. On Fodor's nomic-informational semantics, by contrast, a term like "cat" carries information only by satisfying certain counterfactuals: "cat" refers to cats because I *would* token "cat" if I were in the presence of cats. This subtle difference betrays a huge difference in outlook when we consider the consequences for intentionality. Take the case of Davidson's swampman, the molecule for molecule replica of Davidson who one day springs from the swamp.[41] On the causal story, the swampman would (initially) not be in any intentional states, since nothing of what he means or believes is actually caused by the outside world. Dretske accepts this consequence, and he thinks that it is telling against various views of artificial intelligence that seek to construe meaning and belief in terms of internal organization (factoring out the external component). Fodor, however, argues that it is intuitively very plausible that the swampman would have a mental life, and in any case he seeks to defend the artificial intelligence perspective. Construing meaning and content in nomic terms rather than causal terms seems to do the job: for the swampman can refer to cats given that he *would* say "cat" in the presence of cats. His own tokenings of "cat" do not have to be actually caused by cats in order for him to refer to cats (and hence carry information bearing contents about cats). The nomic view has other advantages as well in addressing certain problems for causal theories of reference, such as "the *qua*-problem": in virtue of what does "cat" refer to cats, given that tokenings of "cat" are also caused by other things, such as spatial/temporal parts of cats, felines, mammals, etc.?[42] Putnam himself will employ his Model-Theoretic argument (Section 2.4) against the idea that causal relations themselves can uniquely determine the reference relations between words and things. Fodor's nomic view at least offers the promise of sidestepping these thorny problems while preserving the goal of naturalizing semantics.

The key notion to Fodor's account is the idea of *asymmetric dependence*. As in standard causal theories of reference, we want our terms to be related causally to the things in the world they are about. We want to safeguard the following law:

(1) Cats cause "cat" tokenings.

But there are many other things that can cause "cat" tokenings: pictures of cats, statues of cats, even meows and pictures of dogs! The idea is that (1) will be basic in the way that other potential causes will not be. There is a dependence relation expressed by the following counterfactual:

(2) If cats didn't cause "cat" tokenings, then the other things that cause "cat" tokenings (picture of cats, statues, meows, etc.) wouldn't cause "cat" tokenings either.

Thus, take the following covariation law:

(3) Pictures of cats cause "cat" tokenings.

Fodor's view can be summed up by saying that while (3) depends on the truth of (1), (1) doesn't depend on the truth of (3). While there may be various things that covary with the tokening of "cat," (1) will express the basic law at the top of the hierarchy. Fodor uses the terminology of possible-world semantics to flesh out his point: if cats didn't cause "cat" tokenings then the closest possible worlds in which cats didn't cause "cat" tokenings would be worlds in which "cat" referred to something else.

Putnam's strategy is to point to various counterexamples which prove that Fodor has not shown asymmetric dependence.[43] While it is indeed true that (3) depends on (1), Fodor has not succeeded in showing that (1) doesn't depend on (3). In order for the dependence to be asymmetric, Fodor would need to show that "it is not the case that *if cat pictures didn't cause 'cat' tokenings, then cats wouldn't cause 'cat' tokenings either*" (p. 39). But the closest possible worlds in which cat pictures don't cause "cat" tokenings would presumably be ones in which people do not know what cats look like. In those worlds, it would be evident that cats wouldn't cause "cat" tokenings either, so that the above counterfactual would actually be *true*, not false. Fodor's theory also has a difficult time with analytically defined words like "superbillionaire" and nonreferring terms like "witch." If we define a "superbillionaire" as someone who has at least a hundred billion dollars, we could easily imagine scenarios where "superbillionaire" would refer to superbillionaires even though no superbillionaire has ever heard of or used the term, in which case no superbillionaires would ever cause any "superbillionaire" tokenings. Nonreferring terms also reveal an evident problem: how could there be a law that witches cause "witch" tokenings if there are no witches (at least none defined as "females with superhuman powers")? Fodor could say that the counterfactual here should rather be "if there *were* witches, then they would cause 'witch' tokenings." But this would be a rather strange counterfactual to appeal to in the context of providing a *naturalistic* reduction of reference.

Perhaps the main problem with Fodor's account, aside from these technical problems, is that he is surreptitiously appealing to an ordinary, intentional, and context-sensitive notion of causation in framing his causal laws, when a true naturalistic reduction would require a nonintentional, context-independent notion. Unlike our ordinary notion of cause, physics defines the total cause of an event mathematically in terms of all the factors that led up to the event. But when we say something like cats cause "cat" tokenings we are evidently selecting only one of the factors out of the many contributing causes and labeling it as "the cause." What Fodor really means then when he says that cats cause "cat" tokenings is that the presence of a cat is a *contributory cause* of many "cat" tokenings. But since there are many other contributory causes of "cat" tokenings, Fodor will fail to establish asymmetric dependence: for example, it would also be true that cats wouldn't cause "cat" tokenings if English had never become a language. The only way to rule these other causes out is to appeal to some intentional, context-sensitive notion of causation: we want to say, in this context, that the presence of cats is *more relevant* than the adoption of the English language. Putnam's own example is inquiring into the cause of someone's heart attack. If we are interested in what would have happened if he had obeyed the doctor's orders, then we would focus on bad eating habits and lack of exercise as "the cause." But if we are interested in what would have happened if John did not have high blood pressure, we would look to the high blood pressure as "the cause." This notion of "relevant cause" is one that depends on our interests which itself has an intentional dimension. Since this is the notion of cause that Fodor is appealing to in formulating his counterfactuals, it is evident that he will not be able to provide a *reduction* of reference to nonintentional notions, as was his stated goal.

Putnam himself does believe that there is a causal element involved in reference: it is in part because "water" on Earth is causally related to H_2O and not XYZ that we can say "water" has a different reference on Earth than it does on Twin Earth. But the notion of "cause" here is mediated by the intentions of speakers in deferring to experts, and the intentions of experts in constructing their theories. Furthermore, the notion of "cause" is itself a fluid one in theory construction, and we should not be mislead into thinking that the same notion of "cause" in physics can be applied to the notion of "cause" in semantics or intentional psychology. Putnam's point here will assume greater significance in the next chapter when we consider metaphysical realism and its view of truth as correspondence between thought and reality. Putnam will argue, along Kantian lines, that the notion of "cause" depends on its use within a conceptual scheme, and therefore cannot be appealed to as some superglue to connect our words to the mind-independent world.

1.6. CONCLUSION

In this chapter we have traced the route from Putnam's early critique of Positivism to his semantic externalism as presented in "The Meaning of 'Meaning.'" We have defended Putnam's externalism against various criticisms by Fodor, Searle, Chomsky, and others, by divesting it of its appeal to indexicality and rigidity (and naturalistic versions of the causal theory of reference) and instead playing up the importance of Putnam's thesis of the division of linguistic labor. We shall see that calling attention to the social nature of reference and meaning has special significance when applied to the question of truth and the realism debate. In the next chapter, we shall chart Putnam's move away from metaphysical realism toward internal realism. This move makes sense when considering the practice-based nature of Putnam's externalism, for it suggests that our concepts of reference (and therefore truth) are immanent to our total theory of the world, and not metaphysical primitives that could establish a relation between language and reality as if from some "God's Eye" or Absolute perspective.

CHAPTER 2

EXTERNALISM, REALISM, AND SKEPTICISM

2.1. RENEGADE PUTNAM?

In his now historic 1976 Presidential Address to the American Philosophical Association, Putnam shocked the philosophical community by repudiating "metaphysical realism"—a position he had allegedly helped to rehabilitate in the post-Positivist era—in favor of "internal realism." Despite the many attempts to make sense of Putnam's so-called turn, there is little agreement and still less appreciation of the motivations underlying it. According to an erroneous but widely held opinion, Putnam simply woke up one morning a changed man. "Let me ditch everything I have been committed to and see what happens," he must have thought, on this interpretation.

Some critics then go on to conflate the realism issue with that of the externalism/internalism debate, claiming that Putnam must have given up his previous externalism along with metaphysical realism. The Model-Theoretic argument, for example, is read as a repudiation of his earlier causal theory of reference, and the "externalism" that Putnam rejects in *Reason, Truth and History* (1981) is linked with his previous externalism (even though it is clear that the "externalism" he rejects there is a metaphysical thesis and not *semantic* externalism). Michael Devitt sums up the opinion of many philosophers by simply dubbing him "Renegade Putnam."[1] Putnam is deemed to be a traitor to naturalist philosophers like Field, Fodor, and Devitt, and he is welcomed with open arms by anti-realists like Richard Rorty (even though Rorty is one of the main *targets* of Putnam's internal realist writings).

If my interpretation of Putnam's externalism in the previous chapter is correct, however, Putnam's move toward internal realism should not appear so dramatic or even unsurprising. There we saw that Putnam's early views in the philosophy of language are guided predominantly by an attempt to make sense of our ordinary linguistic and scientific practices. Putnam's theory of reference and consequent semantic externalism is best seen not as a naturalistic or metaphysical attempt to pin down the word-world relation, as though from some God's Eye perspective. Externalism is rather a sociolinguistic proposal which tries to make best sense of our ways of speaking—it attempts to account for our ordinary practices of interpretation and translation by bringing to light the norms that guide a speaker's actual language use. From this point of view, the only realism that externalism argues for is a broad realism according to which "water" refers to an actual liquid in the world, and "electron" refers to a real subatomic particle. To make sense of features of scientific practice, we need to also say that "electron" refers to electrons independently of its being provable within any particular scientific theory. But this does not by itself point to metaphysical realism: it is to simply capture how scientists speak, for purposes of communication and rational criticism. Bohr, for example, took his 1934 model of the electron to be an *improvement* over his 1904 theory. But any thesis as to the successive improvement of theories implies that the referents of the theory by and large remained the same, even while the nature of these referents became better understood.

In this chapter we will see that Putnam's scientific realism can be conjoined with his semantic externalism to present a compelling unified vision. Looked at from this vantage point, Putnam's early scientific realism cannot be equated with metaphysical realism, just as his semantic externalism cannot be equated with the causal theory of reference. When Putnam realized that this is what his views imply, he announced his advocacy of "internal realism," which is predominantly a practice-based view of reference and truth. But, unfortunately, Putnam made two mistakes at this juncture. First, he misled other philosophers by saying that he was abandoning his previous metaphysical realism—a position he was never really committed to. Secondly, he was led precariously in the other direction, into a kind of Kantian transcendental idealism. This move, highlighted by the designation of "internal" realism (and the use of *a priori* arguments against skepticism such as his BIVs argument), marked an insufficient understanding on Putnam's part of the pragmatic or practice-based nature of his own basic commitments in the philosophy of language and science. Thus, Putnam failed to capitalize on the real insight into the realism debate that was within his grasp at the time. This failure will be remedied by Putnam's more recent pragmatic or natural realist outlook.

2.2. SCIENTIFIC REALISM AND METAPHYSICAL REALISM

According to Putnam's early theory of reference, theoretical terms like "electron" and vernacular natural-kind terms like "cat" continue to refer to the same entities before and after theory change. This idea formed the backdrop to Putnam's *scientific realism*: if we add to this theory of reference a Tarski-style theory of truth whereby truth is defined in terms of reference, then it follows that truth cannot be reduced to the provability of sentences within a particular theory. This is enough for early Putnam to also conclude that he was committed to the correspondence theory of truth. At the beginning of his 1975 article, "What is Realism?" he writes that "whatever else realists say, they typically say they believe in a correspondence theory of truth." Putnam concludes without further ado that he is a realist, without qualification. Indeed, in this article Putnam is concerned to show that the acceptance of scientific convergence lends credence to the idea that statements in science are true because they correspond to a mind-independent reality.[2]

However, because Putnam had not yet distinguished between scientific and metaphysical realism, we cannot conclude that he was committed to metaphysical realism at the time. First of all, Putnam is rather ambiguous about the status of these "theory-independent" entities. Sometimes he uses the phrase to only signify "transtheoretical" entities; in this case, scientific terms refer independently of the particular theory they are couched in, but not independently of *all* theory. At other times, he does appear to baldly state that they refer to a mind-independent reality, but this doesn't tell us much until we know exactly what he means by "mind-independent."

In any case, Putnam soon came to realize that his scientific realism need not have the loaded metaphysical commitments that many (including notably himself) took it to have. According to Richard Boyd, scientific realism is committed to the following four theses:

(1) Theoretical terms in scientific theories (i.e., nonobservational terms) should be thought of as putatively referring expressions.

(2) Scientific theories are confirmable and in fact are often confirmed as approximately true by ordinary scientific evidence interpreted in accordance with ordinary methodological standards.
(3) The historical progress of mature science is largely a matter of successively more accurate approximation to the truth about both observable and nonobservable entities.
(4) The reality which scientific theories describe is largely independent of our thoughts or theoretical commitments.[3]

Compare and contrast this characterization of scientific realism with Putnam's definition of metaphysical realism, according to which:

> the world consists of some fixed totality of mind-independent objects. There is exactly one true and complete description of the way the world is. Truth involves some sort of correspondence between words or thought-signs and sets of things.[4]

As far as I can see, only Boyd's fourth thesis can be directly linked to metaphysical realism, while the first three theses need not be seen as implying or presupposing the fourth thesis. For we could say that the existence of theoretical entities like electrons is indeed posited, but only from within a conceptual scheme of language users. Furthermore, we can uphold semantic commensurability insofar as we maintain that successive theories are improvements over their predecessors. But this does not imply that the entities a scientific theory refers to are "mind-independent," for improvement can be account for intratheoretically. Suppose we construed truth, not as correspondence to a mind-independent reality but as what is rationally acceptable at the end of scientific inquiry. Then we could say that our present theories are "approximately true" insofar as they are converging toward this final consensus. The same goes for the reference of scientific terms: there is an identity of reference through theory change because these theories are, by and large, about the same things, but these "same things" are *not* mind-independent insofar as they are *ideal-theory dependent*.

The internal realist position that Putnam will try to articulate can be seen as steering between two extremes: the first is a kind of provincialism which holds that there is nothing more to truth than what our current scientific theories say it is; the second a kind of metaphysical skepticism according to which even our best scientific theories can be completely wrong about reality. We do not want to be provincial given what we know about the history of science. Many well-entrenched scientific theories—Newton's for example—were subsequently shown to be mistaken, and it is plausible to believe that we stand to the future as the past stands to the present.[5] But we don't want to be too skeptical either, for we want to say that our present scientific theories are at least "approximately true" and that our terms by and large refer, even if the exact nature of these referents is still not fully understood. In good Aristotelian fashion, Putnam wants to adjudicate between two views which each have a kernel of truth but are equally exaggerated.

One way of charting this middle course is to provide a new characterization of truth. The metaphysical realist's construal of truth as correspondence to a mind-independent reality is supposed to capture the idea that the statements of science are *objective* (i.e., that they answer to something in the world independently of our present beliefs), but it actually undermines this objectivity by espousing the possibility that our statements *don't* answer to anything (we could, for example, be BIVs or deceived by an evil demon). But if we construe truth as rational acceptability from the standpoint of an ideal science, we can maintain the objectivity without the fear that the world might be for some reason out of our reach. Truth is certainly not cheap: science is a laborious enterprise and much needs to be done before we can claim any kind of "Theory of Everything." But there is no reason to think that truth is so hard that our very best efforts will never be good enough to unravel it. One motivation of Putnam's linkage of the concept of truth with the concept of rationality is just this: to get us to appreciate that our very natures as rational beings enable us to come to correct beliefs about the world. Indeed, a rational animal can also be conceived as a *truth-detecting* animal. If so, truth cannot be so radically severed from rationality.

Putnam's internal realism then is motivated by a felt need to articulate a conception of truth that can explain scientific progress within the context of our practices of rational inquiry. It asks us not to adopt Thomas Nagel's "View from Nowhere," where we project into some absolute perspective from which we humans could be no more than BIVs, radically out of touch with the objects we think make up the actual world. Adopting such a perspective is a chimera, for no matter how alienated it is, it still reflects *our* concepts and *our* rationality (if even to formulate it). At the same time, Putnam's internal realism enjoins us not to conclude that "everything is relative" or "truth is ideological," as postmodernism and other radical versions of anti-realism claim. Such views would entail that rationality itself is a chimera, and that our cognitive powers are unable to tell the true from the false (or the good from the bad, Putnam would add significantly). Clearly we *can* tell the true from the false, at least on many occasions, and in large part because of our ongoing methods of empirical investigation and rational deliberation.[6] The relativist or subjectivist creed obviously fails to explain not only the success of science but the success of our ordinary commerce with the world.

In order to see how Putnam arrived at this nuanced position, however, we have to investigate in more detail his struggles to come to terms with the concept of truth. This will also put us in a much better position to evaluate his two most famous arguments against metaphysical realism—the Model-Theoretic and BIVs arguments.

2.3. THE PROBLEM OF TRUTH

The problem of truth in Western thought was raised long before Pontius Pilate's rhetorical "What is Truth?" at least as far back as Aristotle, who defined truth as follows: "to say of what is that it is or of what is not that it is not, is to speak truly, and to say of what is that it is not, or of what is not that it is, is to speak falsely."[7] Contemporary philosophers would stand in universal agreement with Aristotle's statement—the problem begins when we try to interpret it. The general dilemma is this: the Aristotelian formulation is too weak to give an adequate explication of truth, and yet any further explication of truth proves too strong to be acceptable.

We have seen that early Putnam advocated a correspondence theory of truth, which interprets the Aristotelian adage to mean that statements are true insofar as they correspond to reality and false if they do not. The trouble is to define "correspondence" and "reality" in a philosophically justifiable way. Early Putnam equivocated on "reality": at times he writes that this refers to a "mind-independent" realm of objects, and at other times he means only that terms like "electron" refer to real things in the world, electrons. This equivocation is reflected in his attitude toward Tarski's theory of truth: on the one hand he believes that it captures the main idea behind the correspondence theory; and yet he certainly goes beyond Tarski when he claims that truth can play an explanatory role in accounting for the success of science. If truth can play such a role, then it is manifestly *not* philosophically neutral, as Tarski himself claimed.

This confusion comes about largely because early Putnam had not yet come to terms with the concept of truth. Early Putnam takes the question as to the existence of commonsense and theoretical entities to be identical to the semantic question of truth. That is, to say that electrons exist is to say that "there are electrons" is true. This identity follows the Tarskian T-schema: "P" is true if and only if P. Yet it is clear that Putnam does not construe truth in a deflationary way, as others who follow Tarski do. For early Putnam, to say that "there are electrons" is true is to ascribe a substantial property to the sentence, the property *of being true*. This property is not merely a predicate relative to language or theory T—rather, it is a property of the way things are in the world. On this account of truth, however, it would appear that Putnam is a strong realist; indeed, he would qualify as a "metaphysical realist" since it would follow that if truth is a property of the world and not of our theories, then our theories (even the ideal theory) might be false. This would conjoin with the skeptical possibility implied by metaphysical realism: the threat that the way things are might not dovetail at all with the way things appear.

Sometime in 1976, Putnam realized these consequences of his earlier view on truth. In the spring of 1976, he gave a series of lectures at Oxford University (the John Locke lectures, later published as *Meaning and the Moral Sciences*, 1978) which took up the question of how exactly to interpret Tarski on the question of truth. These lectures were influenced to a great extent by Hartry Field's seminal article "Tarski's Theory of Truth" (1972) and by Michael Dummett (who was ironically conducting his own series of lectures on truth at Harvard at the same time!) This sustained reflection let Putnam to re-evaluate his earlier position with respect to the realism/anti-realism debate. The result was "Realism and Reason," his presidential address to the APA in the fall of 1976, where he came out and announced his "Kantian turn," disavowing metaphysical realism in favor of internal realism (which he also called "empirical realism," following Kant again).

Putnam's main concern in the Locke Lectures is to determine the philosophical significance of Tarski's theory of truth. For Putnam, this resolves into the question of what relevance Tarski's theory has for the realism/anti-realism debate. There are five main positions one could take with respect to this questions:

(1) Deflationist Tarski: Tarski's theory is neutral with respect to the realist/anti-realist debate, which is its main virtue. An adequate definition of truth, captured by Tarski's T-schema, does not have any metaphysical or epistemological significance. It is merely a device for what Quine calls "semantic ascent." This is the view which Putnam says "would have seemed preposterous to a nineteenth-century philosopher." It is equally preposterous to Putnam.
(2) Inflationist Tarski: Tarski's theory is not neutral philosophically, since it captures the realist's basic intuition that statements are true insofar as they correspond to reality and false if they don't. Tarski's T-schema is interpreted strongly: what occurs on the right hand of the biconditional is a state of affairs or fact about a mind-independent reality.
(3) Irrelevant Tarski: Tarski's theory is correctly interpreted to be philosophically neutral, as the deflationists claim, but this is not a virtue but a vice. What we need is a theory of truth that relates us to the world, not a mere formal device for generalizing over statements.
(4) Davidsonian Tarski: Rather than trying to define truth a la Tarski, we should take truth as a primitive and construct a theory of meaning on its basis. Middle Putnam rejects the idea that such an important concept in our linguistic practices can be taken as a primitive notion.
(5) Substantive Noncorrespondence Theories: Tarski's theory is philosophically neutral, but this is a vice not a virtue, since it tells us nothing about what it is to understand the predicate "is true." In order to understand the concept of truth, we need to relate it to other notions such as what is recognizable, or rationally justifiable. This will be the position middle Putnam ultimately adopts.

Tarski himself made it pretty clear that his theory was indeed neutral to the realism/anti-realism debate, at least as this is traditionally conceived. As he writes:

> Thus, we may accept the semantical conception of truth without giving up any epistemological attitude we may remain naïve

realists, critical realists or idealists, empiricists or metaphysicians—whatever we were before. The semantic conception is completely neutral toward all these issues.[8]

If we take Tarski at his word, we might be tempted to agree with the deflationists that Tarski's theory is philosophically neutral to the realism debate. The problem however is that, since Dummett and others, the contemporary realism debate is not what it was in Tarski's day; indeed, the present debate between realists and anti-realists has been reconstrued as the semantic one concerning whether or not the notion of truth should be "cashed out" in some other terms, such as assertability conditions. Hence it would be disingenuous to claim that Tarski's theory is philosophically neutral. If one interprets truth along Tarski lines and then goes on to say that is *all* there is to the concept of truth, this is a quite strong philosophical claim indeed and one laden with metaphysical implications.

In the Locke Lectures, Putnam vacillates between (2) and (3). Against Field, he argues that Tarski's theory *can* be seen as philosophically neutral if we look at it simply as a formal scheme allowing us to generate further truths from truths already taken for granted (how exactly this works will be shown below). However, he also argues that we can interpret Tarski's theory as a correspondence theory if we connect the theory with an account of the role of the truth in scientific explanation. Although Putnam vacillates between (2) and (3) in the Locke Lectures, by the time he gives his "Realism and Reason" address he comes to clearly reject both (2) *and* (3) for the sake of (5): contrary to the deflationists, the concept of truth is in need of explication, but the notion of correspondence will not do (it is fraught with paradox). Putnam is led from these considerations to his internal realist characterization of truth.

It is not necessary to enter into all the technical details of Tarski's theory here. What is important is Tarski's basic idea: to define truth in terms of reference, and reference in nonsemantic terms. Tarski assumes we have a finite stock of predicates entering into satisfaction relations with various objects. By way of illustration, Putnam assumes there are only two predicates in language L—"is a moon" and "is blue." The satisfaction conditions can be defined for this language as ®:

> ® "is the moon" refers to x if and only if x is the moon; "is blue" refers to x if and only if x is blue

Reference is defined in nonsemantic terms (what is to the right of the biconditional), and truth is defined in terms of reference, as the T-Schema:

(T) "P" is true (in L) if and only if P

The meaning of "is true" is given by an understanding of the object-level sentence "P" which is itself understood in terms of the satisfaction conditions of its parts, as in ®. The triviality of Tarski's procedure evaporates when we begin to generalize over sentences. Consider, for example, the following sentence:

(1) If Socrates is a man, then Socrates is a man

If we wish to generalize on "Socrates," we get the following in first-order logic:

For all x, if x is a man, then x is man

But what if we wanted to generalize on the sentence "Socrates is a man?" There is no way of doing this in first-order logic; but we can do so if we introduce the truth predicate. If so, then (1) becomes:

(2) If "Socrates is a man" is true, then Socrates is a man

And we can now generalize to:

(3) For all sentences x, if x is true, then x is true.

Combining this aspect of Tarski's theory with the definition of truth via reference relations, we can say that Tarski's theory provides a conservative extension of the object language by which all true sentences in L can be generated from a finite base of predicates.

The debate which interests Putnam concerns whether or not Tarski has succeeded in capturing the meaning of "is true" by defining it in terms of conditions of satisfaction as in ®. Field contends that Tarski has not done this, since the primitive reference relations at the heart of Tarski's theory are defined in terms of a list—but what we want these reference relations to do for us is to hook us up to the world. Take Putnam's example of a language L with 2 predicates, "is the moon" and "is blue." We could give a definition for primitive reference in L by giving the following list:

DF = P primitively refers to x is and only if (1) P is the phrase "is the moon" and x is the moon, or (2) P is the phrase "is blue" and x is blue.

This definition can be generalized to allow for quantifiers and logical connectives (and this inductive generalization can be turned into a proper definition by logic). But, Field objects, if we want an appropriate *physicalist reduction* of truth,[9] we cannot rest content with a mere list; we must account for the *causal relation* which actually links the objects and predicates with the real world. Hence we need to amend Tarski's reference relations as follows:

"is blue" refers to X if and only if "is blue" bears Y to X
"is the moon" refers to X if and only if "is the moon" bears Y to X

Where Y is the "appropriate causal relation"; Field indicates that he has in mind here Kripke's causal-historical account, whereby the terms of the language refer directly to entities in the world unmediated by any conceptual information.

Putnam responds that Field's criticism of Tarski depends on what we want a notion of truth *for*. If we want to generalize over sentences as in (3) above, we cannot do without Tarski's theory, and we certainly don't need Field's physicalist concept of truth for those purposes. Furthermore, not reducing truth to a physicalist notion does not mean, as Field seems to think, that Tarski's theory is inapplicable to the real world. This would only follow if it were shown that the *only* way to speak about the world would be in physicalist terms. But Putnam argues that some of the core physicalist notions that Field appeals to, such as "causal relation," are actually interest-relative notions that cannot be given a physicalist treatment. Rather, we can accept Tarski's theory as "inflationist" to the extent to which it *does* depend on relations between words and things, and insofar as it appeals to a notion of truth that can have explanatory value in our theories, but we can do so without seeking to reduce truth to a physicalist notion.

At the end of the second lecture, we see the seeds of Putnam's "Kantian turn." After defending Tarski as giving a sufficiently "realistic" view on truth contrary to Field's remonstrations, he warns that this is *not* to endorse the view of truth as some sort of correspondence between language and a mind-independent reality. The following passage is revealing:

> "Electron" refers to electrons—how else should we say what "electron" refers to from within a conceptual scheme in which "electron" is a primitive term? Given the Quinean (Kantian predicament?) that there is a real world but we can only describe it in terms of our conceptual system (Well? We should use someone else's conceptual system?) is it surprising that primitive reference has this character of apparent triviality?[10]

This is the first time, as far as I know, that Putnam uses the phrase "conceptual scheme"; not only that, but it is the first time that he makes reference to a "Kantian predicament." What the passage reveals is a new epistemological dimension entering Putnam's thought. As Putnam will put it, to say that Tarski's theory of truth upholds a "realist" conception of truth is not to say that it vindicates a metaphysical realist conception of truth, since once can hold that Tarski's theory links our terms with objects, but only within a conceptual scheme of language users.

Although Putnam has not yet identified the difference between internal and metaphysical realism, the difference is implicit in the above passage. Thus we see another reason why Putnam's turn toward internal realism was not as sudden and unexpected as many have believed: it was born out of an attempt to make sense of Tarski's theory of truth in light of the extremes of both deflationist and metaphysical realist reactions to it. It will be seen however that the position that Putnam ultimately adopts (in his middle period) will move further away from Tarski and toward a Dummettian concept of truth. Field, with his physicalist agenda, seeks to revise Tarski to vindicate a metaphysical realist view of truth, whereas Putnam, concerned with how our concept of truth is linked to actual practices of assertion and justification, will be led to an internal realist conception of truth. Both philosophers are semantic externalists: both take seriously the referential aspect of language use. But whereas Field believes that reference needs to be construed in terms of causal relations, Putnam comes to the view that reference need not be clarified at all. "Cat" refers to cats, not because of some extraconceptual casual relation that hooks up words with mind-independent objects, but because a speaker uses "cat" with the intention to refer to cats (and we might add, with the intention to refer to cats as determined by experts in the greater sociolinguistic community). That is, given verificationist semantics, we need not get mired in the problem of how our words "hook on" to things. It is within the context of this general perspective that we should view Putnam's controversial Model-Theoretic argument, to which we now turn.

2.4. THE MODEL-THEORETIC ARGUMENT

One of the crucial aspects of semantic externalism is the idea that reference to the world is an essential feature of meaning. When I say "elms are trees," the meaning of the statement depends on what "elm" refers to. If the words "elm" and "beech" are switched in my linguistic community, when I say "elm" I actually mean *beech*. But whether I am referring to elms or beeches, there is a presumption that there is a determinate *something* that I am referring to when I use "elm." The fact that the referents of our terms are not always known to us is important epistemologically but less important semantically. Putnam's semantic externalism thus implies *semantic realism*, which holds that that by and large our terms (and by extension our statements) have determinate meanings. But suppose Putnam could cook up an argument to show that metaphysical realism implies semantic *irrealism*. Then, assuming the truth of semantic externalism, we could prove that metaphysical realism is false. This is at least one way to view Putnam's Model-Theoretic argument.

The Model-Theoretic argument then works as a *reductio*: it begins with the assumption of metaphysical realism and seeks to derive an absurd conclusion from it. Two metaphysical realist assumptions incorporated into the argument are: (1) that the World consists of a totality of mind-independent objects, and (2) that reference is a matter of one-to-one correspondence between terms and these mind-independent objects. If we add Tarski's theory of truth, where truth is defined in terms of reference, we get (3) the radically non-epistemic nature of truth: our statements about the world might fail to correspond to the way the world is "in itself." This implies the skeptical thesis (4): it is possible that even our ideal scientific theory of the world is false. So Putnam's metaphysical realist is saddled with the following:

(1) there is a fixed totality of mind-independent objects (uniqueness)
(2) reference is a relation between terms and these objects (correspondence)
(3) truth is radically nonepistemic
(4) possibility of global skepticism.

This way of construing metaphysical realism sees it as a primarily ontological doctrine: it is committed to there being some unique set of objects that make up the world, and that truth consists in determinate one-to-one correspondence relations between our words and these objects. Anyone familiar with Kant could immediately detect a serious problem with this view. (Kant asked, "what could make such an attachment to a mind-independent world possible?" And he concluded: *nothing, except an intellectual intuition we humans do not possess!*) Perhaps there is a more epistemic way of describing metaphysical realism which doesn't commit one to either uniqueness or correspondence; if so, it could be argued that the Model-Theoretic argument is powerless against it. I believe that Putnam's argument works against both epistemic and ontological versions of metaphysical realism, though it is easier to show how it works against the ontological (classical) version. We shall return to this question later.

Putnam's original argument was couched in model-theoretic language, employing certain logical theorems such as the Lowenheim-Skolem theorem, according to which every consistent theory has an enormous number of different possible interpretations, even nonisomorphic interpretations. In later discussions of the argument Putnam presented it without the formal apparatus, and drew attention to parallels it has with Quine's argument for the Inscrutability of Reference and Wittgenstein's Rule-Following Paradox (of course the main difference between Putnam's argument and those two arguments is that Putnam's is a *reductio against* the skeptic). The key idea behind Putnam's argument is that it is possible to preserve the truth of our sentences, even while shifting or "permuting" the referents of our terms. Suppose, for example, we have a theory that contains only the following three sentences:[11]

(1) the flea is on the mat
(2) the cat is on the mat
(3) the mat is on the floor.

Suppose now we shift or permute the reference relations of these terms in the following way:

"the flea" refers to the number one
"the cat" refers to the number two
"the mat" refer to the number three
"the floor" refers to the number four
"is on" refers to the relation of being numerically less then.

This "nonstandard" interpretative schema will make (1–3) come out true just as the standard interpretation:

"the flea" refers to the flea
"the cat" refers to the cat
"the mat" refers to the mat
"the floor" refers to the floor
"is on" refers to the relation of being on.

By virtue of what can the metaphysical realist rule out the nonstandard interpretation? The realist, it seems, is landed in an embarrassing predicament, since according to her, so long as truth is defined a la Tarski in terms of reference, we should be able to account for the *truth* of (1–3) in terms of the reference relations between words and mind-independent objects. But how can we retain this idea if the truth of (1–3) can be preserved while changing these reference relations to *different* objects?

There have been three main responses by metaphysical realists: (1) "bite the bullet" and acknowledge the indeterminacy of reference but hold that this does not affect the metaphysical claims of realism;[12] (2) Explain the reference relation in some rationalist manner, such as a primitive "grasping" relation;[13] (3) Explain the reference relations in terms of extraconceptual causal connections. For example, since tokens of "the flea" are appropriately caused by fleas rather than the number one, we can rule out the nonstandard interpretation.

Obviously (3) would be the preferred tactic by naturalist philosophers such as Field, and it is quite surprising that such philosophers have accused *Putnam* of not sufficiently considering this response given his previous papers on Field and Putnam's explicit critique of the appeal to "causal relations."[14] Be that as it may, the idea is to appeal to Field's physicalist definition of reference:

© X refers to y if and only if x bears R to y

Where R is "the appropriate causal relation," definable in a natural science vocabulary without using any semantic notions. Putnam's response is disarmingly simple: "how 'causes' can refer is as much a puzzle as how 'cat' can, on the metaphysical realist picture." That is, if we add "the appropriate causal relation" to our description of the reference relation we have just added more words to our theory, and we are still free to permute the reference while preserving truth-value just as before. Commentators have labeled this the "just more theory" response on behalf of Putnam.

A careful look at the debate between Putnam and naturalists reveals an impasse here which is not likely to be settled.[15] Naturalists insist that causation is not just another term in the language—it is an extralinguistic relation in the world by virtue of which terms are linked to their bearers. However, once again we should be aware of the "Kantian predicament" that Putnam is now sensitive to. Kant himself argued that causality could hardly relate us to mind-independent objects; at best, causality is a relation between objects of *experience*. To appeal to some primitive notion of causality that could link us to a mind-independent world would then beg one of the major questions in the realism debate. Furthermore, Putnam "ups the ante" against the realist by arguing that we could still perform reference permutations on an *ideal* theory of the world that satisfied all observational and theoretical constraints. The causal relations that link us to objects of experience are satisfied by the observational constraints of the theory, but this would not affect semantic indeterminacy at all. Hence appealing to causality is either too weak to challenge the conclusion of the argument or it is too strong to be appealed to without begging the question.

It might be thought that Putnam's argument has force only against those ontological metaphysical realists who uphold the theses of uniqueness and correspondence. But there are various epistemic versions of metaphysical realism that define the thesis holistically, framing the realism debate in terms of the truth or falsity of a class of sentences or whole theories of the world, rather than ontologically as about a class of entities.[16] These philosophers would acknowledge that even from the standpoint of science itself, the idea of there being a unique set of objects (and therefore only one true description of the world) is implausible. A case in point would be the characterization of light as waves or particles: both are correct descriptions of an objective reality. Here it is not a question of finding the right ontology but rather of seeing which theories about the world are true. Further, two theories that posit different entities can both be true of "the same reality" insofar as they can be mapped onto one another, as is the case in the wave/particle phenomenon.

Perhaps there may be an intelligible way to defend an epistemic version of metaphysical realism, according to which there are no epistemic constraints on truth, and hence no *a priori* arguments that could be given against the skeptic. However, incoherence threatens for the metaphysical realist who rejects a basic ontology of things and yet continues to claim that our best scientific theories, even our ideal theory, could still somehow be false. For we could then ask: by virtue of *what* could the ideal theory be false? If the theory is ideal, it would satisfy all observational and theoretical constraints: it would entail all true observational statements; it would be simple, consistent, elegant, etc. What *further* constraints could one place on the truth of the ideal theory by virtue of which it could be false? The metaphysical realist we are considering here cannot say "because it might not refer to the right set of mind-independent entities" for according to this realist, there is no unique set of mind-independent entities to refer to. And if the metaphysical realist just says that the ideal theory can be false because of some "mind-independent reality" that cannot be specified, then the realist is committed to a Kantian *noumenon* about which nothing can be said (even that it exists!). Surely the realist would not want to be maneuvered into such a position, but if so, Putnam would have scored a serious victory.

Similar reasoning applies if the realist claims that the reference relation to the mind-independent world need not be *specified* for it to obtain.[17] For then we would fall into semantic ineffability regarding not only reference but the contents of our own thoughts (which are determined by these reference relations). Ineffability does not arise for Putnam since he does not take reference to be a primitive, nor does he think it is necessary to find a link (third thing?) between words and objects to secure reference, as if from some perspective we could adopt outside of language. Our judgments that someone refers to the world are made from within our linguistic practices and are subject to norms of translation and interpretation. It is enough that someone use the word "cat" correctly, and be willing to use the term as the community does, to be judged as referring to cats. On this view (curiously similar to Davidson's), interpretation takes care of the problem of referential determinacy. The metaphysical realist, on the other hand, is forced into some kind of Tractarian silence regarding how reference is possible. If we combine the epistemic metaphysical realist with this response, we get the viewpoint that we refer to *something somehow*. If this is not a *reductio* of metaphysical realism, then nothing is!

2.5. VERIFICATIONIST SEMANTICS?

I think it is in light of this discussion that we can best understand Putnam's adoption of "verificationist semantics" which he takes to be implied by the rejection of metaphysical realism. The question of how we are able to grasp truth conditions is another way of putting the question "what makes reference possible?" In order to get away from appealing to brute causal relations or be reduced to semantic ineffability, Putnam is led to agree with Dummett that such a grasp involves an *ability* on our part to recognize when such conditions obtain. Indeed, Dummett's long-standing objection to realism shares some important similarities to Putnam's. According to Dummett, the realist believes that we can make sense of the meaning of a statement in terms of its truth conditions. The trouble posed for the realist concerns those effectively undecidable statements for which we have no means of telling whether they are true or not. Dummett asks a question similar to the one Putnam asks in his Model-Theoretic argument: by virtue of what is there a determinate truth or falsity for such statements? One answer is because of the principle of bivalence, which states that every meaningful statement has either a true or false value. But anticipating Putnam's critique of the "God's Eye Perspective," Dummett argues that this principle can only be justified if we assume some super being, for whom a class of statements M, undecidable to us, would nevertheless be decidable for *Him*. The implication is that, since we need not assume such a super being (or at least, need not for semantic purposes) we need not assume the principle of bivalence.

Dummett's own verificationist proposal is to identify the understanding of a sentence with a speaker's grasp, not of truth conditions, but assertability conditions. Thus, a speaker can be said to understand a sentence like "there is a cow" by correctly asserting that sentence in front of a cow, or by drawing a picture of a cow. In general, there has to be some manifestation of that speaker's understanding if we are to ascribe meaning to her utterance. The concepts of reference and truth conditions do not have any explanatory role to play in this semantics, and thus the question of how to account for the reference relation between words and things does not arise. As Putnam writes:

> Now the puzzle about what singles out correspondence as the relation of reference does not arise. The notion of "reference" is not used in the semantics. We can introduce "refers" into the language a la Tarski, but then
>
> (1) "Cow" refers to cows
>
> will simply be a tautology—and the understanding of (1) makes no reference to the metaphysical realist picture at all

For a verificationist semantics, there is no problem with referential determinacy, since extensional concepts like reference and truth are replaced by intensional ones like recognizability and assertability.

Now on a superficial level, this adoption of verificationist semantics should strike us as yet another proof that Putnam has had a complete change of heart. Wasn't he the one responsible for debunking all forms of verificationism, whether in philosophy of language, mathematics, and science? Furthermore, his own semantic externalism revolves around the claim that meaning is more intimately connected to the referential use of language than traditional philosophers have supposed. How can Putnam now tell us that reference has no explanatory role to play in semantics? However, if semantic externalism is interpreted the way it has been throughout this book, the inconsistency should dissipate considerably. We have seen that externalism can be plausibly interpreted as a practice-based view of language which does not appeal to metaphysical primitives such as causally specified reference relations. Social externalism rather focuses on how terms are used in the community, and standard practices of translation and interpretation decide questions of whether or not a term refers to the same thing or not (as in the Twin Earth case). We have already seen how Putnam's externalist conclusions can be made without an appeal to the causal theory of reference.

Unfortunately, however, middle Putnam seems to think that the rejection of the causal theory of reference implies the rejection of truth-conditional semantics and the adoption of verificationist semantics. Clearly this would be unfair to philosophers like Davidson, who employ a truth-conditional semantics but do not appeal to any notion of causal reference. And it is not fair to Putnam's own externalism, which I believe is best seen as also supporting a truth-conditional account. That is, we could say with Davidson that the meaning of a sentence is given by its truth conditions *within a linguistic practice that is already taken for granted*. The concepts of reference and truth are no longer causal-explanatory notions, but they do not have to be replaced by assertability conditions. When a speaker says "water is wet" on Earth, we interpret her as referring to H_2O and thus meaning water rather than twin-water. The meaning then can be given by the truth conditions, which would differ in the mouth of our twin on Twin Earth who is referring to a different substance. But this is because of norms that are built into our linguistic practice: among them, the norm of deferring to experts to determine the reference of such terms, and the norm of treating a difference in reference as a difference in meaning. If we assume the normative nature of our practices, we can not only accommodate the truth-conditional semantics but show precisely how and why the attribution of such truth conditions is illuminating and informative.

It is important to note that Putnam's verificationist semantics in his middle period was conjoined with his functionalist theory of mind (thus his use-theory differed significantly from Dummett's Wittgensteinian version). Putnam's claim is that speaker understanding can be accounted for by saying "not that language mirrors the world but that speakers mirror the world—ie their environment, in the sense of constructing a symbolic representation of that environment." On this picture, the external world provides the input which gets filtered through a system of representations (computational in character), resulting in a "model" of the external environment; this model then determines which symbolic outputs will be expressed, whether in language or perceptual representation. Thus there is never a direct connection between language and reality; as Putnam puts it, the idea that we could compare a word to a thing is "the myth of comparing a sign with unconceptualized reality." For this reason too we cannot establish a link between language and reality through causal connections alone, since these causal connections would be mediated by the entire system of internal representations, whereby symbols are compared with other symbols before they are expressible in language.

Putnam now completely repudiates this picture of the relation between language (and perception) and reality, calling it the "interface model of mind," a modern form of Cartesian representationalism that has had disastrous epistemological consequences in the history of philosophy. He now writes that when I perceive a tree, I am actually perceiving *that* tree, not proxy an internal representation of the tree. I perceive the tree directly and can appeal to that "external perception" as a justifier in my beliefs about the tree. Similarly for my utterances: they are directly about facts in the world and not mediated by any inner representations. Quoting Wittgenstein approvingly, Putnam remarks, "when I say or think that things are thus and so, I do not stop anywhere short of the fact but I mean: *that things are thus and so.*"[18] Of course, Putnam would hardly doubt that there is background system of beliefs that my current perceptions and utterances are informed by (which is why labeling it "direct perception" is slightly misleading). The crucial point is that the facts that are presented to us via perception are already conceptualized—they are not unorganized "bare" percepts that stand in need of being taken up and synthesized by our internal system. Because perceptual facts are already conceptualized, they can be appealed to in justifying our other conceptual states, such as our beliefs and desires. If they were nonconceptual causal inputs, then we could not justify our beliefs and desires by appealing to our perceptions, which would create the worry that we stand in a precarious inferential relation to our environment.

More will be said about Putnam's recent view in Chapter 3; for now, it should be simply pointed out that so long as we drop the emphasis on "direct" perception, Putnam's view can be made to cohere pretty well with what Davidson says about speaker understanding. For Davidson, we do not need to posit internal representations (or anything "hidden") in order to account for speaker understanding.[19] As interpreters, we pair sentences with truth conditions, given an understanding of language already in place (and thus given a holistic network of beliefs expressed in language). A speaker asserts "that is a tree" and we take that sentence to be about trees, given that the speaker would reliably produce that sentence in the presence of what we interpreters take as trees. Social externalism would add to this the division of linguistic labor, according to which we interpret the meaning of a person's utterances to be in compliance with the wider meaning in that person's linguistic community. What results is a truth-conditional semantics, but one where the concepts of reference and truth do not figure as causal-explanatory notions. Thus it is possible to agree with Putnam's critique of naturalist views that appeal to the causal theory of reference, and also to agree with him that such views go hand in hand with an ontological metaphysical realism that is called into question by the Model-Theoretic argument. But we can say all this without being tempted into a version of verificationist semantics, whether this is construed in Dummettian or functionalist terms.

2.6. INTERNAL REALISM

Putnam's professed aim in *Reason, Truth and History* is to "break the stranglehold which a number of dichotomies appear to have on the thinking of philosophers and laymen. Chief among them is the dichotomy between objective and subjective views of truth and reason" (p. ix). Putnam picks up where the Model-Theoretic argument left off, building a case against metaphysical realism and its notions of "correspondence" and "mind-independent reality." He seeks to articulate a view of truth and rationality that gives up on the attempt to fashion some "objective" perspective outside our linguistic practices, without falling prey to the self-refuting and world-renouncing errors of various forms of anti-realism, postmodernism, subjectivism, and relativism. To this end he employs the following strategy: in chapter one he presents his famous BIVs argument, which utilizes certain basic intuitions about reference to undermine the possibility of global skepticism implied by metaphysical realism. In the second chapter, he gives a new version of the Model-Theoretic argument. In chapter three, he contrasts metaphysical realism with his own internal realism, and he fleshes out what he takes to be the "Kantian" element in his position. In chapter four he argues that certain considerations in the philosophy of mind support his perspective. In chapters five and six he extends the discussion to moral philosophy, arguing that the collapse of metaphysical realism coincides nicely with the safeguarding of moral objectivity. The structure of this last argument mirrors Kant's move from epistemology to ethics from the first to the second *Critiques*. The various ways this parallel can be played out, and the limitations to it, are drawn out in Putnam's next published book, *The Many Faces of Realism* (1984).

As Putnam's BIVs argument deserves separate treatment, we will postpone that discussion until the next section and begin here with the third chapter, where he contrasts two approaches that philosophers have taken with respect to the concepts of truth and rationality: the "externalist" and "internalist" perspectives. The choice of these terms is somewhat unfortunate, since they bring to mind the debate between externalism and internalism in the philosophy of language/mind, or the debate between externalists and internalists in epistemology. In fact, the distinction Putnam draws here is *not* the one in either of those debates, but rather a *metaphysical* distinction as to the nature of reality. On the one hand, there are externalist philosophers who believe that what objects and properties there are in the world does not depend at all on what humans believe or could come to believe; then there are internalist philosophers who hold that "'what objects does the world consist of?' is a question that only makes sense within a theory or description" (p. 49). Putnam will side with the internalist philosophers in this debate, and this should be kept in mind when trying to figure out the "internal" part of Putnam's internal realism.

For the internalist, truth is "some sort of ideal coherence of our beliefs with each other and with our experience as those experiences are themselves represented in our belief system" (p. 50). What makes a statement or belief true is its connection to other statements or beliefs rather than correspondence to a mind-independent reality. Putnam connects this view on truth with a certain picture of how we are able to refer to objects. The mind never actually compares an image or word with an object, but only with other images and words. In order to compare representations with mind-independent objects, as the externalist perspective requires, the mind would have to occupy a position outside of itself, which is impossible. One recalls here the Tractarian image of the eye trying to see itself, or

Davidson's statement that "no confrontation makes sense, for of course we cannot get outside our skins to find out what is causing the internal happenings of which we are aware."[20] The internalist faces no such problem, since for him there is no question of the mind confronting something outside of itself. Rather the objects that we refer to are objects that are already conceptualized, or carved out of our total theory of the world. As Putnam puts it:

> "Objects" do not exist independently of conceptual schemes. We cut the world into objects when we introduce one or another scheme of description. Since the objects and the signs are alike internal to the scheme of description, it is possible to say what matches what. (p. 52)

As it stands, this passage is in need of clarification. First of all, the language of the passage suggests what Putnam explicitly denies elsewhere in the book, that we "create" objects (similar to the criticism leveled against Nelson Goodman that according to him we have "created the stars"). The reference to "conceptual schemes" might also suggest a picture criticized by Davidson, that there is some noumenal world "out there" which then gets schematized and organized by our theories and descriptions to result in the empirical world of objects and properties we perceive and talk about. It is natural to fall into this kind of language, but I will argue that Putnam is not trying to rehabilitate this *bad* reading of Kant.[21] One step toward clarifying these remarks is to follow Putnam in sketching a brief history of representationalist philosophy that culminates in Kant's critical philosophy.

Putnam notes that before Kant, philosophers basically held a "similitude" view of truth, according to which truth was a literal similarity (or "copying") between external objects and our representations of them. This view was modified by Descartes and Locke with the distinction between primary and secondary qualities: judgments like "the leaf is green" reflect not an objective property of the leaf but rather a disposition or power in the leaf to give rise to the sensation of green. Berkeley's contribution was to extend the argument to primary as well as secondary qualities: judgments about so-called objective properties like length and shape themselves depend on the perceiver and can differ from person to person. But if all we can have are subjective representations, what makes us think that there is an independent object that these are representations *of*? The inference from a 3-foot mental image of a table to there actually being a 3-foot table is patently invalid. Putnam draws the following conclusion from Berkeley: "nothing can be similar to a sensation or image except another sensation or image" (p. 59).

Next comes Kant. Putnam sees Kant as basically accepting Berkeley's argument but drawing a different conclusion. Berkeley concluded that we should reject the notion of objectivity and restrict knowledge to simple, subjective qualities. But Kant argued that even these simple, subjective qualities are appearances; thus, there is no way to privilege them over external objects, which are *also* appearances. If all properties and objects are secondary, then we cannot make the contrast between what is internal and what is external that seemed to linger in Berkeley's conception of things. As Putnam puts it,

> it follows that everything we say about an object is of the form: it is such as to affect us in such-and-such a way. Nothing at all we say about an object describes the object as it is "in itself" independently of its effect on us, on beings with our rational natures and our biological constitutions. (p. 61)

There are two consequences to such a view: (1) we have to give up on the idea of correspondence to a mind-independent reality and acknowledge the mind dependence of all knowledge claims; (2) once we give up the epistemological priority of the inner over the outer, there is no reason to suppose that external objects are "reducible" to private subjective sensations (and hence no reason to lapse into forms of anti-realism and Berkeleyan idealism). Our representations of objects are not representations of a mind-independent reality, but nor are they private representations. On this latter point, we do of course see an important difference between Kant and Putnam; for Kant, objects are "mind-dependent" in the sense that they are determined by *a priori* categories of thought and the *a priori* forms of space and time. For Putnam, objects are "mind-dependent" only in the sense that they are posited from within our ongoing linguistic and scientific practices.

It should be clear from this exposition that Putnam is not absurdly claiming that human beings create the external world. Nor does he mention any sort of transcendental ego or Absolute or God that creates the world out of its own consciousness, or any such idealistic conception. Science teaches us that the world existed long before language users came on the scene to talk about the world. Nevertheless, it is *science* which teaches us this, and science is itself a social practice that is theory driven (and we might add, the theories it postulates depend as much on norms that guide inquiry as it does observation and experimentation). From within this social practice we can indeed draw the important distinction between what appears the case and what is the case and thus can safeguard the concept of objectivity. Kant himself distinguished between two ways of talking, the transcendental and the empirical perspectives. From the transcendental perspective, we see that all talk about objects is talk within our conceptual scheme, and that any attempt to refer to something outside this scheme is incoherent. Yet on the empirical level, we must distinguish between our private representations of trees and the external trees that we intersubjectively refer to. In the "Refutation of Idealism" Kant further argued that inner representation is itself only possible on the basis of outer representation—external objects belonging to an objective spatiotemporal order. Now Putnam would not agree with Kant's thesis as to the transcendental ideality of space and time, but he would agree that without the distinction between what appears to be the case and what is the case, we could not make sense of our linguistic practices. This distinction is a fundamental norm that makes agreement, disagreement and hence communication itself possible.

Another way to divest Putnam from charges of anti-realism and idealism is to take a closer look at his positive characterization of truth as idealized rational acceptability. Unfortunately, Putnam doesn't spend nearly enough time in arguing for his own positive view as he does in debunking metaphysical realism. What results is a certain looseness in his account which critics, including his later self, will capitalize on. His position does serve at least to distinguish him from the metaphysical realist who believes that truth is correspondence with reality and anti-realists who simply equate truth with justification. According to Putnam, our beliefs are true to the extent to which they cohere with our other beliefs. However, we also want to preserve the idea that truth is a property of sentences that cannot be lost. Not only that, but there can be statements that are presently justifiable but later on turn out to be false (the history of science is replete with such examples). We can preserve both of these ideas by conceiving of an *ideal final theory* which satisfies all observational and theoretical constraints: it is confirmed by all observational statements and satisfies maximally all the virtues of a good scientific theory (elegance, simplicity, etc.). A statement that could be produced as true according to such a theory would be one which is justified under "ideal epistemic conditions," about which Putnam writes:

> We speak as if there were such things as epistemically ideal conditions and we call a statement "true" if it would be justified under such conditions. "Epistemically ideal conditions," of course, are like "frictionless planes": we cannot really attain epistemically ideal conditions, or even be absolutely certain that we have come sufficiently close to them. But frictionless planes cannot really be attained either, and yet talk of frictionless planes has "cash value" because we can approximate them to a very high degree of approximation. (p. 55)

This emphasis on truth as ideal justification that might never actually be attained would appear to closely approximate C. S. Peirce's definition of truth as "that concordance of an abstract statement with the ideal limit toward which endless investigation would tend to bring scientific belief."[22] The emphasis on the communitarian aspect of truth, or truth as an actual consensus among rational participants who are not biased by power, privilege, or other distortions to ideal communication, has been made into a sophisticated consensus theory of truth by Jurgen Habermas.[23]

Putnam, however, has in no uncertain terms disavowed the Peircian interpretation.[24] For one thing, the talk of "frictionless planes" and the idea that inquiry might never come to an end (or might somehow halt!) suggests that truth might never be attained, and Putnam acknowledges that this "is the first step on the slide to skepticism, and my talk of 'idealization' was unfortunate if it suggested such a view."[25] Secondly, the Peircian definition of truth does not make an important distinction between different kinds of statements, some of which may indeed be true even though we may never be in a position to justify them. Historical statements are paradigm cases of statements that clearly have a truth-value even though, barring time travel, it may be impossible to ever verify them. Consider the statement "dinosaurs roamed the earth three millions years ago." Since this is a statement about the past, commonsense says that the roaming either did or did not occur, regardless of what our theories state about it. If we interpret truth as actual consensus at the end of scientific inquiry, then we have the strange result that the truth about a statement about the past depends on the truth about a statement in the future. Putnam demurs: the truth of such statements does *not* depend on our ability to verify *them*. However, being able to ascribe truth to historical statements *is* parasitic on our ability to ascribe truth to our present-tense statements, and these *are* verifiable. That is, I know what it would mean for me to now verify that "dinosaurs roam the earth" and it is because I have this ability that I can conceive the possible truth of "dinosaurs roamed the earth three million years ago." Thus while it is not required for any *particular* statement that it be justified in order to be true, its truth does depend (in general) on our justificatory abilities.

To take another example, consider the following two statements:

(1) There is intelligent extraterrestrial life
(2) There is no intelligent extraterrestrial life

Clearly (1) is capable of verification, but since we are presently incapable of verifying it, we can say that its truth depends on some notion of ideal verification. But we may never be in a position to verify (2), and yet it may nevertheless be true. Putnam writes, "what makes us consider (2) a possible truth is not that we have any clear notion of what would make it warrantly assertible [but rather] that it is the negation of an empirical statement."[26] Thus, (2) may be true even though we may never be in a position to verify it, but nevertheless our conception of what makes it possibly true depends (1) on our understanding of what makes an empirical statement like (1) true, which is our ability to verify it, and (2) our concept of negation, which is endemic to our logical practice. As Putnam would now put, language and logic allows us to extend our conceptual powers in ways that do go beyond verifiability. Nevertheless, language and logic are still aspects of our conceptual scheme, so that the truth of such recognition-transcendent statements does not imply a metaphysical realist concept of truth.

It is worth pointing out in this regard that Putnam never intended to provide a *definition* of truth, as many have erroneously believed.[27]

For suppose we considered the following the internal realist definition of truth:

(3) A statement p is true if and only if p is justifiable under epistemically ideal conditions

But Putnam gives the following characterization of "an epistemically ideal condition":

(4) An epistemically ideal condition is one which would best enable us to determine if a given statement p were true or false.

Clearly (3) cannot be a definition of truth, since it depends on (4) which already *presupposes* the notion of truth. Putnam's goal then is *not* to give a definition of truth: even in *Reason, Truth and History* (1981) he states clearly "I am not trying to give a formal definition of truth" (p. 56) and "I am not offering a reductive account of truth, in any sense" (p. 115). Putnam's point is rather that our concepts of truth and rational acceptability are interdependent, insofar as we cannot possess one concept without possessing the other. We have already shown this in the case of historical and certain other recognition-transcendent statements: even while the truths of these statements may outrun our ability to verify them, our being able to conceive of their possible truth *does* depend on our ability to verify *other* statements. Truth, then, is not *radically* nonepistemic, as metaphysical realism holds, but it can be *locally* nonepistemic, depending on the particular kind of statement being made.

To this, the metaphysical realist would probably respond that the resulting position is still too anti-realistic, and she might enlist what I will label the "Master Realist Argument" (MRA) against Putnam's internal realism. Surely, the metaphysical realist reasons, there existed a world *long before* the evolution of any rational species. Long before language, logic, or any ability of a sentient being to verify *any* statement, there were still facts about the world, such as, *that dinosaurs roamed the earth*, or *that neutrino stars had such-and-such mass.* Surely anyone in their right mind would agree that such facts were obtained before there were any conceptual schemes or language users. Thus it would also make sense to say that our present statements such as "dinosaurs roamed the earth" or "neutrino stars have such-and-such mass" are made true by these same facts, and *not* by our ability to verify facts, or our ability to conceptualize facts, etc. I believe that it is this MRA that fuels the metaphysical realist's refusal to grant Putnam's arguments, however ingenious they may be. To this, however, I believe that Putnam has a compelling response. First of all, as we shall see in Section 2.8, "Conceptual Relativity," Putnam does not believe that we can make sense of the notion of a "totality of facts" prior to the adoption of a conceptual scheme or a decision *we make* as to how to carve the world into separable "facts." Thus, while we might agree that there was a world prior to the evolution of rational beings or conceptual schemes, it is not quite as *obvious* that there were clearly demarcated "facts," as the metaphysical realist assumes. Secondly, it might be helpful to recall that while the world exists independently of language, the world itself is neither true nor false. *Sentences* (or thoughts) are true and false, and "while it is true that the stars would still have existed even if language users had not evolved, it is not the case that sentences would have existed. There would have still been a world, but there would not have been any truths."[28] Thus, there are no truths until language users evolve, and we cannot make sense of a notion of "fact" as something "out there" independently of our choice of a conceptual scheme. Given our *current* conceptual scheme, of course, we can say that stars existed prior to the evolution of language users and conceptual schemes. But it would not make any sense to say that stars existed independently of any conceptual scheme whatsoever.

The qualifications that Putnam has made to his internal realist view of truth has, however, pulled him away from Kant to a more realistic perspective. In his next book, *The Many Faces of Realism* (1987), Putnam states that he should have called his view "pragmatic realism," and he is concerned there to defend a commonsense realism about objects in the external world. And in a series of writings after that, he abandons the verificationist semantics of his middle period, returning to a fully truth-conditional account of meaning, but one interpreted through a realist reading of the later Wittgenstein. This move will be discussed in the Section 3.3, "Problems of Perception." For now I want to turn to two of Putnam's arguments against metaphysical realism that he has clearly *not* rejected—the BIVs argument, and the argument from Conceptual Relativity.

2.7. THE BRAINS IN A VAT ARGUMENT

The BIV scenario is an illustration of global or Cartesia skepticism: you are told to imagine the possibility that at this very moment you are actually a brain hooked up to a sophisticated computer program that can perfectly simulate experiences of the outside world. Here is the skeptical argument. If you cannot now be sure that you are not a BIV, then you cannot rule out the possibility that all of your beliefs about the external world are false. Or, to put it in terms of knowledge claims, we can construct the following skeptical argument. Let "P" stand for any belief or claim about the external world, say, that snow is white.

(1) If I know that P, then I know that I am not a BIV
(2) I do not know that I am not a BIV
(3) Thus, I do not know that P.

The BIVs Argument is usually taken to be a modern version of René Descartes' argument (in the *Meditations on First Philosophy*) that centers on the possibility of an evil demon who systematically deceives us. The hypothesis has been the premise behind the movie *The Matrix*, in which the entire human race has been placed into giant vats and fed a virtual reality at the hands of malignant artificial intelligence (our own creations, of course).

In Putnam's eyes, the significance of the BIVs scenario consists in the fact that the global skepticism it illustrates is implied by metaphysical realism: for it depicts a situation where all of our beliefs about the world could be false, even though they are well justified. Thus if one can prove that we cannot be BIVs, by *modus tollens* one can prove that metaphysical realism is false. Or, to put it in more schematic form:

(1) If metaphysical realism is true, then global skepticism is possible
(2) If global skepticism is possible, then we can be BIVs
(3) But we cannot be BIVs (BIVs argument)
(4) Thus, metaphysical realism is false (1, 2, 3).

In what follows, I will focus mostly on claim (3), though as we shall see there are some philosophers who would question (2), insofar as there may be ways of presenting the skeptical thesis even while granting Putnam's argument.

2.7.1. Putnam's Argument

The major premise that underwrites Putnam's argument is what he calls a "causal constraint" (CC) on reference:

(CC) A term refers to an object only if there is an appropriate causal connection between that term and the object

To understand this criterion we need to unravel what is meant by "appropriate causal connection." If an ant were to accidentally draw a picture of Winston Churchill in the sand, few would claim that the ant represented or referred to Churchill. Similarly, if I accidentally sneeze "Genghis Khan," just because I verbalize the words does not mean that I refer to the infamous Mongolian conqueror, for I may have never heard of him before. Reference cannot simply be an *accident*: or, as Putnam puts it, words do not refer to objects "magically" or intrinsically. Now establishing just what *would* count as necessary and sufficient conditions for a term to refer to an object turns out to be tricky business, and there have been many "causal theories" of reference supplied to do just that. Many have taken the virtue of Putnam's constraint (CC) to be its generality: it merely states a necessary condition for reference and need not entail anything more controversial. Sometimes it is claimed that endorsing (CC) commits you to semantic externalism but the issues are more complex, since many internalists (e.g., John Searle) appear to agree with (CC). The relation between externalism and Putnam's argument will be considered in more detail later (in Section 2.6.3, "Brains in a Vat and Self-Knowledge").

With the (CC) established, Putnam goes on to describe the BIV scenario. It is important to note exactly what the thought experiment is, for failure to appreciate the ways in which Putnam has changed the standard skeptical nightmare has lead to many mistaken "refutations" of the argument. The standard picture has a mad scientist (or race of aliens, or AI programs) envatting brains in a laboratory then inducing a virtual reality through a sophisticated computer program. On this picture, there is an important difference between viewing the brains from a first- or third-person viewpoint. There is the point of view of the BIVs, and the point of view of someone outside the vat. Clearly when the mad scientist says "that is a brain in a vat" of a BIV, he would be saying something *true*, no matter the question of what the BIV means when *it* says it is a BIV. Furthermore, presumably a BIV could pick up referential terms by borrowing them from the mad scientist. Thus when a BIV says "there is a tree" referring to a simulation of a tree, it would be saying something *false*, since its term "tree," picked up from the mad scientist to refer to an actual tree, in fact refers to something else, like his sense impressions of the tree. Putnam thus stipulates that *all* sentient beings are BIVs, hooked up to one another through a powerful computer that has no programmer: "that's just how the universe is." We are then asked, given at least the *physical* possibility of this scenario, whether we could say or think it. Putnam answers that we could not: the assertion "we are brains in a vat" would be in a certain sense self-refuting, in the same way that the general statement "all general statements are false" is.

The thought experiment stipulates that BIVs would have qualitatively identical thoughts to those unenvatted or at least, they have the same "notional world." The difference is that in the vat-world, there are no external objects. When a BIV says "there is a tree in front of me" there is in fact no tree in front of him, only a simulated tree programmed by the computer. However, if there are no trees, there could be no causal connection between a BIV's tokens of trees and actual trees. By (CC), "tree" does not refer to tree. This leads to some interesting consequences, however. A standard reading of a BIV's utterance of "there is a tree" would have the statement come out false, since there are no trees for the BIV to refer to. But if "tree" does not refer to tree, then the semantic evaluation of the sentence becomes unclear. Sometimes Putnam suggests that a BIV's tokens refer to images or sense impressions. At other times he agrees with Davidson who claims that the truth conditions would be facts about the electronic impulses of the computer that are causally responsible for producing the sense impressions. Davidson has a good reason to choose these truth conditions: through the principle of charity he would want to interpret the BIV's sentences to come out true, but he would not want the truth conditions to be phenomenalistic. Thus it turns out that when a BIV says "there is a tree in front of me," he is saying something *true*—if in fact the computer is sending the right impulses to him.

Another suggestion is that the truth conditions of the BIV's utterances would be empty: the BIV asserts nothing at all. This seems to be rather strong, however: surely the BIV would mean *something* when it utters "there is a tree in front of me," even if its statement gets evaluated differently because of the radical difference of its environment. One thing is clear, however; a BIV's tokening of "tree" or any other such referential term would have a *different* reference assignment from that of a nonenvatted person's tokenings. According to (CC), my tokening of "tree" refers to trees because there *is* an appropriate causal link between it and actual trees (assuming of course I am not a BIV). A BIV however would not be able to refer to trees since there are no trees (and even if there *were* trees somewhere in the universe there would not be the appropriate causal relation between its tokenings of "tree" and real trees, unless we bring back the standard fantasy and assume it picked up the terms from the mad scientist). Now one might be inclined to think that because there are at least brains and vats in the universe, a BIV would be able to refer to brains and vats. But the tokening of "brain" is never actually caused by a brain except only in the very indirect sense that its brain causes *all* of its tokenings. The minimal constraint (CC) then will ensure that "brain" and "vat" in the BIV language does not refer to brain and vat.

We are now in a position to give Putnam's argument. It has the form of a conditional proof:

(1) Assume we are BIVs
(2) If we are BIVs, then "brain" does not refer to brain, and "vat" does not refer to vat (via CC)
(3) If "brain in a vat" does not refer to BIVs, then "we are brains in a vat" is false
(4) Thus, if we are BIVs, "we are brains in a vat" is false (1, 2, 3).

Putnam adds that "we are brains in a vat" is *necessarily* false, since whenever we assume it is true we can deduce its contradictory. The argument is valid and its soundness seems to depend on the truth of (3), assuming (CC) is true. One immediate problem is determining the truth conditions for "we are brains in a vat" on the assumption we are BIVs, speaking a variation of English (call it *Vatese*). From (CC) we know that "brains in a vat" does not refer to BIV. But as suggested already, it doesn't follow from this alone that "we are brains in a vat" is false. Compare:

(A) "Grass is green" is true iff grass is green
(B) "Grass is green" is true iff one has sense impressions of grass being green
(C) "Grass is green" is true iff one is in electronic state Q

On the assumption that we are BIVs, (CC) would appear to rule out (A): "grass" does not refer to grass since there is no appropriate causal connection between "grass" and actual grass. Thus the truth conditions for the statement "grass is green" would be nonstandard. If we take them to be those captured in (B), then "Grass is green" as spoken by a BIV would be *true*. Consequently the truth conditions for "we are brains in a vat" would be captured by (D):

(D) "We are brains in a vat" is true iff we have sense-impressions of being BIVs

On this construal of the truth conditions, "we are brains in a vat" as uttered by a BIV would indeed be *false*, since a BIV would *not* have sense impressions of being a BIV: recall a BIV's notional world would be equivalent to the unenvatted, and he would appear to himself to be a normally embodied person with a real body etc. However, if we follow Davidson and adopt the truth conditions of (C), we would have the following:

(E) "We are brains in a vat" is true if and only if we are in electronic state Q

Now it is no longer clear that "we are brains in a vat" is false: for if the brain is in the appropriate electronic state, the truth conditions could well be fulfilled.

There are other reconstructions of the argument that do not depend on specifying the truth conditions of a BIV's utterances. What is important is the idea that the truth conditions would be nonstandard, as in:

(F) "We are brains in a vat" is true if and only if we are BIVs*

Now since being a BIV* (whatever that is) is not the same as being a BIV, we can construct the following conditional proof argument:

(1) Assume we are BIVs
(2) If we are BIVs, "we are brains in a vat" is true if and only we are BIVs*
(3) If we are BIVs, we are not BIVs*
(4) If we are BIVs, then "we are brains in a vat" is false (2, 3)
(5) If we are BIVs, then we are not BIVs (4).

Notice that the argument leaves the antecedent of the conditional open, what Wright calls an "open subjunctive." We do not want the premises of the argument to be counterfactual, following the train of thought "If we *were* brains in a vat, the causal constraint would entail that my words 'brain in a vat' would come to denote something different, BIV*." For then we would be assuming that we are not BIVs, when that is what the argument is supposed to prove.

Nevertheless, there are still problems with the appeal to disquotation (DQ) to get us from (4) to (5). Even if, by virtue of the (CC), the sentence "We are brains in a vat" is false, an intuitive objection runs that this change of language should not entail falsity of the proposition *that we are BIVs*. As we shall see, many recent reconstructions of Putnam's argument are sensitive to this point and try to account for it in various ways. In the following section, I shall focus on two of the more popular reconstructions of the argument put forward by Brueckner (1986) and Wright (1994a).

2.7.2. Other Reconstructions of Argument

Brueckner (1986) argues that even if we grant the reasoning of the above argument up to (4), the most the argument proves is that if we are BIVs, then the sentence "we are brains in a vat" (as uttered by a BIV) is false, and that if we are *not* BIVs, then "we are brains in a vat" is false (now expressing a *different* false proposition). If correct then the argument would prove that whether or not we are BIVs, "we are brains in a vat" expresses *some* false proposition. Assuming the truth conditions of a BIV would be those captured in (D) above we could then devise the following constructive dilemma type argument:

(1) Either I am a BIV or I am not a BIV
(2) If I am a BIV, then "I am a brain in a vat" is true iff I have sense-impressions of being a BIV
(3) If I am a BIV, then I do not have sense impressions of being a BIV
(4) If I am a BIV, then "I am a brain in a vat" is false (2, 3)
(5) If I am not a BIV, then "I am a brain in a vat" is true iff I am a BIV
(6) If I am not a BIV, then "I am a brain in a vat" is false (5)
(7) "I am a brain in a vat" is false (1, 4, 6).

If "I am a brain in a vat" expresses the proposition that I am a BIV, and we know from the argument that "I am a brain in a vat" is false, then it follows that I know I am not a BIV, thus refuting premise (2) of the skeptical argument. However, can I know that "I am a brain in a vat" expresses the proposition that I am a BIV? If I am a BIV, then "I am a brain in a vat" would, via the (CC) on reference, express some different proposition (say, *that I am a BIV in the image*). So even if "I am a brain in a vat" is false whether or not I am a BIV, I might not be in the position to identify *which* false proposition I am expressing, in which case I cannot claim to know that my sentence "I am not a brain in a vat" expresses the true proposition *that I am not a BIV*.

Some philosophers have gone even further, claiming that if the argument ends here, it actually can be used to strengthen skepticism. The metaphysical realist can claim that there are truths not expressible in any language: perhaps the proposition *that we are BIVs* is true, even if no one can meaningfully utter it. As Nagel puts it:

> If I accept the argument, I must conclude that a brain in a vat can't think truly that it is a brain in a vat, even though others can think this about it. What follows? Only that I cannot express my skepticism by saying "Perhaps I am a brain in a vat." Instead I must say "Perhaps I can't even think the truth about what I am, because I lack the necessary concepts and my circumstances make it impossible for me to acquire them!" If this doesn't qualify as skepticism, I don't know what does. (Nagel, 1986)

Putnam makes it clear that he is not merely talking about semantics: he wants to provide a metaphysical argument that we cannot be BIVs, not just a semantic one that we cannot assert we are. If he is just proving something about meaning, it is open for the skeptic to say that the bonds between language and reality can diverge radically, perhaps in ways we can never discern.

There is yet another worry with the argument, centering once again on the appropriate characterization of the truth conditions in (2). If one claimed in response to the above objection that in fact I do know that "I am a brain in a vat" expresses the proposition that I am a BIV (whether or not I am a BIV), one may have in mind some general DQ principle:

(DQ): "Grass is green" is true iff grass is green

If it is an *a priori* truth that any meaningful sentence in my language homophonically disquotes, then we can *a priori* know that the following is also true:

(F): "I am a brain in a vat" is true iff I am a BIV

Here is the obvious problem: if we are not to beg the question, we have to be open to the possibility that we are BIVs, speaking Vatese. Then we would get:

(G): If I am a BIV, then "I am a brain in a vat" is true iff I am a BIV.

(G) however gives us truth conditions that differ from premise (2) of Brueckner's argument:

(2) If I am a BIV, then "I am a brain in a vat" is true iff I have sense impressions of being a BIV

If we assume (CC), then (G) and (2) are inconsistent, since the term "brain in a vat" would refer to distinct entities. No contradiction ensues if we assume we are speaking in English: for then (G) would presumably be false (appealing to CC). But the problem is that we cannot beg the question by assuming we are speaking in English: if we assume that, then we know in advance of any argument that we are not speaking in Vatese and hence that we are not BIVs. But if we do not know which language we are speaking in, then we cannot properly assert (2).

One response to this might be to formulate two different arguments, one whose metalanguage is in English, the other whose metalanguage is in Vatese, and show that distinct arguments can be run to prove that "I am a brain in a vat" is false. Even if successful, however, these arguments run into the objection canvassed before: if I do not know which language I am speaking in, even if I know "I am a brain in a vat" is false, I do not know which false proposition I am expressing and hence cannot infer that I know that I am not a BIV.

Similar worries plague Crispin's Wright's popular formulation of the argument (1994a):

(1) My language disquotes
(2) In BIVese, "brains in a vat" does not refer to brains in a vat

(3) In my language, "brains in a vat" is a meaningful expression
(4) In my language, "brains in a vat" refers to BIVs
(5) My language is not BIVese (2, 4)
(6) If I am a BIV, then my language is BIVese
(7) I am not a BIV.

There are several virtues to this reconstruction: first of all, it gets us to the desired conclusion without specifying what the truth conditions of a BIV's utterances are. They could be sense impressions, facts about electronic impulses, or the BIV's sentences may not refer at all. All that is needed for the argument is that there is a *difference* between the truth conditions for a BIV's sentences and those of my own language. The other virtue of the argument is that it clearly brings out the appeal to the DQ principle that was implicit in the previous arguments. If indeed (DQ) is an *a priori* truth, as many philosophers maintain, and if we accept (CC) as a condition of reference, the argument appears to be sound. So have we proven that we are not BIVs?

Not so fast. The previous objection can be restated: if I do not yet know whether or not I am a BIV before the argument is completed, I do not know which language I am speaking (English or Vatese). If I am speaking Vatese, then so long as it is a meaningful language, I can appeal to (DQ) to establish that "brains in a vat" does refer to BIVs. But this contradicts premise (2). The problem seems to be that (DQ) is being used too liberally. Clearly we do not want to say that *every* meaningful term disquotes in the strong sense required for reference. If so, we could take it to be an *a priori* truth that "Santa Claus" refers to Santa Claus. But "Santa Claus" does not refer to Santa Claus, since there is no Santa Claus. We could introduce a new term "pseudo-reference" and hold that "Santa Claus" *pseudo-refers* to Santa Claus, and then attach further conditions on reference in order to establish what it would take for the term to truly refer. One proposal (Weiss, 2000) is the following principle:

W: If "x" psuedo-refers to x in L, and x exists, then "x" refers to x in L

Thus, given the DQ principle we know that in my language "Santa Claus" pseudo-refers to Santa Claus. Supposing to the joyful adulation of millions that Santa Claus is discovered to actually exist, then given (W) "Santa Claus" refers to Santa Claus. Now this also seems too simplistic: as Putnam pointed out, in order for a term to refer to an object we must establish more than the mere existence of the object. There has to be the *appropriate* causal relation between the word and object, or we are back to claiming that in accidentally sneezing "Genghis Khan" I am referring to Genghis Khan. But whether we accept (W) or attach stronger conditions to reference, it is clear that any such move would make Wright's formulation invalid. For then we would have:

(1) My language disquotes
(2) In BIVese, "brains in a vat" does not refer to BIVs (CC)
(3) In my language "brain in a vat" is a meaningful expression
(4) In my language, "brain in a vat" pseudo-refers to BIVs (DQ)
(5) My language is not BIVese (2, 4)
(6) If I am a BIV, then my language is BIVese
(7) I am not a BIV.

(5) no longer follows from (2) and (4) given the ambiguity of "refers" in (2) and (4). If on the other hand we insist on a univocal sense of reference, then either (2) will contradict the (DQ) principle, or we are not entitled to appeal to (1), insofar as it would beg the question that we are speaking English, a language for which the (DQ) principle applies.

2.7.3. Brains in a Vat and Self-Knowledge

Ted Warfield (1995) has recently sought to provide an argument that we are not BIVs based on considerations of self-knowledge. He defends two premises that seem reasonably true then argues for the desired metaphysical conclusion:

(1) I think that water is wet
(2) No BIV can think that water is wet
(3) Thus, I am not a BIV (2, 3).

Premise (1) is said to follow from the thesis of privileged access, which holds that we can at least know the contents of our own occurring thoughts without empirical investigation of our environment or behavior. Warfield's strategy is to present each premise as nonquestion begging against the global skeptic, in which case at no point can we appeal to the external environment as justification. Since the thesis of privileged access is said to be known *a priori* whether we are BIVs or not, premise (1) can be known nonempirically.

Premise (2) is a little trickier to establish nonempirically. The main argument for it is by analogy with other arguments in the literature that have been used to establish content externalism. The main strategy is derived from Putnam's Twin Earth argument: if Oscar and his twin mean different things by "water" then they have different concepts and beliefs: Oscar would believe *that water is wet* whereas Twin-Oscar would believe *that twin-water is wet*. If we accept content externalism, then the motivation for (2) is as follows. In order for someone's belief to be about water, there must be water in that person's environment: externalism rejects the Cartesian idea that one can simply read off one's belief internally (if so then we would have to say that Oscar and his twin have the same beliefs since they are internally the same). So it doesn't seem possible that a BIV could ever come to hold a belief about *water* (unless of course he picked up the term from the mad scientist or someone outside the vat, but here we must assume again Putnam's scenario that there is no mad scientist or anyone else he could have borrowed the term from). As Warfield puts it, premise (2) is a conceptual truth, established on the basis of Twin Earth style arguments, a matter of "armchair" *a priori* reflection and thus able to be established nonempirically.

The problem with establishing (2) nonempirically though is that the externalist arguments succeed only on the assumption that our own use of "water" refers to a substantial kind, and this seems to be a matter of empirical investigation. Imagine a world where "water" does not refer to any liquidy substance but is rather a complex hallucination that never gets discovered. On this "Dry Earth," "water" would not refer to a substantial kind but rather a superficial kind. The analogy to the BIV case is clear: since it is not an *a priori* truth that "water" refers to a substantial kind in the BIV's language, it cannot be known nonempirically that "water" is substantial or superficial; if it is a superficial kind, then a BIV could very well think that water is wet so long as it has the relevant sense impressions.

2.7.4. Significance of Putnam's Argument

A close analysis of Putnam's argument has revealed that its appeal to disquotation is question begging, and hence that its attempt to provide an a priori argument against the global skeptic fails. Some philosophers have claimed that even if Putnam's argument is sound, it doesn't do much to dislodge Cartesian or global skepticism. Crispin Wright (1994) argues that the argument does not affect certain versions of the Cartesian nightmare, such as my brain being taken out of my skull last night and hooked up to a computer. Someone of a Positivist bent might argue that if there is no empirical evidence to appeal to in order to establish whether we are BIVs or not, then the hypothesis is meaningless, in which case we do not need an argument to refute it. While few philosophers today would hold onto such a strong verifiability theory of meaning, many would maintain that such metaphysical possibilities do not amount to real cases of doubt and thus can be summarily dismissed. Still others see the possibility of being a BIV an important challenge for cognitive science and the attempt to create a computer model of the world that can simulate human cognition. Dennett (1991), for example, has argued that it is physically impossible for a BIV to replicate the qualitative phenomenology of a nonenvatted human being. Nevertheless, one should hesitate before making possibility claims when it comes to future technology. And as films like the *Matrix*, *Existenz*, and even the *Truman Show* indicate, the idea of living in a simulated world indistinguishable from the real one is likely to continue to fascinate the human mind for many years to come—whether or not it is a BIV.

2.8. CONCEPTUAL RELATIVITY

We have seen that on Putnam's construal, metaphysical realism is committed to a "fixed totality of mind-independent objects," what Bernard Williams calls the "absolute conception of the world" and what Nagel calls the "objective perspective." The view goes hand in hand with scientific naturalism which supposes that there is a unique set of physical facts "out there" waiting to be uncovered by the methods of the natural sciences. Gilbert Harman perhaps speaks most eloquently on behalf of this perspective:

> I confess that I still feel the attraction of metaphysical realism. I can't help but think that yes, there is a single world out there,

a single causal explanatory order, a world which is as it is, quite apart from what anyone says or thinks about it . . . indeed truth involves a relation between a remark or thought and the way things are in the world.[29]

This reference to a "single causal explanatory order" confirms Putnam's description of metaphysical realism as adhering to the "uniqueness thesis," according to which there is a determinate set of things that exist independently of the human mind. Elsewhere Putnam calls this a "ready-made world": a world that has clearly demarcated objects and properties that do not depend in any way on human description or classification.

This uniqueness thesis is directly challenged by Putnam's arguments for conceptual relativity. Putnam argues that there can be no sense attached to a "basic ontology of the world" given that there are a number of incompatible ways to divide the world into objects, reflecting conceptual choices made from different background theories. Putnam's tactic is to refer to specific examples: in "Realism and Reason" he takes the example of a "straight line." There are two different stories we can tell: first, we can say that the line consists of points from which line segments are constructed, or we can say that the line consists of line segments and that points are logical constructions out of these segments. Is there some determinate fact of the matter as to what the line really consists of? No, for there is no justification for privileging one true description over the other. Another example Putnam gives from *Representation and Reality* (1988) concerns mereology, where he imagines taking "someone into a room with a chair, a table on which there are a lamp and a notebook and a ballpoint pen, nothing else, and I ask 'How many objects are there in this room?' My companion answers, let us suppose 'five'" (p. 110). But suppose we take a mereological view according to which for any two particulars there is an object which is their sum. Then there would be an object that is the mereological sum of my nose and lamp—in which case there would be more than five objects in the room. Given these different ways of counting how many objects there are, there is no nonarbitrary way of settling exactly *what* objects there are in the room.

Given the fact that "object" itself is theory relative, Putnam would not accept the standard metaphysical response that we could talk about "the same thing" by giving two different descriptions. Related to this is what Putnam calls the "cookie cutter" response of the metaphysical realist, according to which there is one noumenal dough "out there" but different cookies depending on the shapes and sizes of our cookie cutters (concepts). This is just a metaphor, but it teeters on incoherence once we ask "what are the pieces of the dough?" If the realist answers this question, then she is privileging one story over another, against the phenomenon of conceptual relativity. If the realist just continues to insist there is a mind-independent reality but cannot specify at all what it is, then reality becomes an unknowable and indescribable *ding an sich*. If that is the corner the metaphysical realist is driven into, then Putnam has clearly won this round.

Perhaps this point could be thrown into bolder relief if we consider Barry Stroud's recent argument in his *The Quest for Reality* (2001). Part of the "metaphysical quest" Stroud draws attention to concerns whether or not ordinary objects are *really* colored. According to commonsense, objects really do have the colors they appear to have; hence, leaves are typically green, oranges are yellow, and the sky is blue. However, according to the "absolute conception of the world," or from the standpoint of physics, secondary qualities like colors are not objective features of the world and would not be mentioned as legitimate properties of objects (unlike measurable qualities like momentum and frequency). Stroud believes that the question of whether commonsense or science is correct on this point is a significant one and he criticizes the view of P. F. Strawson, who claims that there is no contradiction between commonsense and science.[30] Echoing Putnam's argument for conceptual relativity, Strawson argues that commonsense and science can both be correct, since they populate the world with objects from different perspectives (Putnam's "conceptual schemes"). The question as to whether objects are *really* colored makes no sense, for it *assumes* that there is some point of view independently of these different perspectives which could decide the case. Stroud responds that we can't say of the *same objects* in the world that they are both colored and not colored—it has to be one or the other, hence there is a real conflict between commonsense and science.[31] But this ignores Putnam's point that we cannot ask whether a thing is colored at all without specifying a discourse or scheme whose objects we are talking about. If the very notion of an object is relative to a scheme, we cannot appeal to some neutral concept of object from which to say that the commonsense and scientific perspectives contradict one another.

Putnam's claim that objects are "relative to a conceptual scheme" can easily lead to misunderstandings, however. We find Donald Davidson, for example, arguing that Putnam's conceptual relativity falls prey to his criticism of the scheme/content distinction (Davidson's "third dogma of empiricism"). As Davidson writes, his own "coherence theory of truth" is "not Putnam's internal realism nor his metaphysical realism. It is not internal realism because internal realism makes truth relative to a scheme, and this is an idea I do not think is intelligible." However, it seems that Davidson's viewpoint simply reiterates Putnam's *rejection* of the cookie cutter metaphor, according to which there is some external world of things "out there" which then gets carved up into different descriptions depending on different internal schemes. As we have seen, Putnam rejects this metaphor since it presumes that there is some intelligible notion of an "external thing" independently of our descriptions. For Davidson, the scheme-content distinction is unintelligible since it suggests that there can be schemes that are so different as to be untranslatable. Putnam, however, has been one of the biggest critics of "incommensurable schemes" in the philosophy of science and we have seen elsewhere that he affirms the norm of the principle of charity,[32] which aims to maximize agreement when interpreting another person's utterances. More recently Putnam has argued that there is still a sense in which we can talk about "different conceptual schemes," since, while no two languages are completely untranslatable, there may be elements of those languages that are.[33] Putnam gives as an example the Shawnee term which gets translated as "fork-shaped pattern." When we say "I have an extra toe on my foot," the Shawnee would express this by saying something like "I fork-tree on toes (have)." Here interpretation is not simply a matter of translation, since English had no expression for "fork-shaped pattern" prior to the discovery of the Shawnee language. What Davidson assumes is that translation leaves the language into which we translate unaffected, which seems incorrect. The Shawnees *do* have a different ontology, as reflected in their language, even if this ontology can indeed be grasped by us once we add it to our own language.

Seeing that his comments on "conceptual schemes" could lead to misunderstanding, Putnam has endorsed Jennifer Case's suggestion that "what Putnam refers to as 'conceptual schemes' are not really schemes of distinct concepts but rather linguistic schemes distinguished primarily by their divergent ways of extending shared concepts."[34] The reference to "shared concepts" here is meant to imply that there is a basic language we all speak given our common linguistic practices, but that we can extend this language in various ways given different contextual purposes to create what Case calls "optional languages." This clarification puts to rest the criticism that on Putnam's view, every conceptual scheme has an incompatible alternative, such that conceptual relativity would apply to *every* statement we make. In keeping with his more pragmatic perspective, Putnam states that we are *not* free to abandon our common discourse about everyday objects like trees and tables. Rather, optional languages include various scientific images of the world, including mereology and the language of particle physics—but we can use ordinary language *and* such scientific descriptions "without being required to reduce one or both of them to some fundamental and universal ontology." This is part and parcel of Putnam's pragmatic pluralism, according to which we can adopt various vocabularies—scientific, religious, aesthetic, and moral—without requiring to judge or criticize them from some perspective outside those discourses.[35] It is important to note, however, that there can be rational criticism from *within* an optional language—hence there can be a debate within religion over the best way to characterize the nature of God. What we should not do is take the method of the natural sciences—a different and incommensurate optional language—and use that to judge the claims of another optional language.

2.9. CONCLUSION

In this chapter I have argued that Putnam's semantic externalism, with its emphasis on the social nature of reference, is more consistent with internal realism than metaphysical realism, and that this is one of the reasons that Putnam adopted the former and abandoned the latter. Furthermore, we can retain the most important features of scientific realism—reference to theoretical entities and arguments against incommensurability—without appealing to a notion of truth as correspondence or as a causal-explanatory notion. Putnam's first two arguments against metaphysical realism—the Model-Theoretic argument and BIVs—are problematic insofar as they are seen as *a priori* arguments against the skeptic.

Putnam's best argument, and one that points to his newfound pragmatic pluralism, is the argument from conceptual relativity. All of our statements about the world, even those that can be called metaphysical realist, are made from a particular perspective, and there is no sense in being able to peer at the way things "really are" outside the veil of language and its various norm-governed discourses. In the next chapter, we shall see that exactly the same criticisms can be launched against those who believe that they are capturing the "essence" of the mind. As Kant showed long ago in his Paralogisms, the collapse of the absolute perspective applies equally to inner sense as it does to outer sense.

CHAPTER 3

MIND, BODY, AND WORLD

3.1. THE RISE OF FUNCTIONALISM

When Putnam first came on the philosophical scene in the late 1950s, there were basically two respectable options one could take in the philosophy of mind—behaviorism and type identity theory (also called "central state materialism" and now sometimes called "Australian materialism") Both of these positions were formulated as scientific alternatives to Cartesian dualism and both of them were forms of reductionism: logical behaviorism sought to reduce talk about the mind to talk about overt behavior, and type identity sought an ontological reduction of mental states to neurophysiological states of the brain. Both of these theories had problems concerning their particular brands of reductionism, and also with the notoriously intractable problem of phenomenal states (such as feeling pain or sensing the color red). The most serious objection to type identity theory did not come until Putnam's "multiple realizability argument" in his 1967 "The Nature of Mental States." And the main alternative to these two theories was also not formulated until Putnam outlined his computational functionalism in that same article and others. Functionalism quickly became the dominant viewpoint in the philosophy of mind, though it is currently in decline due partly to Putnam's own critique of his earlier theory. To chart the rise and fall of functionalism is particularly instructive in the context of Putnam's recent critique of scientific naturalism, but we will also ask what, if any, picture of the mind can be salvaged from this critique.

In the late 1950s behaviorism as a theory within psychology and linguistics was under heavy attack by Noam Chomsky, Jerome Bruner, and other pioneers of what has been called the "cognitive revolution." Chomsky famously remarked that defining psychology as the study of human behavior was like defining physics as the study of meter readings.[1] His own syntactic theory in linguistics drew attention away from performance (verbal behavior) toward competence (those grammatical rules in the mind that explained the verbal behavior). Simultaneously, psychologists were turning toward the computer as a possible model for explaining certain cognitive processes. These efforts perhaps reached a crescendo in the conference on artificial intelligence in 1956 attended by Claude Shannon, Marvin Minsky, John McCarthy, and others—also, Chomsky's *Syntactic Structures* was published in the same year. The idea of using the computer as a model of the mind was appealing from a psychological point of view, due to the phenomenon of "reverse engineering." In short, if we could program a computer to carry out an intelligent piece of reasoning, that could shed some insight into how the human mind is able to intelligently reason. It didn't take long before someone realized that the computer model could prove instructive not just in psychology but in philosophy as well. Perhaps it could even solve (or dissolve) the mind/body problem, one of the great philosophical puzzles since at least the time of Descartes.

One formulation of the mind/body problem is a variant of the old saw that you can pour water on the brain but not on the mind. That is, mental states seem to have properties that are radically different from physical states—they are invisible, introspectable, and nonlocalizable—occurring in time but not in space. Since one and the same thing cannot have contradictory properties, mental states cannot be identified with physical states. On the other had, if mental states are ontologically distinct from physical states, by virtue of what mechanism can they interact with one another? How can something that is not in space causally affect something in space, as it presumably does when our beliefs and desires cause us to act in various ways? To put the problem in Cartesian terms, various commonsense arguments support the view that there is a "soul" or mental substance in addition to the physical body, but our current understanding of science seems to allow no role for such souls to exist within or interact with, the physical world as we know it.

This alleged problem, however, can seem to dissolve when we think of the computer as a model of the mind. And in Putnam's "Mind and Machines," first published in 1960, Putnam uses an analogy between minds and machines to argue that "the various issues and puzzles that make up the traditional mind-body problem are wholly linguistic and logical in character . . . all the issues arise in connection with any computation system capable of answering questions about its own structure" (p. 362). The machine model that Putnam takes as analogous to the human mind is a Turing machine. A Turing machine consists of a long tape divided into squares and a scanner that can move one square at a time: it has four basic functions; it can move to the left or right, print a symbol, or erase a symbol. Despite the rudimentary nature of such a machine, it can be proven that it can perform any computation whatsoever, if given enough time.[2] A simple example of a Turing machine would be a program which writes out the sequence "111" after scanning three blank squares. The behavior of such a machine can be completely characterized by the following flow chart or "machine table."

	State 1	State 2	State 3
B	write 1; stay in state 1	write 1; stay in state 2	write 1; stay in state 3
1	go right; go to state 2	go right; go to state 3	[halt]

The table states that if the machine is in state 1 and scans a blank square (B), it will print a *1* and remain in state 1. If it is in state 1 and reads a *1*, it will move one square to the right and go into state 2. If it is in state 2 and reads a *B*, it will print a *1* and stay in state 2. If it's in state 2 and reads a *1*, it will move one square to the right and go into state 3. Finally, if it is in state 3 and reads a *B*, it prints a *1* and remains in state 3. The important thing to emphasize here is that behavior of the machine is accurately captured by giving the machine table, and yet we have not specified any part of the machine's physical hardware in doing so. Putnam believes there is an important analogy between a machine and the human mind. The machine itself can be described in two different ways: first there are the physical parts that compose it—the electronic components that enable the machine to carry out its program, that is, the "hardware level" of description. Then there is the machine table or its program, the "software level" of description. But the human being also can be described in analogous terms: there is the hardware level of the brain with its neuron firings, but "it would be possible to seek a more abstract description of human mental processes in terms of 'mental states' . . . a system which would specify the laws governing the succession of the machine's logical states" (p. 373). In other words, it would be possible to construct a machine table to explain human behavior as well as a machine's behavior. It is a short step from here to machine functionalism, and in Putnam's subsequent articles he explicitly identifies a mental state with a functional state of a system which is causally responsible for producing a certain output given a certain input and other states that the system is in. For example, the state of being in pain could be characterized by that internal state which produces "ouch" when there is a physical damage to the body and no occurrent pain-suppressing desires. In principle we could characterize every mental state by its place in the machine table, and we could add a rational preference matrix to make the model probabilistic rather than deterministic, thus more realistically accounting for actual human behavior.

In "Minds and Machines" Putnam did not yet outline a theory of the human mind—his main point in making the analogy between the mind and the machine is to cast doubt on the mind/body problem as traditionally conceived. Suppose I observe an orange afterimage and at the same time I observe a brain scan showing my neurons being stimulated. It would seem that I am observing two different facts here, not one. This could be used as an argument for dualism, insofar as it seems we cannot identify the sensation with the neuron stimulation. However, a Turing machine would be in a similar situation: it could state "I am in state A" and at the same time print out "flip-flop 32 is on," referring to its hardware. If the dualist argument were successful in the human case, by analogy it would be successful in the machine case, and then we will "have to be prepared to hug the souls of Turing machines to (our) philosophical bosoms" (p. 376). Surely something has gone wrong with the dualist argument to produce such an absurd conclusion! Against Putnam, one could insist that the machine is simply printing out "I am in state A": it isn't *really* experiencing anything. But this misses the whole point of Putnam's argument, which has nothing to do with the problem of consciousness. The point is that any argument a human being can give for distinguishing between sensations and brain states, a robot could give for distinguishing between its "sensations" and brain states.[3] Regardless of whether it "really is" conscious or not, the robot can correctly say something like "I am in internal state A but I do not know that flip-flop 72 is on." Psychological predicates are not the same as physical predicates, but this is not a point that argues for any ontological conclusion since it really only has to do with the "logic" or "language" of psychology. In his 1967 articles "The Mental Life of Some Machines" and "The Nature of Mental Events," Putnam takes this analogy between minds and machines one step further and outlines the theory of mind that has since come to be known as "machine functionalism" or "computational functionalism." Putnam presents his theory as one that can incorporate the strengths of behaviorism and type identity theory while avoiding their shortcomings. Consider the metaphysical question "what is a pain?" The dualist answers that it is an unpleasant conscious experience taking place in an immaterial soul. The behaviorist says that pain is a disposition: a disposition to say "ouch" when pricked by a sharp object, for example. The identity theorist responds that pain is in fact a brain state, and that such an identity can explain why pain states are correlated with certain C-fiber stimulations. Neither behaviorism nor identity theory *need* deny that pain is accompanied by a subjective conscious experience.[4] They could concede the obvious phenomenology, while insisting that pain *ontologically* does not refer to any internal state (behaviorism) or that it refers essentially to an internal brain state (identity theory). Functionalism falls in with these theories to the extent that it also does not identify pain with some inner experience (though it too can hold that pain *involves* conscious experience). Rather, it identifies pain with an internal state, as identity theory does, but it argues that identity theory has picked the wrong kind of internal state. Thus Putnam writes, "I shall argue that pain is not a brain state, in the sense of a physical-chemical state of the brain (or even the whole nervous system), but another kind of state entirely. I propose the hypothesis that pain, or the state of being in pain, is a functional state of the whole organism."[5] As we shall see, identifying pains with brain states fails because it seeks reduction at the hardware or physical level, while a satisfactory theory of the mind will seek reduction at the software or functional level of organization.

Putnam's most famous argument against identity theory, his "multiple realizability" argument, also serves as an indirect argument for functionalism. To lay the context for this argument, it is important to see exactly what kind of identity is being proposed by the identity theorist. On a weak construal, to say that "every mental event is a physical event" is simply to say that every event that has a mental property has some physical property. Thus, to say that I am in pain means that I am in some physical state, but it is not specified *what* kind of physical state. This is called "token physicalism" insofar it holds that every tokening of a mental event type can be identified with a tokening of a physical event type. A stronger identity thesis would hold that every type of mental event is identical with a type of physical event. Thus, the property of being in pain is identified with a specific physical property, such as the property of C-fiber stimulation. Unlike token identity, which only claims that the mental event is identical to some physical event, type identity specifies what this physical event is (by specifying the property instantiating the event). If type identity is true, then whenever an organism x is in a state of pain, there is some specific neurophysiological state it must be in. Note that most mind/brain identity theorists advocate this stronger kind of identity, insofar as they hold that mind/brain identity is analogous to other "theoretical identities" in science, such as "water is H_2O" or "lightning is electrical discharge."[6] The virtue of this proposal is that we can retain the *conceptual* distinction between the mental and physical while retaining the important *ontological* reduction of the mental to the physical. That is, someone can know that water is wet without inferring that H_2O is wet, despite the fact that water is H_2O, if they do not *know* that water is H_2O. The meaning of "water" is different from the meaning of "H_2O" even though "water is H_2O" is a true identity statement. Similarly, I can be in pain without knowing that I am in a certain brain state. This does indeed show that the meaning of "pain" is different from the meaning of "brain state." But for all that it may still be true that, ontologically speaking, pain *is* a brain state.

Putnam showed however that this ontological reduction is on shaky ground. The hypothesis that every psychological state is a brain state sets itself up for plausible counterexamples. As Putnam puts it, "if we can find even one psychological predicate which can be clearly applied to both a mammal and an octopus (say 'hungry') but whose physical-chemical 'correlate' is different in the two cases, the brain-state theory has collapsed" (p. 435). We can thus construct the following "multiple realizability" argument against the identity theorist:

(1) If mind/brain identity-theory is true, then whenever two organisms are in the same mental state they must be in the same brain state
(2) But it is possible for two organisms to be in the same mental state and in different brain states
  (a) An octopus and a human being may both be in pain but have different biochemistries
  (b) An alien and a human being may be both in pain but aliens do not have anything that even appears brain like
  (c) A robot and a human being may both share a certain belief but the robot is composed of inorganic, silicon materials
  (d) Two human beings may be in the same mental state and yet in different brain states
(3) Therefore, mind/brain identity-theory is false.

The problem with type identity is that it is overwhelmingly probable that there can be (and are) organisms or systems that have similar psychological constitutions but very dissimilar physical constitutions. There are various ways to explain this, from an empirical point of view. For example, if we accept the doctrine of evolutionary convergence, psychological similarities among different species may often reflect convergent environmental selection rather than underlying physiological similarities.[7] In response, type identity theorists suggested that we could construe identity as holding between a mental state and a brain state *within a species*. Thus, as David Lewis puts it, "a reasonable brain-state theorist would anticipate that pain might well be one brain state in the case of men, and some other brain (or non-brain) state in the case of mollusks. It might even be one brain state in the case of Putnam, another in the case of Lewis."[8] However, this response fails to address (d) above, the plasticity of the brain even within a species. It is well known that certain parts of the brain can take over the function of other parts when there are injuries or accidents to the brain. And in any case, it has proven difficult if not impossible to localize specific mental events in the brain even if there has been success in localizing more general cognitive functions. These empirical facts suggest that the kind of one-to-one correlations between mental states and brain states are not forthcoming. On the other hand, if we take up Lewis's suggestion that mind-brain identities can only be had within each individual, we give up the idea that there can be a general theory of mind at all—there would only be psychological theories for each individual! Surely this is not a good result for psychology as a scientific discipline.

The multiple realizability objection to type identity leads to a positive argument for functionalism, insofar as the basic idea of functionalism is that the mind should not be described in terms of the physical stuff that realizes it, but in terms of what it does (what its function is). The idea is taken from other concepts that are defined functionally: take a hammer, for example. Something can be a hammer whether it is made out of plastic, metal, or wood, so long as it performs its function, banging in nails. Or something is a kidney if it fulfills the role in filtering blood and maintaining certain chemical balances: if an artificial kidney can do that, it is a kidney. The same thing is true of a mental state: it does not matter what physical stuff carries out the functional role, it's the functional role itself that is definitive of the state: thus if you replaced a neuron with a silicon chip, but the same inputs and outputs and other states of the system remained the same, functionalism would say that the mental state remained unchanged. The mind-brain identity theorist would have to say, implausibly, that there was a change merely because of the difference in the underlying physical composition.

Putnam's specific brand of functionalism, computational functionalism, is not only compatible with, but entails multiple realizability. As Putnam puts it,

> our mental states, e.g., thinking about next summer's vacation, cannot be identical with any physical or chemical states. For it is clear from what we already know about computers etc., that whatever the program of the brain may be, it must be physically possible, though not necessarily feasible, to produce something with that same program but quite a different physical or chemical constitution.[9]

If thinking is what makes a mind, and thinking is computation, then a mind may be best conceived of as a software program that can run on any number of different machines. If we are to have a general theory of the mind, then, it would be about this software level of programming, and not about the hardware level where the program states are physically realized in the machine. This is the basic program of cognitive science: we can have a science devoted to cognition because cognition has its own properties that can be studied independently of the other sciences (biology, chemistry, physics). In this way, then, Putnam's computationalism formed an integral part of the cognitive science revolution, and some have gone so far as to claim that computationalism provides the "foundation" for cognitive science.[10]

Putnam's computational functionalism allows psychology to be a more or less autonomous field of inquiry, whereas type identity theory in effect reduces psychology to biology and chemistry. At the same time, Putnam's brand of functionalism is able to do justice to certain insights of type identity theory, at least when contrasted with behaviorism. First of all, computational functionalism affirms that behavior is to be explained in terms of internal states of the organism. And while these internal events are functional states of the organism and not brain states, functionalism can preserve at least a weak version of the identity theory, namely, token physicalism. The functionalist can affirm with physicalism that all events are physical events. Thus, every mental event is identical with some physical event (this token identity implies Davidson's notion of the supervenience of the mental on the physical: there can be no mental change without a corresponding physical change). However, various physical events can serve as realizers of one and the same mental property. On the computational model, we can explain how mental events can cause physical events while still preserving the distinction between the mental and the physical.[11] In effect, computational functionalism preserves the commonsense aspects of the Cartesian picture (the causal interaction of the mental and physical, the autonomy of the mental), while avoiding its pitfalls (the mind as an immaterial substance).

Computational functionalism can also be seen to incorporate some of the strengths of behaviorism without suffering any of its weaknesses. Compare and contrast the following characterizations of behaviorism and functionalism:

Behaviorism: mental state is a disposition to produce a certain output (say "ouch") given a certain input (say, a pin prick)
Functionalism: mental state is that internal state that produces a certain output (say "ouch") given a certain input (say, a pin prick), and given other internal states.

Like behaviorism, functionalism explicitly characterizes mental states in terms of inputs and outputs. Unlike behaviorism, functionalism holds that mental states are internal states and that these internal states are the key *explanans* in explaining behavior. This delivers it from one of the main problems of behaviorism, that it cannot explain behavior in terms of mental states, since mental states are themselves explained in terms of behavior. Furthermore, mental states are characterized not merely in terms of stimulus/response, but also in terms of other states that the organism or system is in. This "holism of the mental" responds to some fatal defects of behaviorism that Putnam pointed out in his article "Brains and Behavior" (1967). According to behaviorism, someone is in a state of pain if and only if they are disposed to produce typical pain behavior given typical pain stimuli. However, we can well imagine a community of "super Spartans" who are trained to never display any pain behavior when they feel pain. Furthermore, it is possible to imagine an actor who can display all the behavioral dispositions of pain and yet feel no pain at all. These counterexamples to behaviorism are handled by functionalism, since the behavioral outputs depend not merely on the input but other states the system is in. The super-Spartan's pain is related to other mental states (such as the desire to suppress his pain), hence his behavior would differ accordingly. And the pain behavior of the actor is explained by other mental states, such as his desire to fool the audience.

It is no surprise that functionalism quickly became the leading theory of the mind, since it seems to remedy the deficiencies in Cartesian dualism, type identity theory, and behaviorism, while retaining salient features from all three. However, Putnam's particular brand of computational functionalism soon came under attack, with some of the most penetrating criticisms coming from Putnam himself. As we shall see yet again, Putnam's own semantic views, especially his semantic externalism, prove to be of central importance in this issue as well. More specifically, externalism will imply that intentionality cannot be characterized in functionalist terms.

3.2. THE FALL OF COMPUTATIONAL FUNCTIONALISM

The most common objections to functionalism can be grouped into three categories: (1) *Phenomenal Critique*: functionalism cannot adequately account for qualitative properties or "raw feels" like experiencing pain, or sensing the color red; (2) *Semantic Critique*: functionalism cannot provide a reductive account of intentionality due to certain features of meaning (in particular, meaning holism and semantic externalism); (3) *Realization Critique*: functionalism is too "liberal" a theory insofar as many (if not all!) systems can be said to realize functional organizations and yet not possess any kind of mentality. Unsurprisingly, it is Putnam himself who is most responsible for original formulations of each of these objections.

3.2.1. Phenomenal Critique of Functionalism

Standard criticisms of behaviorism and type identity theory involved the problem of phenomenal properties like experiencing pain or sensing a certain color. It was deemed wrong by many to identify a sensation like pain with a behavioral disposition or a brain state, since the essence of such a state seems to be the conscious experience itself.[12] The same criticism can be directed against functionalism insofar as it identifies the "essential nature" of a state like being in pain with a functional state rather than the unpleasant conscious experience. To motivate this objection, various thought experiments have been proposed. Here is one conceived by Putnam himself in *Reason, Truth and History* (1981): suppose that you wake up and everything that once appeared red to you now appears blue. However, in order to conform to society's usage, you continue to call red things "red" even though they now appear qualitatively blue. If someone asked you and another person "what does this sweater look like?" you would both give the same answer: "it is a red sweater." According to functionalism, both of you would be in identical functional states, and yet by hypothesis you would be experiencing different *qualia*: he is experiencing red while you are experiencing blue. Putnam then writes:

> Now suppose we adopted the following functionalist theory of subjective color: a sensation is a sensation of blue (i.e. has the qualitative character that I now describe in that way) just in case the sensation (or corresponding physical event in the brain) has the role of signalling objective blue in the environment. This theory captures one sense of the phrase "sensation of blue," but not the desired qualitative sense. If the functional role were identical with the qualitative character, one couldn't say that the quality of sensation has changed . . . But the quality has changed. The quality doesn't seem to be a functional state in *this* sense. (pp. 80–81)

This conclusion is actually consistent with what Putnam has said all along, even as far back as "Minds and Machines." Recall that in that article Putnam only presents a Turing machine as a "machine analogue" of a human mind, and he makes it clear that talk of a machine's "sensations" has to be taken in scare quotes, since the machine may "be in a sensation" in the sense of being able to report on its own internal states, but *not* in the sense of actually consciously experiencing anything. Nevertheless that seems to beg one of the most important questions in the debate: how *are* we to handle phenomenal properties of mental states? And if functionalism *cannot* handle them, as cases like the inverted spectrum show, does that constitute a refutation of functionalism (just as the super-Spartan counterexample was considered by Putnam to be a refutation of behaviorism)?

In *Reason, Truth and History*, Putnam was still a committed functionalist; however, he argues that in the case of phenomenal properties we should revert back to identity theory after all. The most plausible way to make sense of physically possible scenarios such as the inverted spectrum is to say that some wires got "crossed" in the brain, such that the inputs from the blue sensation that used to go to one mechanism in the brain now go to a different mechanism. However, it may be possible to simply reproduce the inverted spectrum case at the physical level: that is, it may be logically possible for two people to have inverted spectra even while remaining *physically* identical to one another. If we can conceive of such cases, or if there is no self-contradiction involved in describing such cases, then it follows that facts about conscious experience are not reducible to any physical facts about the organism. Indeed, David Chalmers' more recent "zombie argument" basically makes the same point insofar as it argues that it is logically possible for there to be two physically identical entities (and therefore also functionally identical), while one has conscious experience and the other does not. Thus there is something essential to the mind that is left out by functionalist accounts.

There are two possible replies the functionalist can make to this problem: (1) deny that cases like the inverted spectra or zombie world are logically possible, or (2) deny that the *qualitative content* of a mental state is essential to it (mental states do not require qualitative content of any kind). The issues over (1) are complex, but suffice it to say that some functionalists who assume the truth of physicalism would argue that it only *seems* that we can conceive of such scenarios, and in any case conceivability is not a reliable indicator of logical possibility. Other functionalists have opted for (2): thus, the Churchlands have argued that we should construe the two people in the inverted spectrum case as having the same sensations insofar as they both *say* they are having the same sensations.[13] However, if we extend this to the zombie example, the Churchlands would have to say that the zombie *does* have conscious experiences after all simply because he *says* that he has them. But this would contradict the whole assumption of the thought experiment, that there could be physically identical *doppelgangers* of us who do not have conscious experiences. Thus it would seem that (2) really falls back upon (1).

More recent Putnam is neither a physicalist nor a reductive functionalist, so he would not be interested in formulating either of the above responses. He does hold however that zombie-like scenarios, while logically impossible, are not "fully intelligible." In his Royce Lectures of 1996, Putnam argues that formulating the zombie scenario presupposes that we know what we mean when we talk about the *independence* of mental properties from physical properties. That would suppose we had some implicit notion of "identity" that could decide when such properties were identifiable or independent of one another. But this kind of "identity" would only make sense if we could make sense of the notion of reducing the whole body of laws involving mental properties to the body of laws involving physical properties. This is impossible in the case of folk psychology, as Davidson noted in his argument for the "anomalism" of the mental. Hence we cannot formulate any clear notion of what it would mean for some entity to possess all the "same" physical properties while not having the "same" mental properties, though we are tempted into *thinking* such a scenario is conceivable given our inheritance of the religious language of disembodied souls. It is only due to this religious tradition that we are mislead into thinking that there is anything "mysterious" about consciousness. Recent Putnam would no doubt happily countenance the existence of nonreducible qualitative properties, but go on to warn that this should *not* lead us back into Cartesian dualism, anymore than acknowledging the existence of other nonreducible properties like *being a homerun ball* should require us to postulate the existence of ghostly baseballs. We will say more about Putnam's new alternative picture of the mind later in this chapter, but for now we should note that in this area as well he will bring to bear his newfound pragmatic pluralism.

3.2.2. Semantic Critique of Functionalism

According to the standard view of computational functionalism, it holds a reductive theory of mind: every mental state, intentional or qualitative, it can be identified with a computational state, where this state is captured by the role it plays in that organism's machine table. In *Representation and Reality*, however, Putnam provides a sustained argument to show that "mental states cannot be identified with computational states, although they may be emergent from and supervene upon them" (p. xii). Note here that Putnam does not deny that there are computational states of the brain, nor does he deny that there is much of value in cognitive science in studying these states (he mentions David Marr's work in this regard). What he denies is the metaphysical thesis which identifies mental states with computational states, though it becomes clear that Putnam is going to focus exclusively on intentional states to make the point.[14]

Putnam's argument is made in three stages: first, he argues that meaning holism shows that the same thought can be realized in different computational structures. Second, semantic externalism shows that there can be different thoughts realized in the same computational structure. Third, both arguments show the need for a more sophisticated version of functionalism, the crucial notion being formalizing an equivalence relation among similar computational structures. However, Putnam argues (fascinatingly along Godelian lines) that this is a utopian project—more a matter of "science fiction" than "cognitive science." The upshot is that "functionalism doesn't work. That is to say, it doesn't fit the phenomena. But much has been learned, I feel, for trying it on for size" (p. 105).

Recall that one of the main reasons functionalism emerged victorious over identity theory was due to Putnam's multiple realizability objection: organisms can be in the same mental state (such as being hungry) and yet in very different physical states. But it is worth asking if the same objection can be directed at functionalism: is it possible for there to be two people in the same mental state and yet in different computational states? Putnam argues that because of meaning holism, this is highly likely. Consider a Thai speaker using "meew" to refer to cats and saying something in Thai that we translate as "the cat is on the mat." Given how we interpret the meaning of his words, we would similarly ascribe him the belief *that the cat is on the mat*. However, "meew" does not have the exact same use as "cat" does in English—among other things, the perceptual prototype for "meews" is a Siamese cat, and there may be other beliefs about these "meews" (say, that they are divine creatures), that no English speaker has. It follows that the functional states involving "meew" are going to be rather different than the functional states of an English speaker involving "cat."[15] Putnam concludes that mental states are computationally as well as compositionally plastic. It turns out then that functionalism does *not* signal an improvement over identity theory in this regard after all.

Putnam then turns his own semantic externalism against functionalism. According to functionalism, if two organisms have the same functional organization, they should be in the same mental states. However, consider the Twin Earth argument, where by hypothesis my twin and I are in the same physical and functional states. When I say "water is wet" I mean (and believe) *that water is wet*, and when my twin says "water is wet" he means and believes *that twin-water is wet*. The elm and the beech case make a related point: when Putnam says "elms are trees" his belief is about *elms*. And yet it is impossible to see how there is anything in his computational structure that would yield his belief being about *elms* rather than about *beeches*, since he is unable to differentiate them (they are both described merely as "common deciduous trees"). Putnam focuses on Fodor's version of functionalism, according to which there are innate mental representations, and where "sameness and difference of mental representations is what sameness of meaning is about." However, even if there is a language of thought, we cannot assume that its representations have a definite reference built into them. This would ignore the social and worldly nature of reference that externalism calls attention to. But reference is certainly an ingredient in meaning: and for some terms (such as natural-kind terms), it is the *main* ingredient in meaning (insofar as it is the ingredient that gets preserved in translation). Any theory of the mind that cannot account for reference and meaning will not be able to account for intentionality, and Fodor's version of functionalism is just one version that fails this crucial litmus test.

There have been two main responses made by functionalists to these challenges. The first, led by Fodor and Ned Block, proposes to divide intentional content into two components, narrow/wide, and argue that narrow content can be identified with internal functional states, while wide content is a function of the narrow content plus causal relations to the outside environment. The second, led by Frank Jackson and Philip Pettit, proposes that the inputs and outputs characterized by functionalism be extended out into the environment—this has been labeled "global functionalism" or "sociofunctionalism." Putnam does not believe that either of these responses will work. We have already seen some of the problems with the notion of "narrow content" in Section 1.4.2, chief among them being that it is very difficult if not impossible to provide identity-conditions for such contents. Fodor has suggested that narrow contents are sentences in the language of thought and that they only become semantically evaluable when contextualized—thus "water" is the same mental representation (narrow) for me and my Twin, but becomes a different *concept* (wide) when we determine what the representation causally refers to. One problem here is seeing in what sense "narrow content" is any kind of content at all, insofar as the intentional states are characterized wholly in terms of the wide content.[16] On Block's version, the narrow content is to be identified with the conceptual role of the representation, where conceptual role is defined by how it is used in making inferences, etc. The idea here is that "water" has the same conceptual role for me and my Twin insofar as it is used by us in the same way (it factors into all the same inferences, etc.), thus it should be considered to "mean the same thing." This seems however to completely sidestep Putnam's externalism, insofar as externalism argues that meaning is primarily determined by the reference of the term and *not* by its conceptual role (which closely relates to Putnam's stereotype vector). In any case, both Fodor's and Block's versions would still fall prey to the meaning holism argument: it would be a hopeless task to try to specify scientifically whether an English speaker and a Thai speaker shared the same narrow content when they used "cat" and "meew" respectively. But if we cannot give identity-conditions for narrow contents, then the scientific project of identifying computational states with intentional states collapses.

Putnam presents global functionalism as proposing that one can be a reductionist without being a methodological solipsist, insofar as one tries to explain reference in terms of computational structures *and* causal relations to the physical environment (now taken to provide the inputs and outputs to the system). Putnam concedes that at least superficially, this response meets the externalist objection to functionalism. However, it would still fall prey to meaning holism: on global functionalism, since it is a reductive version of functionalism, we would still have to provide identity conditions for mental states that would make my statement "the cat is on the mat" and a Thai's statement "the meew is on the cat" express the same belief, *that the cat is on the mat*. Given that the Thai has different beliefs about "meews" than I do about "cats," we will be in different computational states and therefore have different beliefs. The only way out of this is to scrap the idea of "identity" between computational states and instead try to formalize some "equivalence relation" whereby certain computational structures will be deemed "the same" in some computationally definable sense of "the same" that has explanatory value. We are free to define this "equivalence relation" not only in terms of the dispositions of the speakers, but also in terms of the physical science of the environment. The idea might be to say that *biology* shows that "meews" and "cats" are the same animals, and that since we both have the same speech dispositions to pick out these animals with "meew" and "cat," we could define ourselves to be in "equivalent" computational states. But Putnam argues that things cannot be this simple, for reasons Quine long ago pointed out. If we are trying to scientifically specify "sameness," we cannot assume that the Thai has the same ontology as we do: he may be referring to temporal slices of cats rather than cats. And even if we assume similar ontologies, the Thai might still use "meew" deviantly, to refer only to "Siamese cats" in a way that would be hard to detect unless we were able to survey all of the speaker's *possible* speech dispositions—how he would react, for example, when put in new situations that could not be fully anticipated.

The problem is not whether we can interpret the Thai as believing *that the cat is on the mat*. We indeed do this, but we do so according to norms of charity and reasonableness that cannot be defined in a formal theory. The problem is that "sameness of meaning" cannot be computed by a finite-state automaton, since it would have to in some way survey all possible theories in order to decide finally on "the correct one." In any case, this is not possible for a human being, for if we are given any human society there is another possible future society which is more sophisticated, possessing certain theories that the previous one could not anticipate. Putnam relates this to a Godelian theme regarding the open-textured nature of our theories—no theory can be said to be "complete" since there is always a metatheory that can prove statements the contained theory cannot prove. The same applies to our being able to produce an algorithm to determine for any possible language whether its terms are synonymous with our own. Putnam calls this "science fiction" but it may be even worse than that, for at least one can conceive a fantastic science fiction scenario. Due to the Godelian limits on computability, the finite-state automaton may not be able to conceive what certain theories would look like and hence what terms in those theories would refer to.

3.2.3. The Realization Objection

One of the early objections to functionalism was the charge of "liberalism," first pointed out by Ned Block and then formulated somewhat differently by John Searle. Block argued that if mentality were simply a matter of producing the right outputs given certain inputs and other states, then it would follow that many other obviously nonmental systems would have minds. His famous example was the "Chinese Nation": suppose we took a billion people in China and gave them walkie-talkies. Each person is assigned a role that reproduces something in the human functional network. When we get it all right, the billion Chinese people could be situated to reproduce—on a very large scale—the functional states of some given person for an hour. Block observes that it is very hard to believe that as soon as the Chinese line up correctly (and reproduce the functional states) the whole Chinese nation will suddenly start to experience "raw feels" that are associated with having qualitative experiences. But if not, then just having the right kind of functional organization alone is not sufficient for qualitative experience. Searle's "Chinese Room" thought experiment can be said to make a similar point for intentional states. It would be possible to put a man who knows no Chinese in a room and have him replicate the function of a computer by producing the right answers to a series of Chinese questions. But all he is doing is syntactic manipulation; the man in the room does not understand what those symbols mean. In short, we could produce functional organizations that have the same kind of complexity of that as a human being, but that would not be sufficient for the possession of any intentional states which are bearers of semantic information.

Putnam's own realization objection is along these lines, but it is much stronger: it attempts to prove that *every* ordinary open system is a realization of *every* abstract finite-state automaton. It would follow from this that nearly anything, such as a rock, could be said to have a functional organization and therefore have a mind. If Putnam's theorem were true, it would also follow that every human brain realizes an infinite number of different functional organizations, each constituting a different mind. Since these absurd conclusions follow from the functionalist characterization of mentality, Putnam argues, functionalism should be rejected.

Putnam's proof applies only to finite-state automata (FSA) with no inputs and outputs—this would seem to severely limit the applicability of his proof but we shall see that it really doesn't. In brief the proof can be summed up as follows: every FSA is characterized by a machine table that defines a certain sequence of states, say ABABABA. Suppose we are given a physical system (such as a rock) that can go through seven physical states during a seven-minute interval. Assuming certain noncontroversial principles, we can associate the initial physical state of the system with an initial state of a finite-state automaton, and subsequent physical states with states of the FSA according to its state-transition rules. Since we could perfectly map the physical states of the rock onto the functional states of the FSA, the rock can be said to implement or "realize" the FSA. But there are no limits to what kind of FSA could be realized by the rock or any other system for that matter. Hence, every system can be said to realize every FSA.

Putnam's proof only applies to FSA without inputs and outputs. The obvious reply then is that functionalism defines a mental state not only in terms of the internal states of the system but also in terms of its inputs and outputs. If we define the "right" kinds of inputs and outputs in terms of an organism's perceptual/motor organs, we can argue that a rock does not have a mind since it lacks these organs. However, Putnam replies that this misses the force of his proof, for if that is the only response on behalf of functionalism, it has in effect lapsed into behaviorism. For now we are being told that what makes something a mind is not the internal computational organization, but rather the inputs and outputs. But the idea that inputs and outputs are constitutive of mentality has already been repudiated, by his own super-Spartan argument among others. Another line of response, made by David Chalmers, is that Putnam's proof only applies to simple kinds of automata, but that the kinds of automata that we would take for minds would be more complicated, having a combinatorial internal structure that could not be mimicked by something like a rock.[17] The details of Chalmers' proposal are technical and complex and there has been no consensus as to whether his combinatorial automata can really escape Putnam's proof. But it is worth pointing out that even if Chalmers' counterargument succeeds, it would still have to meet the other consequence of Putnam's theorem, which could now be restated as implying that every *human* brain implements every kind of combinatorial state automata (and therefore every possible mind). Nothing in Chalmers' argument addresses *this* absurd consequence.

A major question we are left with after this dismantling of functionalism is what Putnam now believes to be the correct philosophical view of the mind. Putnam does not spend nearly enough time presenting a positive picture as he does negatively criticizing other wrong pictures. It would seem though that he would retain something in the spirit of functionalism, minus its reductionism: the mind is basically what the mind does, but these capacities can only be fleshed out in intentional terms. What emerges is a picture of the mind not unlike Aristotle's (minus *his* metaphysical assumptions!), and indeed in his article "Changing Aristotle's Mind" in *Words and Life* (1994a) written with Martha Nussbaum, Putnam fleshes out what he sees as essentially correct in Aristotle's view—the mind as an irreducibly intentional, embodied system of capacities, where thinking and perception are interconnected in ways that make it less of a mystery as to how we as *living beings* are able to have cognitive contact with our environment. As we shall see in the next section, Putnam also comes to see that the Pragmatists had a better picture of the relation between the mind, perception, and environment, one that can do much to dismantle the traditional antinomies that infect ongoing discussions in the philosophy of mind.

3.3. PROBLEMS WITH PERCEPTION

Many functionalists have since come to see the force of Putnam's critique: thus Jerry Fodor raises the "Eponymous Question" as the crucial challenge for himself and other functionalists: "how could a computational process, which is merely a syntactic device for transforming symbols, guarantee the causal relations between symbols and the world that a content-externalism calls for?"[18] We have seen Putnam's answer to this: if all we have are computational processes and causal relations, we *cannot* guarantee reference to external things. As Putnam puts it in his Dewey Lectures, the problem with modern forms of materialism, functionalism included, is that epistemologically they revert back to the old problems of representationalism that plagued modern philosophy from Descartes to Hume. Instead of "ideas" or "sense-data" as the intermediaries between the cognitive agent and the external world, we now have "mental representations" but the same problem persists: if we set up an interface between the mind and the world, this threatens the very idea that we have cognitive contact with the world at all. For, as the internalist (or "methodological solipsist") has it, all of our mental representations could remain the same even if there wasn't any external world. And if we insist on reference to the external world, Putnam's Model-Theoretic argument shows that we could hold fix these representations while radically altering the reference relations. The "Cartesian-cum-materialist" model of the mind, then, either cuts us off from referring to the world at all, or it makes reference radically indeterminate.

In the Dewey Lectures, Putnam frames this point in terms of perception. For it would seem that the most basic kind of contact we have to the world is through perception: for example, I believe that there is a tree outside my window because I perceive it is there, or I recall perceiving it there on other occasions, etc. But according to modern materialist theories of the mind, my perception of the tree is really a mental representation—something my mind has constructed, a mental "model" of the tree if you will. Materialists hasten to add that this representation of the tree is (normally) caused by the tree, but in this they are no different from Descartes' indirect realism, where we infer the existence of external things as the cause of our ideas. The problem is that the mental representation of the tree cannot justify me in believing that it is there, for (according to these theories) I would have the same mental representation if I were dreaming. On the other hand, if we bring in the causal relation to the actual tree, that also would not justify my belief, since a mere causal relation has no cognitive relation to my beliefs. As Putnam puts it, "this philosophy of perception makes it impossible to see how we can so much as refer to external things." In its place, Putnam urges that we adopt a version of direct realism (or preferably, natural realism), and he sees this as part and parcel of a defense of commonsense realism—for after all, commonsense says that when I am perceiving the tree, I am perceiving *the tree* and not merely my own representation of it. However, from a philosophical point of view (especially given our inheritance of the representationalist tradition), direct realism can seem to be a horribly naïve position. Putnam's strategy then is to utilize some arguments from his "philosophical heroes," among them William James and J. L. Austin, in order to show that direct realism is a hard-fought philosophical victory, and not merely a "reinfantilization of philosophy."

I will focus on Putnam's reconstruction of James' argument, for we can also see in it a useful segway to Putnam's pragmatic perspective that will be discussed in more detail in the next chapter.[19] James sets himself the monumental task of refuting one of the oldest empiricist dogmas, namely, that in perception, we do not really perceive the environment, but rather our own images or sense-data. According to the representationalist tradition going back at least to Descartes, in perception we immediately perceive only our own ideas or sense-data, and the object is either inferred as the cause of these ideas (Descartes), or is logically constructed out of them (Russell). James points out that this view conflates two separate questions: (1) Do we immediately perceive external things? and (2) Do we perceive things incorrigibly? One can agree with Descartes and others that we do not have incorrigible perceptions (due to familiar possibilities of hallucinating, error, dreaming, etc.), while not concluding from this that we must *therefore* perceive the sense-datum rather than the thing itself. An alternative possibility is that when we are *not* deluded, dreaming, or hallucinating etc., we do perceive the external thing and not merely our idea of it. As James writes, "when I have a veridical perception of a fire I don't see a private sense-datum of the fire and infer the fire; I just see the fire." And when I have a hallucination, according to James, what I see is a fire that isn't really there.

Of course, this view seems equally problematic, for what does it mean to say that "I see a fire that isn't really there?" Does this lead us to postulate Meinongian entities, an ontology in which hallucinatory fires exist alongside real fires? Putnam admits that James sometimes appears to flirt with such a "nutty metaphysics," but he also defends James by appealing to his distinction between "adjectival" and "intentional" attributions. For example, in the case of the hallucinatory fire we can say "the fire is hot" where "is hot" is not used adjectivally to qualify a real fire, but only intentionally to qualify an intentional object. This should be no more perplexing than our use of such predicates in fictional discourse, as when we say "a unicorn is fast" where "is fast" is used intentionally to refer to a fictional animal rather than adjectivally to refer to something real. Furthermore, James makes a distinction between those objects which have "general validity" and those which do not. The real fire, unlike the hallucinatory one, has "general validity" because it can be seen, touched, and felt by others: it is a public fire, one might say. What James is claiming, then, is that the difference between the hallucinatory and the real fire is that one is public and the other private. The difference is not to be explained by saying that in both cases that same sense-data are seen but that one mistakenly infers the object in one case and not in the other. James is here offering us a *redescription* of the events which do not involve mentioning sense-data at all.

On the traditional argument, the only way to explain the similarity between my hallucination and the veridical experience is to posit some common factor, namely, that in both cases I perceive the same sense-data. James however suggests the intriguing alternative that the hallucinatory fire simply *looks like* the real fire. Our mistake arises when we are fooled by this resemblance and proceed to use "is a fire" adjectivally when it should only be used intentionally. The motive for this redescription of the situation should be obvious: it is to vindicate a commonsense realism with respect to perception. When two people stand side by side looking at Memorial Hall, commonsense would say that they both perceive the same object, whereas the sense-datum view would say that they perceive two numerically distinct objects. The sense-datum view in effect cuts the agent off from the public realm of observable objects and confines our experience to representations in our subjective mental realms. Putnam adds that this view is essentially unaltered in modern materialist versions of functionalism, where "mental representations" simply replace the old "sense-data." James's critique of the traditional sense-datum theory then equally applies to these theories as well.

Putnam believes that this Jamesian or "pragmatic" perspective can be developed into a rehabilitation of the concept of experience, a concept which has been much maligned in analytic philosophy. Wilfred Sellars presented what has since become the classic argument against the explanatory value of experience, which he called "the given."[20] Sellars argued that epistemology deals with issues of justification, which is the giving of warranted reasons for a certain claim or belief. If we think of experiences as "bare presences," some kind of uninterpreted raw data that our perceptual apparatus takes in from the environment, it is hard to see how they can play this kind of role. Bare presences or "sensory impressions" by themselves cannot tell me why anything is the case, since that would entail some degree of conceptualization and interpretation. My pointing to a kitten, for example, does not by itself provide a reason for why I believe the kitten is on the table. If I talk about my perception of the cat in ways others can understand (thus do so in intentional terms), it is evident that I am no longer talking about my sense-data but rather fitting this data under concepts shared by others. Issues of justification are dependent on a community of speakers and thus are concerned with intersubjective propositional contents. To a degree, then, Sellars agrees with James: they both want to get rid of sense-data as explanatorily useless constructs in epistemology. However, since Sellars is wedded to the idea of experience as uninterpreted sense-data, he is forced to conclude that experience is explanatorily useless in epistemology. But this seems counter to commonsense. As James pointed out, it seems perfectly natural and explanatorily relevant to say that my perception of Memorial Hall helps explain why I believe that it is on the Harvard campus. The appropriate response to Sellars' critique of the "myth of the given" should be not to throw away the concept of experience, but rather to articulate a different concept of experience which could enter into justificatory relations with our beliefs and desires.

Unfortunately, James himself never fully articulated such a view, despite some promising references to perception as "sensation fused with thought." This project was taken up by John McDowell in his 1992 Locke Lectures, now published as *Mind and World* (1994), about which Putnam writes, "although I do not wish to hold McDowell responsible for my formulations in the present lectures, I want to acknowledge the pervasive influence of his work, which has reinforced my own interest in natural realism in the theory of perception—an interest first reawakened by thinking about the views of William James."[21] McDowell's target is not the sense-datum theorist but naturalist minded philosophers like Davidson and Quine who, following Sellars, still think of experience as some kind of brute causal relation between the mind and the world. McDowell argues for a Kantian view, according to which the objects that we perceive in perception are conceptually as well as causally related to us. Since the objects we perceive are already conceptualized, they can serve as reasons, and hence play a role in justifying our beliefs, desires, and other empirical judgments.

McDowell's view is a rehabilitation of Kant's famous slogan that "concepts with intuitions are empty, intuitions without concepts are blind,"[22] and McDowell explicitly links Kant's distinction between the sensibility and the understanding to Davidson's scheme/content distinction, where "content" concerns "bits of experiential intake" and "scheme" refers to our conceptual capacities, which organize what is passively drawn in by the senses. McDowell's agenda is to articulate a notion of experiential content which (1) provides a constraint on our thinking by connecting us to an external world, and yet (2) provides a way to link these experiences rationally to our beliefs, desires, and other empirical judgments. The problem is that these criteria pull in opposite directions, resulting in what McDowell calls an "interminable oscillation." On the one hand, focusing on (1), we might be led to link experience with an independent extraconceptual reality, for example, treating experiences as sensory stimulations, susceptible to scientific analysis. This does justice to the independence criterion, but then (2) becomes impossible, since the notion of an extraconceptual reality can provide no justificatory role (a la Sellars). Alternatively, seizing on (2), we might assimilate the notion of experience to "experiential belief" and treat it just as another kind of conceptual content (as Davidson does). The problem here is that we lose sight of the independence criterion: we need a notion of experience which connects not merely beliefs with one another, but beliefs with the world. McDowell often puts this tension in terms of responsibility: on the one hand, our thoughts need to be grounded in an external reality insofar as they have any content whatsoever. On the other hand, we want our thoughts to be free from the coercion of the external world if we are to be held responsible for them. In short, we want our thoughts to be free from external control and yet rationally grounded in the external world. Recent views on experience fail to bring these two sides together, either emphasizing our freedom at the expense of the world, or the world at the expense of our freedom.

McDowell's solution to this dilemma is to argue that in experience, we draw upon the same conceptual capacities that are operative in our nonexperiential judgments. Crucially, these capacities are "drawn on in receptivity, not exercised on some supposedly prior deliverances of receptivity" (p. 10). What this means is that when I experience something as a cat, for example, the experience occurs in receptivity (the external constraint) *and* simultaneously as a result of my conceptual capacities (my conceptual scheme). My experience is answerable to the world since it is drawn on in receptivity, but I can use it to justify my other beliefs since it is *at the same time* the work of the spontaneity of my conceptual powers. The latter point is what enables me to exercise some freedom over the deliverances of my senses. I can, for example, reject a certain appearance as deceptive. In such a case, there would be the experience itself and the state of judging that the experience is misleading, and these two contents can enter into justificatory relations with each other. But how experience presents the world to me is not in my rational control, so I am not free to experience what I wish. McDowell uses the example of the Muller-Lyer illusions, where two lines of equal length are experienced as being unequal. One cannot change the experience, but one can reject it as misleading.

McDowell indicates that his views are largely inspired by the Kantian goal of trying to close the gap between the mind and world. As such, McDowell can be read (and has been read by Richard Rorty) as just another attempt to use the language of representationalism (with its distinction between receptivity and spontaneity) in order to provide a transcendental argument against the skeptic. While I do not think this charge against McDowell is entirely fair,[23] it is clear that Putnam's appropriation of McDowell pulls in a more Pragmatist direction. Putnam is more interested in providing a coherent view of perception that would accord with our commonsense ways of speaking and acting than he is with providing a knockdown argument against skepticism. The idea is not to bridge the gap between the mind and world through philosophical argument, but to use philosophical argument to confirm what we already know, *that there is no gap between the mind and the world.* The effect of this can be potentially liberating, insofar as we are no longer blinded by the interface model into thinking, for example, that I am not *really* perceiving this bird outside my window. It may be naïve to simply think the world is more or less as we perceive it to be: indeed, our first lessons in philosophy are designed to upset such naiveté.[24] Yet the second lesson in philosophy, Putnam suggests, is to win our way back to the commonsense picture we began with. He calls this a "second naiveté" and he quotes John Wisdom approvingly when he writes that the goal of philosophy should be to complete the journey "from the familiar to the familiar."[25] Vindicating a natural realist view of perception along the lines that McDowell laid out is one important step in such a journey.

Putnam suggests that McDowell's view of experience can be made sense of in terms of the distinction between merely seeing and *seeing-as*. Consider the difference between my seeing a resistor lying on the table versus someone else seeing the same thing who has no concept of what a resistor is. Despite the fact that we are both causally related to the resistor in the same way, our perceptual states are clearly quite different. I see the object *as a resistor*, and this is not a mere causal taking in of uninterpreted data, but rather involves what McDowell calls "the operation of conceptual capacities in receptivity." The difference is akin to the difference between a 4-year-old and a 14-year-old looking at a newspaper: the 4-year-old just sees a series of marks on a page, but the 12-year-old sees not merely the marks but the *words themselves*. Being able to read, or understanding someone else's speech, are paradigm examples of conceptual powers being operative *in* our experience.

Indeed, Putnam sometimes writes as if this 'second nature' with regard to perception is largely a matter of how the acquisition of language enables us to extend our conceptual powers and thus transform the nature of experience itself. Interestingly, he relates this not only to problems of perception but also to the realism debate. On a typical anti-realist view, the sentences we utter are just mere marks and sounds; a meaning has to be *given* to them depending on whether or not we are able to recognizably assert these marks and sounds. If there is no effective means of telling whether the sentence is verifiable, then there is no way to impart a meaning to the sentence. However, it seems that some sentences are meaningful irregardless of our ability to verify them. Putnam takes the example of the phrase "things too small to see with the naked eye." I can understand the idea of things too small to see simply because

I have the concept of "small," without requiring the use of a microscope in order to give that phrase a meaning. When I hear a sentence like "that person is too small to see," then, I can immediately understand it since the concepts expressed directly key me to that possible state of affairs. As Wittgenstein puts it, "when we say, and mean, that such-and-such is the case, we—and our meaning, do not stop anywhere short of the fact; but we mean this-is-so." Putnam suggests that we think of a statement that we understand not as a series of marks or sounds to which we have to give significance, but rather as something that already has significance built into it. Thus, when we listen to someone else speak in a language we understand, we are directly clued into what they are saying. This idea is found in Wittgenstein's conception of a *Satz*, which is neither a sentence nor a proposition, but best conceived of as a *claim*. Putnam's reading of section 503 of the *Philosophical Investigations* leads him to the following interpretation:

> Wittgenstein makes a similar point about the role of words and sentences in thinking . . . when we hear a sentence in a language we understand, we do not associate a sense with a sign-design; we perceive the sense in the sign-design. Sentences that I think, and even sentences I hear or read, simply do refer to whatever they are about; not because the "marks and noises" that I see and hear (or hear "in my head" in the case of my own thoughts) intrinsically have the meanings they have, but because the sentence in use is not just a bunch of "marks and noises." (p. 46)

Putnam believes (following McDowell and Cora Diamond) that this idea contains the seeds of a realist reading of the later Wittgenstein, and indeed it is this reading which can be said to be most responsible for Putnam's final movement away from internal realism to pragmatic realism. The key idea is that if we think of a statement p as a *Satz*, then we can simply say that "p" is true iff p. To say that something "is true" is not to attribute a substantive property to a sentence (contra metaphysical realism), but nor is it to simply assert a sentence (contra deflationism), since what is being asserted is not a sentence but a *Satz* (which is already world involving). Thus we can be, to use William Alston's term, "alethic realists" insofar as we untie truth from any epistemic notion, without being metaphysical realists, since we do not need to see truth as somehow—magically—*adding* something to the *Satz* that it doesn't already have.

As this last transition from the philosophy of perception to the realism debate shows, Putnam now believes that it is not very useful to decompartmentalize philosophy into various separate fields, as has been the wont of analytic philosophy. It is still required, for example, to list your main areas of specialization on your *curriculum vitae*, as if "Philosophy of Language" could somehow be separated from "Philosophy of Mind" or "Philosophy of Science." In reality, philosophical problems and the dualisms that result from them are intertwined in complicated ways, and it is the goal of the philosopher now as ever to disentangle them. The interface model of the mind that gave rise to both the Cartesian and modern materialist views of the mind is the very same model that is unwittingly presupposed by anti-realists who want to dispose of truth conditions in favor of assertability conditions. Putnam's philosophical analysis manages to expose these interconnections, while at the same time showing us a way out of the dualisms they spawn, back to the "natural realism of the common man." It is a good illustration of what Putnam thinks philosophical inquiry should now be: to illuminate how philosophers have talked themselves into conundrums, and then show how they can free themselves from philosophical perplexity. Having achieved this emancipation, philosophers can now apply their critical intelligence to "live problems" concerning how we are to live in the world in order to make it a better place. This movement of the theoretical to the practical mirrors the one Dewey sought to effect in his *The Quest for Certainty* (1929, 1960) and *Experience and Nature* (1930, 1958), among other writings, and thus it is quite fitting that Putnam would initiate this new philosophical perspective in the "Dewey Lectures" given at Columbia in 1994. Those of us in the audience at those lectures sensed that something grand was being proposed, though we couldn't really specify what it was. I will try to elaborate on this new vision of philosophy when discussing Putnam's pragmatism (or neo-pragmatism) in more detail in the next chapter.

3.4. PRAGMATIC REALISM AND INTENTIONALITY

We have seen (Sections 1.4, 3.2) that according to normal standards of translation and interpretation, semantic externalism (a thesis about *meaning*) implies psychological externalism (a thesis about *content*). According to Putnam's Twin Earth argument, two twins can be phenomenally and physically identical and yet when they utter "water is wet," they mean different things given that the terms have different extensions. But meaning is closely intertwined with our standard attributions of the *content* of what a person believes. Kripke has proposed the following DQ principle to capture this close relationship:

> (D) When a speaker sincerely asserts "a is F" where "a" is a general term, the literal meaning of "a" gives the concept which is expressed by "a"[26]

Thus, when the two twins assert "water is wet," given that "water" has different meanings in their ideolects, (D) would entail that they express different concepts. But concepts are what the contents of our intentional states are composed of. Thus, when the twins sincerely assert "water is wet," we should interpret them as expressing two different beliefs: the one believes *that water is wet*, the other *that twin-water is wet*. Tyler Burge's thought experiments support this psychological externalist conclusion (Section 1.5.2). Thus, when Bert sincerely asserts "I have arthritis in my thigh" we take him to believe *that he has arthritis in his thigh*, even though arthritis is a disease that applies only to the joints. As Burge points out, this attribution makes sense of the fact that we take Bert to make a *mistake*: he could only mistakenly believe *that arthritis is in his thigh* if he has the concept *arthritis*. But nothing "in his head" warrants the attribution of the concept *arthritis* to Bert. We attribute the concept to him because of factors outside of his head: the greater sociolinguistic community and (for standard natural-kind terms) the layout of the physical environment as determined by experts in the community.

Psychological externalism seems to make sense of the following factors that we want a notion of content for:

(a) the close linkage between belief and meaning, as indicated by Kripke's DQ principle
(b) the referential aspect of content: that is, the *aboutness* of our beliefs and desires
(c) the normative nature of content, for example, explaining mistakes as in the Bert case.

Emphasizing these factors, social externalists like Putnam and Burge, and even naturalistic-minded externalists like Dretske, have argued against various proposals that factor content into two kinds—"narrow" versus "wide," arguing that the distinction is unmotivated and that one unified notion of externalist content suffices to do all the work needed of a notion of content in intentional psychology. We have seen that Putnam was initially sympathetic to bifurcationist views of content while he was still committed to functionalism—he believed that in addition to the externalist "wide" content we needed a notion of "narrow" content that could be utilized for purposes of psychological explanation. But with his critique of functionalism, he came to believe that the prospects for making sense of this notion of narrow content were dim, and he concluded in *Representation and Reality* that he "has come to bury the distinction between narrow and wide content, not to praise it." But it is worth asking the following important question: what becomes of the original motivation for adopting narrow content, namely, the role of content in psychological explanation? Can the standard externalist notion of content really explain behavior in a satisfactory way? And if not, it may be that we still need another notion of content, even if it is not to be construed in the naturalistic "narrow" way that Putnam has rightly criticized.

If we think about what we need a notion of content for, we have to add to (a–c) the following criteria:

(d) serve to explain behavior: for example, we explain why I took the umbrella because I believed *that it was raining*, and I desired *not to get wet*
(e) reflect the agent's point of view: attributing content allows us to see *how things are* to a cognitive agent.

Criterion (d) is really what motivated Fodor to push so strongly for an individualistic notion of content, even while he agreed with the standard arguments for externalism. Take his following argument for an individualistic notion of content:

1. My Twin and I are molecular duplicates
2. Therefore our (actual and counterfactual) behaviors are identical in relevant respects
3. Therefore the causal powers of our mental states are identical in relevant respects

4. Therefore my Twin and I belong to the same natural kind for purposes of explanation (and individualism is true).[27]

Now even if we agree with Putnam's arguments against Fodor's naturalistic version of narrow content, I think it would be quite dogmatic not to see that there is *something right* in Fodor's viewpoint here. If the two twins do not know the difference between water and twin-water, that difference is irrelevant in capturing their own cognitive perspectives or points of view. And insofar as we are trying to explain their actions in terms of their beliefs and desires, shouldn't the "relevant" explanation be one that refers to their own cognitive perspectives? On this viewpoint, external factors such as the chemistry of water do not seem to play a role in explaining why, for example, the two twins reach for a cup in order to satisfy their thirst. The standard externalist contents seem to posit a difference that doesn't make a difference, as far as psychological explanation is concerned.

There is yet another closely related argument, one that focuses more on criterion (e), to show that another notion of individualistic content is necessary. On an externalist analysis, we should attribute different beliefs and desires to the twins; however, neither twin (assuming they are chemically ignorant) knows that he has *that* particular belief (say, *that water is wet*) as opposed to the other one (*that twin-water is wet*). Thus, neither twin really knows *what* they are thinking.[28] But ever since Descartes, it has been assumed that there is a special kind of authority that one has over one's own thoughts. As Descartes pointed out, I might not know that I have a hand (since I could be dreaming the hand), but at least I know that I think that I have a hand. Barring cases of self-deception, inattention (and other psychological phenomena studied by Freud, etc.), we can state as a general rule that my own thoughts are directly accessible and known *a priori*, whereas knowledge of the external world is inferential and *a posteriori*. But externalism, by holding that the contents of our thoughts are determined by external factors, seems to upset this alleged self-knowledge of our own thoughts. Since we do not simply want to jettison the concept of self-knowledge, we ought to concede another notion of content that does reflect the agent's point of view.

Burge and others have argued against this conclusion, arguing that we do not need to have individuating knowledge of the contents of our thoughts in order to know these thoughts.²⁹ Burge points out, for example, that whatever goes into the individuation of one's first-order belief that p carries over to the second-order knowledge that one believes that p. Thus, so long as Twin-Oscar believes that twin-water is wet, he knows that he believes that twin-water is wet, and "one need not exercise comparisons between it and other thoughts in order to know it as the thought one is thinking" (p. 656). I think there are problems with this response: it may be that if I think that p, then I know that I think that p, but I still might not know which proposition p I am thinking. The issue of self-knowledge concerns my first-person recognition of my thoughts, and not some third-person appraisal. So while an *interpreter* might be able to attribute me the thought that p (and hence knowledge that I am thinking p), if I am in a situation epistemically similar to the twin, *I* might not know that I am thinking that p. In this case, it would seem, counterintuitively, that the interpreter knows what I am thinking while I do not! Nevertheless, even if Burge's strategy can rescue externalism from the *prima facie* problem of self-knowledge, there is another argument (advanced by Akeel Bilgrami) that is even more damaging.³⁰

On the standard externalist picture, we would attribute the concept *arthritis* to Bert and characterize his belief accordingly:

(1) Bert believes that he has arthritis in his thigh

The key idea behind psychological externalism is that one can be attributed concepts that are not in the head, but are determined rather by the greater sociolinguistic community. That is, Bert's concept *arthritis* **just is** the community concept *arthritis*. But then, since the community concept of arthritis is that of a rheumatoid disease that only applies to the joints, we should be able to substitute to get the following:

(2) Bert believes that he has a rheumatoid disease which affects the joints only in his thigh

But this would attribute contradictory beliefs to Bert, and surely we don't want him to come out as a logical idiot simply because he has an incomplete understanding of the meaning of "arthritis." In order to handle such cases, Burge makes a sensible distinction between concepts, which are word meanings, and conceptual explications, which are conceptions that a speaker associates with the term she is using. The reason why we cannot substitute "a rheumatoid disease which affects the joints only" for "arthritis" is because Bert's conception of arthritis involves no reference to a disease which affects the joints only. But now it seems, as Bilgrami points out, that we need to introduce another notion of content in order to handle these cases. That is, now we are being asked to characterize Bert's belief, not in terms of the community concept *arthritis*, but in terms of his more fine-grained conception of what arthritis is. Based on this revisionist move, we might want to report Bert's belief by the following:

(3) Bert believes that a rheumatoid disease which affects the joints and the thigh is in his thigh

The advantage of this re-write is that it rather than (1) delivers us from belief-puzzles, captures what a person "has in mind" for purposes of self-knowledge, and in many situations, seems more useful in explaining behavior. Bilgrami has generalized from these kinds of examples, arguing that all content attributions should be guided by the following constraint:

© When fixing an externally determined concept of an agent, one must do so by looking to indexically formulated utterances of the agent which express indexical contents containing that concept and then picking that external determinant of the concept which is in consonance with other contents that have been fixed by the agent.

So, for example, suppose we are trying to explain why two people at a picnic reach for a glass of water. In that context, the same concept of water will be attributed to them: that thirst-quenching liquid. In that locality of explanation, chemical beliefs are irrelevant in explaining the behavior and hence will form no part of the concept figuring in the explanation. Note that this concept of content—what may be called "localized content" is not at all Fodor's notion of content, since it is a nonnaturalistically specified intentional notion that can be clearly explicated by the speaker himself. Furthermore, Bilgrami denies that it is an "individualistic" notion of content, insofar as the concepts ascribed to agents, fine-grained as they are, still point to externalistically salient items, such as thirst-quenching water.

As I see it, the main problem with Bilgrami's proposal is that he believes it is the only notion of content we need in intentional psychology. But while localized content seems to satisfy criteria (d) and (e), it does a poor job of satisfying (a)–(c). If, for example, we *only* ascribed (4) above to Bert and not (1), then it turns out that Bert is expressing a *true* belief when he says "I have arthritis in my thigh." If so, then he is not actually making a mistake at all, and when the doctor corrects him, he should respond "you are wrong, doctor, since what I mean by 'arthritis' is a disease that can also apply to the thigh." Surely Bert would be acting like an idiot if he said that, since the meaning of "arthritis" does not depend on his own conception of arthritis. As Putnam would put it, speakers using such terms are obliged to defer to experts when determining meaning, and localized content by its very nature does not capture this normative dimension. Localized content will also not capture the referential aspect of content, which is what we normally preserve in translation and interpretation. If, for example, a Thai would say "meew" when referring to a cat, but believes that meews are divine creatures, we would still translate "meew" as "cat" since it has the same reference as our "cats" despite the difference in beliefs. If we decided to opt for a more fine-grained concept, we would most likely have to introduce a new term in the language, which would confuse rather than elucidate interpretation. It seems then that while there are cases where localized contents are called for, there are other cases where the standard externalist attributions will be more helpful.

It would seem that we have reached an impasse here: Putnam's externalism seems to satisfy (a)–(c), while a more individualistic notion of content seems necessary to explain (d) and (e). Utilizing the insights of Putnam's own pragmatic realism, however, it is possible to argue that there is only a problem here if we insist on *one absolute way to conceive of content*. But Putnam's conceptual relativity should make us wary of any claims considering the "absolute nature of the world," whether we apply this to external objects *or* psychological states. It is clear that most of the participants in this debate are presupposing some view of the "absolute conception of the *mind*," where it is deemed unproblematic to ask what the "true nature" of a psychological state is independently of human purposes and interests. But if pragmatic realism is right to claim that we can make no sense of a fundamental ontology, the point should apply equally to psychological reality as it does to physical reality. This was basically Kant's point in the Paralogisms, that the Cartesian view is mistaken in supposing that reference to mental contents is any less problematic than reference to external objects. However, pragmatic realism strips this Kantian insight of its idealist underpinnings and gives it a pragmatic reorientation. What psychological properties there are and what identity conditions we give for them depend largely on us, not nature. Thus we are free to attribute such properties in a variety of ways, depending on the circumstances and the purpose at hand. For ordinary purposes, we may well indeed attribute (1) to Bert, crediting him with the concept shared by the community at large. Doing so ensures that when we communicate with Bert, we are speaking *about* the same disease, and allows that Bert may be mistaken when he claims that the disease is in his thigh. However, for purposes of psychological explanation, we may seek a more fine-grained account, preferring something like (4), in order to capture Bert's perspective, and deliver him from belief-puzzles. We may even adopt a naturalistic perspective, and try to explain beliefs and desires in terms of underlying causal mechanisms, in order to see how far a scientific analysis may be carried to illuminate a person's psychology. What we must *not* demand is that there is one and only one notion of content that must be employed, given all these varied roles we want the notion of content to play.

Putnam himself has never explicitly applied pragmatic pluralism to mental content, but I think it is perfectly consistent with his general outlook. In his response to Bilgrami, he concedes that the notion of localized content is "an interesting proposal," but he thinks that his own vector theory of meaning can be enlisted to capture cases where the referential content seems to do no work in explaining behavior.[31] Most people who use a word successfully do so because they at least grasp the stereotypical information associated with the word: thus in the case mentioned above, while a speaker may not know that water is H_2O, he may at least know it is thirst quenching, and this enables us to ascribe a water thought to that individual. A general theory of content, then, may not need to go as far as Bilgrami in constructing a theory of content for every speaker and every use of that speaker's language. Or, alternatively, we can construct what Davidson calls "passing theories" in order to make sense of words used by speakers who may have an incomplete understanding of the meaning of their terms. I think that such issues can be resolved by pragmatic criteria and there is no danger in "letting a thousand flowers bloom" and allowing for referential, stereotypical, and localized ascriptions of content, depending on the purpose at hand. Once we give up the monism of content that many analytical philosophers are still hankering for, it is possible to incorporate the insights of all these divergent (but not incompatible) perspectives.

3.5. CONCLUSION

So far we have seen how Putnam takes up each part of the language, mind, world triangle and works it into a comprehensible philosophical viewpoint. The starting point of the discussion was his semantic externalism, which was interpreted in a social sense: the point of a theory of meaning is not to pinpoint the connections between language and reality, but rather to articulate the norms that underlie the use of language. These norms license reference and meaning ascriptions from the point of view of the entire community rather than the individual. This idea was then tied to Putnam's internal realist view of truth, where the concept of truth is seen to be bound up with judgments made through the process of inquiry. Finally, in this chapter, the social aspect of content was taken into account in order to resolve recent debates concerning functionalism and content ascription. It was seen that there are different rationales for the positing of "mental content," depending on whether we are interested in the psychological or referential aspect of a speaker's intentionality.

Throughout, our discussion was punctuated by Putnam's pragmatic methodology: to steer a "middle path" between an alienating metaphysical realism according to which there are facts of meaning and truth "out there" that we may never come to know, and a subjectivism/relativism according to which meaning and truth are merely relative to an individual, that there are no facts over and above a speaker's dispositions. Putnam's point is that if we attend carefully to the normative nature of our linguistic practices, we will see that there is no need to choose between these dualistic extremes.

This middle position, one that is responsible to reality while being sensitive to the ineliminable social nature of our descriptions, is one that was carved out by the pragmatists at the beginning of the twentieth century before positivistic philosophy came into dominance. Exactly how Putnam appropriates the pragmatists in the formulation of a new postanalytical outlook will be the focus of the next chapter.

CHAPTER 4

NEO-PRAGMATISM AND THE REVITALIZATION OF PHILOSOPHY

4.1. THE TURN TO PRAGMATISM

So far in this study, we have seen that despite Putnam's numerous shifts of position, there is an underlying continuity, insofar as his methodology throughout is to begin with certain features of our common linguistic practices and construct philosophical theories that are in accord with, and illuminate, those practices. Thus in the philosophy of science, his arguments for scientific realism largely turned on the appeal to actual features of scientific practice, which reveal that scientists do by and large take themselves to refer to the same entities through theory change. Doing so enables them to communicate and disagree with each other, and also makes possible the view of science as progressing to a more approximately true picture of the world. In the philosophy of language, Putnam's work began as an empirical theory of the usage of natural-kind terms, that is, as an attempt to explain what we actually mean when we use terms like "cat." The full-fledged semantic externalism that was expounded in "The Meaning of 'Meaning'" appeals to the division of linguistic labor—a feature which had never been emphasized by previous philosophers—which essentially involves the norm of linguistic deference to the greater sociolinguistic community in determining the extensions and thus meanings of all our general terms. Even the most naturalist sounding elements of his early philosophy involved an appeal to practice: the argument for realism in mathematics turned on the fact that mathematics is indispensable in scientific practice, and the argument for functionalism was an attempt to explain (or legitimate) our common ascriptions of belief and desire.

As Putnam progressed, he became more and more aware of the ubiquity of our norm-governed discourses, and he explicitly appealed to this normativity in his arguments against metaphysical realism (or any view that seeks an "absolute perspective" irrespective of these norms) and computational functionalism (which seeks such an absolute perspective on the mind itself). In his middle period, he was inclined to label this as a move toward a Kantian kind of "internal realism," and indeed we have seen that his arguments follow Kant in trying to provide transcendental arguments against the skeptic. At the same time, the awareness of the centrality of our linguistic practices, and Putnam's newfound pluralism—the idea that there are many true descriptions of reality and that we should not seek one final absolute ontology—points more in the direction of pragmatism than Kantianism. Indeed, Putnam's later arguments eschew any kind of transcendentalism and rather appeal to some of the most important pragmatic themes—the notion of *experience* (as witnessed in his use of James' critique of the sense-data theory), the primacy of *practice* (all philosophical theories have to relate back to our common practices in order to be "meaningful"), pragmatic *pluralism* (Putnam's arguments for conceptual relativity), and the leading idea of maintaining a *realism* even while espousing *fallibilism* (linking experience to nature (a la Dewey) while acknowledging that all inquiry is open-ended). True enough, Putnam's adoption of pragmatism is rather qualified, since he finds problems with pragmatist theories of truth, as well as elements of fallibilism. But it is evident that Putnam's turn to pragmatism should be neither surprising nor unwelcome: not surprising given the pragmatic element in his thought all along, and not unwelcome, given that it offers us a fresh perspective in this "postanalytical climate," a certain kind of philosophy worth pursuing in the twenty-first century after the demise of linguistic philosophy and epistemology as mere philosophy of science.

This labeling of "postanalytical" needs a bit of explication, since many of those who are included in this movement, such as Rorty, Putnam, Davidson, McDowell, and Brandom, are squarely within the analytic tradition, both in terms of ancestry, writing and argumentative style, and the topics they address. The idea behind it is that classical analytic philosophy began as an attempt to use linguistic methods to resolve the traditional problems of philosophy. The projects of Frege, Russell, and early Wittgenstein were designed to solve certain problems endemic to the representationalist tradition by demarcating between logical and factual questions, and by rehabilitating a thoroughgoing realist outlook in consonance with natural science as against the idealisms of the nineteenth century. Logical positivism can be seen as the culmination of these attempts, insofar as it emerged as a self-conscious program to discredit metaphysics and formulate a coherent place for philosophy as handmaiden to the sciences. However, with Quine's "Two Dogmas of Empiricism," Davidson's appropriation of Quine, and the efforts of thinkers like Putnam and Rorty, a new awareness came into being concerning the limits of the traditional project. It was seen that much of analytical philosophy was still mired in the age-old distinctions between theory and observation, subject and object, scheme and content, mind and matter, and that so long as these distinctions were treated as absolute "problems" to be solved, they were insoluble, even by the most ingenious analytic methods. Perhaps the crescendo of this dawning awareness was Rorty's *Philosophy and the Mirror of Nature* (1979), where he argues that linguistic philosophy, far from resolving the traditional problems, makes such problems simply "optional," or a matter of a choice of vocabularies (with the idea being that we no longer have to choose the traditional vocabulary).

Consequently, the return to pragmatism is motivated by an awareness that many of the debates within analytical philosophy are outdated language-games that have no relevance to our practical lives and thus are "idle." As just a few examples, consider the debates concerning Kripke's "essences," Lewis's "possible worlds," or "the mystery of consciousness" which can be seen as repeats of the scholastic debates concerning "substance" and "universals." Putnam's own injunctions in *The Threefold Cord: Mind, Body, and World* against the "metaphysical fantasies" of metaphysical realism and the recoil to mirror-image forms of anti-realism should be read in this light, as a sense that much of analytic philosophy has been engaged in a kind of "spinning of the webs" that needs to be brought back to earth, back to our actual practices. Doing so will also have a liberating effect, insofar as philosophers are now free to explore other areas of discourse that have been traditionally regarded as either meaningless or at least "soft," such as ethics, politics, aesthetics, religion, and of course (for Rorty) poetry and literature. "Neo-pragmatism" is the label for this general new perspective, and Putnam has been included as one of the major influences on this movement, despite his manifold disagreements with Rorty and Brandom (who uses analytic techniques in the service of a pragmatic account of language rooted in our social practices).

In Section 3.5, we will investigate this phenomenon of "neo-pragmatism" more carefully, teasing out the similarities and differences between Putnam's brand with Rorty's and Brandom's. In the next few sections, the focus is rather on Putnam's appropriation of the classical pragmatists, Peirce, Dewey, and James. In "Pragmatism and Moral Objectivity" (1991), Putnam writes that there are four main theses that best characterize classical pragmatism:

> (1) *antiskepticism*: pragmatists hold that doubt requires justification as much as belief (recall Peirce's famous distinction between "real" and "philosophical" doubt); (2) *fallibilism*: pragmatists hold that there is never a metaphysical guarantee to be had that such-and-such a belief will never need revision (that one can be both fallibilistic and anti-skeptical is perhaps *the* unique insight of American pragmatism); (3) the thesis that there is no fundamental dichotomy between "facts" and "values"; and (4) the thesis that, in a certain sense, practice is primary in philosophy.[1]

In what follows, each of these theses will be taken up and examined in relation to Putnam's thought, though we will reverse the order a bit and begin with what seems most fundamental, the pragmatist contention that practice is primary in philosophy.

4.2. THE PRIMACY OF PRACTICE

According to C. S. Peirce's original formulation, the fundamental feature of pragmatism consists in the following "pragmatic maxim" about meaning:

> Consider what effects, which might conceivably have practical bearings, we conceive the object of our conception to have. Then the whole of our conception of those effects is the whole of our conception of the object.[2]

According to Peirce, there are degrees of meaningfulness depending on how much our ideas are subject to the process of inquiry. The goal of inquiry is to graduate our ideas from the most basic kind of meaning (simply being able to use a word correctly), to scientific meaning (being able to adduce conditional propositions indicating practical bearings the concept has to experience). So, for example, someone may indeed have the concept *vinegar* if she is merely able to identify it on the dining room table. But elucidating the meaning of the concept only happens when we subject the vinegar to the test, for example, when we discover that "if vinegar is an acetic acid, then if I dip litmus paper into it, it will turn red." There is no question that Peirce's original formulation of the pragmatic maxim is very similar to the positivist principle of verification, since by "practical consequences" Peirce has in mind overt empirical observations of the kind that can be intersubjectively verified by practicing scientists. Peirce's later formulation differed sharply from the positivists, however, insofar as he believed we needed to construe the conditionals that elucidate the meaning of a concept as subjunctive rather than indicative. This move effectively introduces a kind of rationalism into Peirce's account, insofar as he holds that such conditionals bring "real possibilities" into nature.

In the hands of James and Dewey, the pragmatic maxim is interpreted in yet another anti-Positivist sense, insofar as the "practical consequences" are construed not only as overt observations, but any kind of experience whatsoever. Thus, James allows that a statement like "the Absolute posits itself" has meaning, insofar as the notion of the Absolute can bring solace to the individual (James actually argues that the "cash value" of idealism consists in its being able to give an answer to the problem of evil, a very "practical" problem).[3] However, the pragmatic maxim would militate against many other metaphysical concepts, such as "substance," whose acceptance or rejection would have no practical consequences whatsoever.[4] Indeed, James uses the pragmatic maxim like the positivists to show that many of the old metaphysical debates (e.g., between materialists and dualists) are "meaningless" insofar as they make no practical difference to experience; but because of his more lenient view as to what makes something "practical," he does not dismiss all metaphysics as meaningless. According to Dewey, the "denotative method" which philosophers should employ pays close attention to "primary experience" in two ways: first, all reflection proceeds out of our prereflective experience, and second, all reflection should refer back to this experience, in order to elucidate the things of ordinary experience. On this view, metaphysical inquiry is permissible to the extent that it explains our concrete experience and gives us certain directives to further enrich this experience. And indeed, Dewey's own worldview that emerges in *Experience and Nature* engages in precisely this kind of "practically applied" metaphysical speculation.[5]

These points are important to make, since Putnam's appropriation of pragmatism clearly does not involve an appeal to a verificationist view of meaning. Indeed, insofar as we take the pragmatic maxim to be a criterion of meaning, it is worth distinguishing two different senses of "meaning." First, we can say that a concept is meaningful insofar as it is "intelligible," that is can be used in a sentence and is not self-contradictory. Thus, "unicorn," "God," and even "substance" is meaningful in this sense, though "round square" is meaningless. Second, we can say that a concept is meaningful in the sense that it is "valuable" or "worthy of further discussion," where "valuable" or "worthy" are understood as bearing practical consequences for experience. It is this understanding of "meaning" which Putnam adopts, and we see it being applied in many of his later arguments. Thus recall his critique of Chalmer's zombie argument, where Putnam argues that the possibility that there is a physical duplicate of myself that is not conscious, while "logically possible" (and hence meaningful in the first sense above), is not "fully intelligible" (and hence meaningless in the second sense). And his critique of metaphysical realism takes on a new cast when seen in this pragmatic light: for even *if* metaphysical realism were a coherent viewpoint, its adoption would make no difference to our concrete practices. It may be that the scientist, and even the "ordinary" person, seeks *truths*, for example, that grass is green and that vinegar is acetic, or that electrons are vibrating strings, etc., but nothing is added by saying "and by the way, these are *really* true, that is, by corresponding to a mind-independent reality." Now it may be that some scientists are still enraptured by absolutist thinking, for example, they might say that they are trying to come to an absolute or "final" theory of the world (one thinks of Steven Weinberg's *Dreams of a Final Theory* in this regard). But I think pragmatists, Putnam included, would respond that this way of looking at science is simply an inheritance of the bad traditional metaphysical way of thinking. As Dewey would put it, actual inquiry proceeds by focusing on "ends-in-view" rather than "fixed ends." Rorty summarizes nicely when he writes:

> In Dewey's sense of the term, discovering The Meaning of Human Life and discovering the True Nature of Physical Reality

are fixed ends. By contrast, curing cancer, fixing a leaky faucet, sending a spaceship to Arcturus, and achieving world peace, are what Dewey called "ends-in-view." These are ends toward which we know how to devise means, and are such that you can tell whether or not you have attained them . . . by contrast fixed ends of the sort that philosophers have envisaged are designed to be unattainable.[6]

This is an interesting way of reading the pragmatic maxim, for it brings out another aspect of Putnam's critique of metaphysical realism. The notion of truth as correspondence in effect offers truth as an unattainable goal—for if truth is correspondence to a mind-independent reality, how could we ever know that we have attained it? The skeptical possibility presents itself that the way the world really is differs radically from how we take it to be. But if we focus on attainable goals and disallow the unattainable, this notion of truth no longer makes any "sense." Rather, we should see truth as what would stand the test of inquiry—or, as Putnam had put it, what would be rationally acceptable under ideal epistemic conditions. Now we have already seen that Putnam has problems with this as a *definition* of truth—and indeed, he takes the pragmatists to task when they sometimes appear to apply the pragmatic maxim to the concept of truth (as when James sometimes carelessly says that truth is the "expedient in action"). But giving up the idea of Reality as some "Superthing" that makes our sentences true is surely part and parcel of applying the pragmatic maxim. It redirects our attention away from metaquestions that do not relate to experience to practical questions that make a difference to our ordinary lives in the here and now.

I think it is instructive to revisit the Twin Earth argument again in this context, since it has been argued that Putnam's argument idly turns on imagining a possible scenario that has no relevance to our linguistic practices.[7] I think the point would be telling against the "physical externalist" or naturalist reading of that argument, according to which even in 1750, prior to *anyone* knowing the chemistry of water, the reference of "water" would differ on the two planets, given that "water" refers to the substance H_2O on Earth and XYX on Twin Earth. In this case we are positing a difference that makes no difference to our linguistic practices. However, if we stick with the social externalist reading of the argument, Putnam's externalism can be seen to be quite consonant with a pragmatic perspective. The key to that reading was that the average speaker typically does not know enough about the reference of a natural-kind term to individuate it from other natural kinds, and would be committed to defer to experts when determining its reference and meaning. Here reference is not some bald word-world relation, but subject to the community of investigators. The pragmatic perspective actually helps to explain how this appeal to linguistic deference is not just a *descriptive* feature of our linguistic practice, but involves a *normative* commitment. Insofar as the average speaker wants to achieve her own ends, or "gain control of the environment" (as Dewey would put it), she too is guided by norms that govern inquiry, among them the distinction between how things appear in prereflective experience, and how things are as objects of refined reflection. Water may have certain superficial characteristics such as being thirst quenching and transparent, but those are not the properties that we need to focus on when seeking to manipulate water to serve our interests (e.g., to warm water to heat our baths). To do this, we need to apply our intelligence to nature and investigate its hidden properties. Consider Peirce's pragmatic maxim again: we know more about the meaning of "water" when we know a certain conditional like "if we heat water, the hydrogen and oxygen molecules will become more diffuse and thus appear as air rather than a liquid." This was part of the kind of educational reform Dewey sought to effect in the classroom: that the method of inquiry would be as explicitly applied by the average person as by the scientist (even if the scientist of course has a more specialized and advanced level). Putnam's externalism does justice to this model of inquiry by suggesting a continuum between average and scientific ways of speaking: the scientist is basically just carrying on the kind of research the average speaker would conduct if he had the time and the specialization in that area of knowledge. The results that the scientist arrives at, then, are not the priestly province of a few elites, but openly shared (and utilized) by everyone in the community.

As these comments suggest, Putnam would emphasize that the "return to practice" does not mean the advocacy of a "mindless activism," as Mussolini supposed when he allegedly jumped on the pragmatist bandwagon. For Peirce, of course, the return to practice simply meant the application of the scientific method, and Dewey states that the goal of pragmatism is to "intellectualize practice" which entails applying this scientific method to all areas of inquiry. This should also be enough to ward off charges of subjectivism, anti-intellectualism, and relativism that are often launched against pragmatism. For it is not up to the individual to arbitrarily decide what the scientific method is, anymore than it is up to the individual to define what a valid argument is. Furthermore, the scientific method is the same for Asians as it is for Americans. Contrary to what Rorty sometimes suggests, the pragmatists did not hold that all vocabularies are "optional," since the scientific method and the norms that guide intelligent inquiry are necessary if human beings are to achieve their ends (and even these ends can be rationally criticized). And as Putnam will stress, the pragmatists were *realists*, at least in the sense that they believed that there was an independently real world that we are held accountable to, even if all of our descriptions of this world depend on our conceptual schemes. This nuanced view—what Putnam calls a "transactional view of perception and cognition" was perhaps most lucidly set out in Dewey's *Experience and Nature*, where Dewey writes that primary experience is a "double-barreled notion" that contains a fusion of subject and object, experience and nature. We can isolate both poles as objects of reflection, but should never lose sight of either of them. As such, any view that obliterates the object in favor of the subject (idealism), or the subject in favor of the object (materialism), is a product of excessive refinement, capturing only one side of our experienced reality.

At this point, however, I can hear the following objection being raised: if the "return to practice" means an adoption of the scientific attitude to all areas of inquiry, isn't this precisely the kind of exaltation of science (or *scientism*) that Putnam had been distancing himself from more and more in his later writings? To this the following points need to be stressed: (1) that the pragmatic application of scientific method to inquiry is not a form of reductive naturalism. Here is where the *pluralistic* side of pragmatism comes in: the common world of objects and properties is to be affirmed and not reduced or eliminated. The pragmatic method is to illuminate common objects (tables and trees, flora and fauna) by seeing how they are related to the more refined objects of scientific inquiry. This will not only enrich our understanding of our own experience, but will also provide the means of manipulating our environment so that it furthers our own ends. (2) Each area of inquiry will be autonomous to a certain degree, and the scientific method as applied to it may take on different forms. A pragmatist would see the scientific method in general terms as: (1) beginning with a problem from experience that prompts inquiry, (2) proposing a hypothesis that may resolve the problem, (3) putting the hypothesis to the test via the experimental method, and (4) after confirming or disconfirming said hypothesis, drawing consequences to other areas of experience. The paradigm for the application of this method is of course the "hard" sciences like physics chemistry, and biology, since there have been so many revolutionary advances in those fields due to the adoption of the experimental method. However, the pragmatists were keen on extending this method to other areas that are not normally considered "scientific" at all. Thus Dewey writes:

> As my study and thinking progressed, I became more and more troubled by the intellectual scandal that seemed to be involved in the current (and traditional) dualism in logical standpoint and method between something called "science" on the one hand and something called "morals" on the other. I have long felt that the construction of a logic, that is, a method of effective inquiry, which would apply without abrupt breach of continuity to the fields designated by both of these words, is at once our needed theoretical solvent and the supply of our greatest practical want. This belief has had much more to do with the development of what I termed, for lack of a better word, "instrumentalism," than have most of the reasons that have been assigned.[8]

In the next section we will discuss the pragmatic approach to ethics as a case in point, but Dewey's words can apply even to a field that would seem radically disconnected from science, such as religion.[9] First, we identify the problem in our experience that gives rise to the utterance of religious statements. We might say with the Buddhists that it is *dukkha*, the sense that existence is pain and suffering, or with the Christians that human nature is sinful. We then proceed to form certain hypotheses in order to explain these features of experience: the Buddhists would say that suffering is caused by desire or craving, the Christians that sin is created by self-centeredness as opposed to God-centeredness. The next step would be to apply the experimental method in order to resolve the problem: the Buddhists claim that following their eight-fold path will rid one of desire and craving and thus eliminate suffering, the Christians that confession and repentance will eliminate their felt sinfulness. This new understanding is achieved through communal confirmation and can then be applied to other areas of experience (e.g., we could devise new forms of artistic expression to aid in the goal of eliminating desire, or raising the mind from the ego to God). Of course applying this method to religious experience has some notable differences from traditional scientific applications; the Buddhist, for example, may come up with different descriptions than the Christian (indeed, even the initial experiences which serve as data may be described differently), so there will inevitably be more disagreement here than in physics, where there is typically one common language (though I think we would actually find more agreement among religious traditions if we look behind the language to the common themes or motifs). But that does not negate the point that even here we have what Dewey would call the application of intelligence in order to resolve a concrete problem of experience. Whether this is called "scientific method" or "method of effective inquiry" is really a semantic decision that should not elide the basic point being made.

This is not to say that Putnam himself would go so far, for he often writes as if religion and science do indeed form two incommensurable domains,[10] and there are times also where he seems to stress the autonomy of commonsense ways of thinking without keeping in mind the connection between commonsense and science.[11] A pragmatist like Dewey was careful to maintain a precarious balancing act between features of our common experience and the refined objects of scientific reflection. Dewey points out, for example, that our common ways of thinking should not be left simply as they are, but should be *transformed* by science: hence we should no longer think naively that the sun moves, even though it certainly appears to commonsense that it moves.[12] Sometimes Putnam writes as if commonsense and science were simply two different incommensurable ways of speaking and that we should be tolerant in allowing both to state their claims without any infringement of one over the other. This is taking pluralism to a rather unpragmatic extreme. On the other hand, Dewey sometimes writes as if the application of the scientific method would destroy our common understandings—for example, that once we apply anthropology to religion, we will see that it is merely a sociological phenomenon. So long as we do not assume metaphysical materialism, we cannot simply treat religion sociologically. For the religious statements that are made about a nonphysical reality can be seen as hypotheses that have explanatory value to certain features of concrete experience, for example, the phenomenon of evil.[13] In any case, these brief comments at least indicate that applying the pragmatic maxim in order to effect a "return to practice" is not as simple as one may initially think.

4.3. THE FACT/VALUE DICHOTOMY

In a 1991 interview, Putnam says the following about the importance of repudiating the fact/value dichotomy:

> Doubts about whether normative judgments, and particularly ethical judgments, can be "objective" are almost universal nowadays, and clearly connected with the view that there is a fundamental dichotomy between "facts" and "values"—a view that is the product of the philosophy shop. I see the task of undermining this dichotomy as one of the central points at which one can address a real world malaise and a set of theoretical issues at the same time.[14]

It isn't hard to see what Putnam has in mind here. For the greater part of the twentieth century, when analytic philosophy was at its heights, philosophers tended to see scientific and ethical statements on two opposite ends of the cognitive spectrum: scientific statements are descriptive, fact stating, and capable of being objectively true or false (cognitive), whereas ethical statements are evaluative, expressive (or prescriptive), and incapable of being either true or false (noncognitive). Unlike other philosophical issues that remain abstract and meaningless to society at large, this dominant view on ethics found its way from the philosophy classroom to the street. Hence it is now commonplace when debating an ethical or political issue to hear someone interject "well, that's just a value judgment," with the implication being that it is simply an expression of an opinion or subjective preference that is not capable of being rationally discussed or debated. Putnam's point is well taken that here is one area at least where philosophy *can* make an impact on our everyday lives. And, unsurprisingly given their emphasis on philosophy as a practical discipline, the pragmatists rejected the fact/value dichotomy in no uncertain terms, arguing both that cognitive states like *knowing that* . . . are valuable, and that values themselves are hypotheses about the good in action that can be tested. The return to pragmatism in philosophy just may then result in a change in our common practices, a heightening of the awareness that objectivity *can* be achieved in ethics, and that rational discussion and debate on values may produce more agreement on the controversial issues of the day than people typically think possible.

In *Reason, Truth and History* (1981), where Putnam first presents arguments against the fact/value dichotomy, the issue is framed within the context of his repudiation of metaphysical realism, in particular its advocacy of the correspondence theory of truth. If a statement is made true by some fact in the world, this raises a special problem for moral statements, for what facts "in the world" could possibly make those statements true? When I say "the cat is in the yard" I have a good idea of what the fact is that makes the statement true, for I can go into the yard to see if a cat is there. But if I say "it is wrong to sacrifice one person to save five others," where can I find the "wrongness" of the action?[15] If we insist on the viewpoint according to which facts "out there" make our sentences/thoughts true or false, then it would seem that since there aren't any moral facts "out there," our moral statements are neither true nor false.[16] That would in turn support the fact/value dichotomy, insofar as value statements would be a radically different kind of statement.

One way to undermine the fact/value dichotomy, then, would be to undermine the correspondence theory of truth, and we have already seen how Putnam does this in his arguments against metaphysical realism. If what makes a sentence true or false is not correspondence to a mind-independent reality but rather rational acceptability, then moral statements can be true or false to the extent to which they are rationally acceptable. Here we do not have to worry at all about the problem of "moral facts" or how we are to refer to such "ontologically queer" entities.[17] For if Putnam is right, *all* mind-independent facts are ontologically queer, raising the problem of "magical reference" if we are said to have some kind of noetic access to them. The objectivity of morality sidesteps this entire "moral realism" debate (which Putnam takes to be instituted by G. E. Moore and his positing of "nonnatural" properties). Instead, we are directed to the question of how we can rationally justify moral claims, and here the traditional Aristotelian, Kantian, and Utilitarian arguments can compete and perhaps even collaborate in giving us all the objectivity we need in acting in accord with acceptable moral principles.

Now of course it *could* turn out that none of our moral principles are rationally justifiable, in which case none of our moral statements would be true or false, and the fact/value dichotomy would rear its ugly head again. Here is where Mackie's "argument from disagreement" comes in: he argues that we can in principle come to an agreement regarding the truth or falsity of statements like "the cat is in the yard," but not with evaluative statements like "it is wrong to sacrifice one innocent person to save five others." Putnam agrees that there is more controversy in morality than in other discourses, though he thinks this is overplayed (since, for example, there is more disagreement in science than usually thought). In any case, he is confident that rational discussion and debate on basic moral principles would yield pretty universal agreement, and he even enlists Kant's categorical imperative as a method that would give a general form to morality, even while the content when applied to particular cases might vary.[18] To my mind this is a rather weak part of Putnam's argument, since he wants to enlist Kant, Aristotle, Mill, and Levinas all as collaborators in some grand new moral synthesis, which glosses over some rather basic incompatibilities between these different moral perspectives. I think it would have been better for Putnam to focus on a *method* for producing agreement within, say, modern liberal democracies, such as is found in Rawls' *Theory of Justice* or Habermas' *Theory of Communicative Action*.[19] But in any case, these are just details to be worked out in order to provide some content to Putnam's argument. They do not affect his metaethical argument, namely, that there is no principled objection to the objectivity of moral statements.

In any case, if we focus on Putnam's characterization of truth as rational acceptability, there is an interesting argument here to the effect that *every* factual statement is an evaluative statement. For if we say that a statement or theory is "rationally acceptable" we mean that it satisfies certain epistemically ideal conditions, among them, coherence, simplicity, explanatory usefulness, etc. About these conditions Putnam writes:

> To describe a theory as "coherent, simple, explanatory" is, in the right setting, to say that acceptance of the theory is justified; and to say that the acceptance of a statement is (completely) justified is to say that one ought to accept the statement or theory.[20]

Thus, if a statement's truth is equivalent to its rational acceptability, and if rational acceptability means that one *ought* to accept the statement, then it follows that every true statement is equivalent to an evaluative statement. Furthermore, we have also seen that Putnam accepts Tarski's DQ principle, according to which every statement, for example, "Snow is white" is equivalent to the statement that it is true, that is, "Snow is white" is true. It then follows that *every* statement is an evaluative statement. Lars Bergstrom, who otherwise takes exception to Putnam's arguments against the fact/value dichotomy, concedes rather laconically that "this is a pretty remarkable result."[21] Unfortunately, it isn't clear that the argument would now be rationally acceptable to Putnam, since he has repudiated his earlier internal realist characterization of truth. I think however that a version of the argument can still work. Instead of saying that a statement's truth is *equivalent* to its rational acceptability, all we need say is that a statement's truth *implies* its rational acceptability and we can restate the above argument with the revised conclusion "every statement *implies* an evaluative statement." This might not be as "remarkable" a result, but it would still do damage to the traditional fact/value dichotomy.

If successful, this kind of argument would be effective against popular versions of the fact/value dichotomy which deny that there is any *logical connection* between evaluative and factual statements. Hume's claim that one could not logically derive an "ought" from an "is" may be taken to be a version of this thesis. Even if the above argument fails, however, Putnam has another one which does not depend on the characterization of truth as rational acceptability. He writes:

> The strategy of my argument is not going to be a new one. I am going to rehabilitate a somewhat discredited move in the debate about fact and value, namely the move that consists in arguing that the distinction is at the very least hopelessly fuzzy because factual statements themselves, and the practices of scientific inquiry upon which we rely to decide what is and what is not a fact, presuppose values.[22]

Putnam adds that "we must have criteria of rational acceptability to even have an empirical world" and that "without the cognitive values of coherence, simplicity, and instrumental efficacy we have no world and no facts." The leading idea here is to echo Kuhn's insights as to the sociological image of science, as against the naïve empiricism of the positivists and Karl Popper. Scientific theories get accepted or rejected not merely because of predictive accuracy, but also due to whether or not they accord with certain values, such as coherence, comprehensiveness, simplicity, or even the vague "reasonableness." This is especially clear in the case of theory conflict, where we have two or more theories that agree on all the empirical evidence and yet make incompatible claims. Kuhn gives many examples of how theory choice is guided by normative considerations in his *The Structure of Scientific Revolutions*: to mention one, consider that in the late nineteenth century, Darwinian theory lacked predictive power: it was unclear whether or not the empirical evidence corroborated it, and it did not appear to imply any observations that could falsify it. Nevertheless, it quickly became accepted by the majority of scientists because of its explanatory power in accounting for homology, embryology, and the fossil record, among other things. We can say then that evolution was accepted by scientists because it was a "valuable" theory: it not only supplied the missing link (natural selection) in explaining various phenomena, but it also provided scientists with a research program for further applications. Putnam takes this conclusion and goes one step further: every theory that is part of our modern scientific worldview results from these norms that govern theory choice; and since facts cannot be made sense of independently of the theories they are couched in, all facts presuppose values.

Against this, one might argue that the most this shows is that scientific theories or beliefs presuppose values, not that facts *per se* presuppose values. Here one can locate an ambiguity in Putnam's claim that "without no cognitive values we have no world and no facts": does this mean that without cognitive values we can have no scientific beliefs about the world, or rather that without values there is no world at all? One might agree with the first claim and not with the second, and insist that the fact/value dichotomy ought to be read as an ontological thesis and not as an epistemic thesis regarding preconditions to our beliefs. Of course, the problem with this response to Putnam is that it appears to presuppose metaphysical realism, since it supposes that we can attach a meaning to "the world" independently of our beliefs about the world. We have already chronicled the various arguments against this picture of a "ready-made world" said to be independent of conceptualization and classification. In the pragmatic context, this rejection of metaphysical realism takes on a new light, since the notion of a world completely independent of our beliefs would be meaningless to our common practices. Nevertheless, this objection at least brings out the point that Putnam's "argument from science" against the fact/value dichotomy, while not requiring an internal realist view of truth, at least requires the rejection of metaphysical realism (like his previous argument). It does not stand on its own as an independent argument.

Putnam's third argument against the fact/value dichotomy is one he spends most of his time defending in his book *The Collapse of the Fact/Value Dichotomy* (2003). Here he follows Bernard Williams' lead in drawing a distinction between thin and thick ethical concepts.[23] Thin ethical concepts such as "good," "bad," "right," and "wrong" are very general and leave it open as to what precisely constitutes them—in this respect they stand almost as placeholders for a specific theory to be fleshed out later. Thick concepts, on the other hand, carry with them a more substantive (but not necessarily complete) meaning. We may disagree about when "gratitude," for example, is ethically required, but we all understand that gratitude is the appropriate recognition of a good deed toward oneself, family, or group, and that gratitude is morally virtuous. Another example of a thick ethical concept would be "deceit." Deceit is a morally bad form of deception. Although we may disagree as to whether a particular act should be classified as deceitful (or, say, a white lie), the term "deceit" itself carries with it a clear enough idea of what it is and that it is morally bad. But as Putnam points out, we typically use such concepts descriptively, for example, in saying something like "George Bush deceived the American people about the Iraq War," or "John was grateful to his brother for standing by him in his time of need." A close analysis of such concepts reveals that it is impossible to "disentangle" their factual and evaluative components.

An advocate of the two-component theory might respond that even if thick ethical concepts have both a factual and an evaluative component, it may still be possible to uphold a fact/value dichotomy. Consider a statement like "Attila the Hun was cruel." Let us grant that this is meaningful and true. Now if we wanted to justify the statement, the most straightforward way would be to simply list the cruel things Attila the Hun did. This would be purely positive information: Attila killed women and children; he tortured his prisoners, etc. Now suppose someone says: "I know all these facts, but I don't think Attila the Hun was cruel." Is there any factual content that could explain this difference of opinions? The advocate of the fact/value dichotomy could argue there is none: the difference of opinion would be purely a disagreement about values. Thus the statement "Atilla the Hun was cruel" results from putting two components together: the factual information consisting solely of positive information, and the evaluative statement(s), which upon analysis might involve something like "killing women and children is wrong," or "torture is wrong." Unfortunately this response fails to hit its target. At times Putnam backs off his suggestion that *all* statements are evaluative, claiming that while there is a fact/value distinction, there is no fact/value *dichotomy*.[24] Thus it may be possible to describe some of the cruel *things* that Atilla did without bringing in any values. However, the point is that we can no longer describe these as *"cruel* things." There is no way to restate "cruel" in purely factual idioms, and this is Putnam's main point.

While Putnam appeals to Bernard Williams in making this argument against the fact/value dichotomy, there is an important difference between them. Williams is a metaphysical realist and an advocate of what he calls the "objective perspective," according to which science reveals how things are in themselves, completely independent of human perspective. Williams contrasts this with ethics, which concerns concepts that are always formed from a particular perspective. Or better: the general "thin" concepts like "good" or "right" may be universal but have no content, whereas the substantial "thick" concepts, have content but are relative to culture and historical standpoint. In order to use a term like "courage" or "gratitude" we have to adopt the culture's point of view, but there is no compulsion to adopt this point of view for outsiders. Thus while it may be possible to "go native" and understand an alternative culture, there is no culture-independent perspective from which to criticize certain ethical conceptions as better than others. This cultural relativism has some important political implications: Williams goes on to argue that we cannot defend modern democracy in "vindicatory terms," claiming for instance that it is more justifiable than the divine right of kings. For the very terms that we appeal to in order to make such a vindication—concepts of "reason" and "freedom" were not had by ancient regimes and thus there would have been nothing to argue about.

Putnam responds that Williams is falling into the familiar dualist trap by presenting us with a false dichotomy: either we see certain ethical perspectives (like that represented by the Enlightenment) as mere "contingent" products of a particular history, *or* we attempt to justify such perspectives from an "absolute perspective" which would be completely free of history and cultural perspective. This ignores a third possibility, "the possibility of pragmatism."[25] Dewey in particular attempted to bring the experimental method into ethics and politics but in so doing acknowledged there could only be a *situated* resolution of ethical and political problems. The application of intelligence to settle differences implies that there can be better or worse reasons for a particular claim, and so in this sense justifies the idea that argument is possible in ethics (and thus also the possibility of *vindicating* one view over another). On the other hand, there is no way to completely abstract from contingent historical perspective, for it is always from within a concrete problem situation that inquiry arises. This is true for the hard sciences, but of course even more true for ethics and politics. The middle path that Putnam and the pragmatists call for consists in lowering the standard for knowledge and truth in science but raising them in ethics and politics. What results is a more nuanced view where every domain of inquiry is epistemologically on the same level, even if there may still be a difference in degree. Thus, Dewey writes in *The Quest for Certainty* that "a moral law, like a law in physics, is not something to swear by and stick to at all hazards; it is a formula of the way to respond when specified conditions present themselves. Its soundness and pertinence are tested by what happens when it is acted on" (p. 222). Putnam has argued for this Deweyan concept in a number of papers, emphasizing that it allows for criticizing not just the means but the *ends* of inquiry (and thus Dewey should not be read as any kind of instrumentalist, as Rorty tends to read him).

That the cultural relativism Williams defends is a political and not just ethical perspective is made clear when he denies that there can be a "vindicatory" history of the triumph of democracy. Against this, the pragmatists urged that democracy was not merely a new form of government (one expressing "the will of the people"), but rather a method of thinking and of social transformation. In his paper "A Reconsideration of Deweyan Democracy," Putnam seeks to defend the Deweyan thesis that "democracy is a precondition for the full application of intelligence to solving social problems." In a particularly incisive passage, Dewey writes:

> History shows that there have been benevolent despots who wish to bestow blessings on others. They have not succeeded, except when their actions have taken the indirect form of changing the conditions under which those live who are disadvantageously placed. The same principle holds of reformers and philanthropists when they try to do good to others in ways which leave passive those to be benefited. There is a moral tragedy inherent in efforts to further the common good which prevent the result from being either good or common—not good, because it is at the expense of the active growth of those to be helped, and not common because these have no share in bringing the result about.[26]

This suggests yet another way in which facts are enmeshed with values. In order to determine what values a society should pursue (freedom, justice, etc.), we need to know what the interests and needs are of the people in that society. And such interests and needs (descriptive "facts" about one's psychology) are themselves determined through free discussion and exchange of ideas, enshrined and encouraged in a liberal democracy. After such free inquiry, one might come to see a new possibility and hence come to expand one's vision of the good and/or how to obtain it. Despotism, no matter how benevolent, blocks the road to inquiry and hence truncates this vision of the good. A vision of life based on one person's interests and needs will pale in comparison to the vision afforded by thousands of actively seeking and discussing members of a society. But of course, this reference to "the good" should be taken with a grain of salt, for the ultimate ends for which we act are not known prior to inquiry, and they can always be changed with further inquiry and as new problem situations arise. To dissolve the fact/value dichotomy is to make possible objectivity in ethics, but it is not any sort of return to moral absolutism.

4.4. ANTISKEPTICISM AND FALLIBILISM

To recall, Putnam claims "that one can be both fallibilistic and antiskeptical is perhaps *the* unique insight of American pragmatism."

It was characteristic of the pragmatists to constantly strive for a "middle path" between extremes, and nowhere is this so clear as in their approach to the traditional epistemological "chestnut" of skepticism. On one extreme we have Cartesian skepticism, which asks us to begin by doubting all of our beliefs until we finally arrive at a belief that cannot be doubted. Peirce's early articles were focused on attacking this method, and indeed he believed it quickly founders once we ask "what is the justification for doubting?" If our common beliefs are providing roadblocks to inquiry, they can be corrected, but if we simply doubt them in order to obtain some elusive goal of certainty, then there is no point to it. Dewey put the point by saying that in philosophy we should "start where we are at," rather than try to fashion some epistemologically privileged anchor to support all of our beliefs. This can be seen as an application of the pragmatic maxim, insofar as Cartesian doubts are paper doubts that cannot possibly stimulate anyone to real inquiry.

In combating skepticism, the pragmatists did not try to present transcendental arguments against the skeptic, nor did they seek to replace the uncertainty of skepticism with the equally mistaken eternal veracities of *a priori* philosophy. Indeed, skepticism and the *a priori* method are both flip sides of the same coin: for skepticism only results when philosophers assume the *a priori* standard and conclude that no knowledge can meet it. Instead of searching for certainty, philosophy should model itself on real inquiry, which focuses on real problems, allows doubt only when it is real, and offers solutions that resolve these problems, even when falling well short of certainty. Anyone with an iota of comprehension of the scientific method understands this approach: no scientist claims that he has "proven" his theory, only that it is more or less confirmed. Ironically, by lowering the epistemic standards and not demanding certainty, the pragmatists raised the possibility of objectivity. For now it is open for us to claim that certain truths or even perspectives of the world *are* true, provided we add "provisionally true," until some other real problem is encountered that would force us to revise that truth.

Oddly enough (considering this appeal to scientific method to defray skepticism), modern forms of skepticism avert not to the Cartesian *a priori*, but rather to science itself to open up a gap between how things appear and the way things are. As we have seen, this is the perspective typical of metaphysical realism, called the "Objective Perspective" by Williams, the "View from Nowhere" by Nagel, and the "God's Eye Viewpoint" by Putnam. As Nagel puts it, "realism makes skepticism intelligible," because once we open the gap between truth and epistemology, we must countenance the possibility that all of our beliefs, no matter how well justified, nevertheless fail to accurately depict the world as it really is.[27] Donald Davidson also emphasizes this aspect of metaphysical realism: "metaphysical realism is skepticism in one of its traditional garbs. It asks: why couldn't all my beliefs hang together and yet be comprehensively false about the actual world?"[28] (1986, 309). Realists often appeal to science in making this argument, for it is science itself that has taught us that our commonsense picture of the world is radically mistaken. Not only that, but the march of science tends to destroy every theory and thus every so-called truth: for just as present theories have destroyed past theories once thought not only true but indubitable (e.g., Euclidean geometry), future theories will show that our present theories are all false. The Objective Perspective takes no prisoners, and this is so not because of *a priori* views about foundations of knowledge, but because of our *a posteriori* knowledge of the history of science. Putnam himself used this "metainduction" argument to argue for a realist position in his early work, and indeed we have seen how his internal realism sprung up in part as a response to the skeptical outlook such a view engenders (thus his attempt to give *a priori* arguments against skepticism, most notably his BIVs argument). The leading idea here is that skeptical views are self-defeating in the same way that the statement "all statements are false" is self-defeating. An utterance like "we are brains in a vat" appears to be intelligible, since we think we can conceive such scenarios (e.g., the movie *The Matrix*). But when we draw out the consequences of being a BIV, we realize that if we adopt that perspective, we could no longer *think* we are BIVs. That is, Putnam's strategy is to initially grant the intelligibility of skepticism and then provide *reductio ad absurdums* against it. What results from this exercise is the need to alter our concepts of meaning and truth, to become aware of Kant's Copernican turn, and to realize, as James put it, that "the trail of the human serpent is over everything."

We have also seen the dangers in this approach, for transcendental arguments always appear question-begging against the skeptic.

In short, if we play by the skeptic's rules we will lose, and this has been clear since at least Descartes and his attempt to pull us out of the morass of skepticism via his question-begging proof for the existence of God. There is also a methodological problem in Putnam's middle strategy: for we have to grant the initial intelligibility of the skeptical scenario in order to ultimately show it to be unintelligible. This is very much like the Tractarian problem of being able to say that alternative logics are nonsense from within our own logic. From within our own logic, an alternative logic is unintelligible: but then propositions about an alternative logic are not propositions at all (and hence not negatable!). In his study of Kant, Frege, Wittgenstein, and Putnam on just this problem of being able to express the impossibility of "logically alien thought," James Conant concludes:

> In the end, however, the snake bites its own tail. Our guiding idea—the idea that "we cannot make mistakes in logic" turns out to be nonsense. For if the sentence "we can make mistakes in logic" turns out to be nonsense, then so does its denial. But in order to make sense of either of these sentences we have to make sense of "the possibility of illogical thought." Each rung of the ladder depends on its predecessors for support. The collapse of one rung triggers the collapse of the next . . . The aim is not to take us from a piece of apparently deep nonsense to a deep insight into the nature of things, but rather from a piece of apparently deep nonsense to the dissolution of the appearance of depth.[29]

Conant's "the snake bites its own tail" is a fitting rejoinder to James' "the trail of the human serpent is over everything." For we are led to make these "deep philosophical" claims about "the mind-dependence of truth," or "the revisability of logic" only when we grant the intelligibility of realism and skepticism, and then proceed to negate these ways of speaking. From this vantage point, the best response to skepticism is not to refute it, for that would be to simply negate what is an already unintelligible possibility. This would appear to be more in keeping with the pragmatic perspective, which refuses to play the skeptical game and simply accepts that our common beliefs are true until some real problem prompts doubt. But as James' quote indicates, even the pragmatists fell into the trap of making totalizing remarks, negations of absolutist ways of thinking deeply integral to the tradition of philosophy. For they were led to make general statements like "every belief is revisable," when even this lapses into unintelligibility when we countenance the possibility of a "logically alien language." That is why Putnam no longer wishes to be considered a "fallibilist," without qualification. For fallibilism begins to look suspiciously like the negation of infallibilism, and thus will inherit the very same incoherence.

One last point must be made when discussing the issue of skepticism vis-a-vis the pragmatists. While someone like James was definitely a pluralist and fallibilist, he also held that when one commits to a belief, one should do so passionately. One shouldn't always go around hedging one's bets, or suspending judgment just because there is a possibility that one could be wrong. James famously upheld this viewpoint for religious belief, where he argues against the idea that one should always proportion the belief to the evidence. As he writes:

> Our passional nature not only lawfully may, but must, decide an opposition between propositions, whenever it is a genuine option that cannot by its nature be decided on intellectual grounds, for to say under such circumstances, "Do not decide, but keep the question open," is itself a passional decision—just like deciding yes or no—and is attended with the same risk of losing the truth.[30]

This aspect of James's pragmatism at least forges an interesting connection to existentialism, particularly Kierkegaard's concept of "subjective truth" where the truth of one's belief can sometimes only be ascertained after you commit to what may at first seem absurd. But I think there is also a clear connection to Richard Rorty's ironism here as well. For Rorty, the ironic attitude consists in being committed to certain beliefs even while knowing how contingent and interest relative they are. Because beliefs are action guiding rather than world directed, we do not need to adopt a skeptical attitude to them, for we cannot escape acting in the world. On the other hand, all our beliefs are made from a limited contingent point of view and can be given up once they are no longer deemed useful in the satisfaction of our concrete ends. Fortunately for us, being a product of liberal democratic societies enables us to commit passionately to democratic beliefs, which encourage the free discussion of ideas and the right of diverse ways of life to coexist. All of this is merely the product of ethnocentrism, but our ethnocentrism includes the values of diversity and tolerance and hence ironically undermines itself. In the next section, however, we shall see that Putnam is not a full-fledged ironist. The key to unraveling the differences between Putnam and Rorty on this issue as well as others will consist in their diverging interpretations of the classical pragmatists.

4.5. NEO-PRAGMATISM: PUTNAM VERSUS RORTY AND BRANDOM

Neo-pragmatists can be described loosely as disillusioned analytic philosophers who have turned back to the pragmatists in order to initiate a new philosophical perspective, one that seeks to go beyond the traditional aspirations of analytic philosophy while nevertheless preserving certain aspects of its methodology, in particular the focus on language. Here is how Rorty himself describes this transition:

> Analytic philosophy, thanks to its concentration on language, was able to defend crucial pragmatist theses better than Dewey and James themselves. . . . By focusing our attention on the relation between language and the rest of the world rather than between experience and nature, post-positivistic analytic philosophy was able to make a more radical break with the philosophical tradition.[31]

Rorty basically sees Quine and Davidson as inaugurating the breakdown of analytic philosophy's traditional goals (e.g., using linguistic methods to solve traditional metaphysical problems or to provide a foundation for knowledge). One then sees that the classical pragmatists were in an imprecise way trying to do what Quine and Davidson did in a more precise way. But returning to the pragmatists has the additional value of opening up other areas of inquiry that Quine and Davidson never ventured into—art, literature, ethics, religion, etc. The idea is that the pragmatic perspective has a twofold liberating effect: first, it can get us to stop reconstructing what should not be reconstructed, and second, it encourages us to come up with new reinventions in order to serve whatever "concrete ends" we deem best.

Neo-pragmatists can perhaps be distinguished from other varieties of "postanalytic philosophy" through its emphasis on language. We have already seen how Putnam's semantic externalism is crucial toward understanding his thought as a whole, and how it is one of the main commitments he has preserved and reapplied throughout his entire career. True enough, he has recently discussed the importance of "experience" as providing a justificatory role in linking us up to the world, and this might seem to be a lapse into some prelinguistic philosophy that Rorty would balk at. However, as we have seen, even in this context Putnam emphasizes the role of language in enriching experience: recall his claim that I can experience something *as a resistor* rather than merely experience a sense-datum, since I have a concept of "resistor" that is expressible in language. No doubt Rorty goes further than Putnam when he claims:

> I linguisticize as many pre-linguistic turn philosophers as I can, in order to read them as prophets of the utopia in which all metaphysical problems have been dissolved, and religion and science have yielded their place to poetry.[32]

For Rorty, everything is a matter of adopting a certain vocabulary, and all language is a mere tool that we can pick up or discard as we choose. We have seen that Putnam's pragmatic pluralism agrees with Rorty insofar as we should allow different areas of discourse the autonomy to state their claims without reducing them all to one "higher class" vocabulary. However, he would point out that this very idea would argue *against* Rorty's own privileging of poetry over religion and science, and he would also claim that there are certain aspects of rational inquiry that *can* be preserved in all domains (so that it is not merely a matter of choosing a certain way of speaking—or rather, once we do choose a way of speaking, we are bound to certain norms over and above our speech dispositions to assent or dissent). In Robert Brandom's version of neo-pragmatism, the goal of the philosopher is to articulate the different moves a speaker can make in Sellar's game of giving and taking reasons. This is "pragmatic" insofar as the focus is on what speakers *do* when they use language, but in keeping with the priority of language he basically identifies intentionality with the possession of language. As he writes: "expressing something is *conceptualizing* it . . . in general, addressing it in a form that can serve as and stand in need of reasons, making it *inferentially* significant."[33] Like Rorty and Putnam, Brandom seeks to articulate the social character of meaning and content, though unlike them he appears exclusively focused on the traditional domains of analytic philosophy (philosophy of language and mind).

It isn't always easy to ascertain just what the difference is between Rorty and Putnam, once one goes beyond the rhetoric. Rorty himself does not think Putnam's view is any different from his, saying in an interview "I don't know what he is going on about . . . if I'm a relativist, then he's one too."[34] Rorty basically claims that Putnam's talk about "natural realism" and the need to be "responsible to reality" is mere rhetoric that has no force once we have taken the pragmatic turn and given up the concept of a "superthing" that makes our sentences true or false. Putnam however believes that Rorty's interpretation of the traditional pragmatists is egregiously inaccurate, and that his view spirals off into a dangerous extreme of postmodern relativism. These two criticisms are related, for according to Putnam Rorty's relativism can be seen as following from his flawed reading of the pragmatists.

For Rorty, the pragmatists were chiefly concerned with redefining truth as "success," and "success" in terms of "satisfaction of wants." Thus the pragmatists are seen as instrumentalists, justifying beliefs to the extent to which they satisfy our animal desires. For all Rorty's postmodern pluralism, the picture that emerges is a form of naturalistic reductionism insofar as human beings are viewed as no more than utility-maximizing animals. According to Putnam, this ignores Dewey's insistence that the ends of inquiry are themselves open to rational discussion and debate, and it also ignores the ubiquity of the normative in assessing *what* our interests are (thus it makes no sense to call them "animal desires" at all due to the role of culture in shaping what our interests are). In one of his last articles, "Putnam, Pragmatism, and Parmenides" (2003), Rorty basically concedes to Putnam that, while the pragmatists *can* be read as instrumentalists, instrumentalism itself is a suspect view, nearly as absolute in its pretensions as the Platonism it is seeking to distance itself from. As he writes:

> I was trying to pin down the goal of human life by describing it in terms of the gratification of desire, and thinking of desire

on the model of what Brandom, following Hegel, calls *sinnliche Neigungen*: simple animal urges like the need to stop itching. Brandom's article "Pragmatics and pragmatisms" finally succeeded in making me see that my analogy between the ideal beaver dam and the ideal set of human beliefs would be appropriate only if I were trying to develop a reductionist view of human beings of the sort currently being pursued by people like Steven Pinker and E.O. Wilson, who are dismissive of the idea that "culture" is of any great importance in understanding human beings. That is about the last thing I want to do.

On this reading, the pragmatists were not trying to seriously answer the question "what is truth?" by talking about success or the attainment of our interests, but rather simply mocking that question by giving a naturalistic, reductive answer. There is a connection to Rorty's ironism here: the postmodern pragmatist realizes how central words like "truth" and "goodness" are to our culture, so instead of simply giving them up he continues to use them, but in ways that undermine their traditional meaning. One unfortunate consequence of this strategy, however, is that it leads critics to take such statements too seriously, and what results are the familiar charges of "self-refutation." Rorty himself has been lumped into this category, being charged with self-refuting positions like the claim that "all truth is relative." But from Rorty's perspective, this misses the whole point of the ironist strategy, which is to make totalizing remarks only in order to call into question totalizing ways of speaking.

Putnam, however, refuses to let Rorty off the hook so easily. First of all, Rorty often writes (particularly in early works such as *Consequences of Pragmatism*) as though truth is nothing more than communal consensus (or "warrant"). Putnam is easily able to criticize this, much as his critics attacked his own internal realist characterization of truth. If truth is simply what is warranted by the majority of people, then since the majority of people are traditional realists, it would follow that realism is true and Rorty's characterization of truth false.[35] Rorty, like Putnam, soon became well aware of the problems with defining truth and following Davidson's lead, he came to explicitly reject any attempt to explicate the notion of truth in terms of other concepts. Rorty's mature position is not that truth is reducible to warrant but that the concept has no deep or substantive criteria at all. Indeed, for Rorty, this is part of what makes the concept so useful, since it ensures that no sentence can ever be analytically certified as true by virtue of its possession of some other property. At the same time, talk about "aiming for the truth" when this is taken in its substantive sense, can usually be "cashed out" in terms of reaching intersubjective agreement. As long as we distinguish the semantic concept of truth from the epistemic one of warrant there is no problem, and definitely no danger of self-refutation.

The deeper criticism that Putnam launches against Rorty is not directed at his concept of truth, but at his concept of *warrant*. For Putnam, we cannot simply identify a warranted belief with what most people believe (or assent to) since this undermines the very concept of warrant itself. Rorty's naturalistic, dispositional account ignores the normativity involved in the concept of warrant: for to say that a belief is warranted implies that one should believe it regardless of whether anyone else does so. This applies to ethical concepts like "being good" as well, as Putnam writes: "it is internal to our picture of reform that whether the outcome of a change is good (a reform) or bad (its opposite) is logically independent of whether it seems good or bad."[36] The main problem with Rorty is his naturalistic outlook which he shares with Quine. Both Quine and Rorty reject the traditional talk about "meaning" and "truth" as mythology, and yet they both help themselves to the notion of "speech disposition" as though that were ontologically unproblematic. In *Word and Object* (1960), Quine writes famously that the only fact of the matter to meaning is "the totality of a speaker's dispositions," and this comes to play again in Rorty's concept of warrant as the disposition of a culture to agree to a set of sentences. But then, as Putnam writes:

> But if the whole project of saying how the world is, as opposed to saying what sentences we utter, has collapsed, then why are dispositions, of all things, in better shape than truth? The philosophical problems associated with disposition talk (including counterfactual talk) are just as formidable as the philosophical problems associated with the notion of truth. It looks—to me at any rate—as if Rorty says "no more metastories" and tries to convince us by telling us a higher level metastory of his own, a cultural relativist or cultural imperialist metastory. But if you go

with Wittgenstein so far as to say "no more metastories," then you had better not tell me a metastory—not even a metametastory![37]

This is where Putnam's talk of "being responsible to reality," his natural realism, comes in as an alternative to Rorty's postmodern relativism. Just because the absolute conception is defunct and there is no "superthing" that makes our sentences true or false does not mean that we can simply jettison the concept of reality, or the distinction between something being the case and seeming the case. Rorty is throwing the baby out with the bathwater or, as Putnam puts it in his Dewey lectures, he is part of the problem of jumping "from frying pan to fire, from fire to a different frying pan . . . apparently without end."[38] The middle line between the excesses of metaphysical realism and relativism lies in attending to the norms that underlie our practices of inquiry, and these norms will require us to be responsible to an independent reality, even while recognizing that our descriptions of this independent reality will be shaped by our concepts. In terms of the pragmatist underpinnings of their views, clearly this was closer to Dewey's conception, who stressed the "objective pole" of our experience as something that often confronts us and compels us to revise our beliefs.

Rorty's response to Putnam is to basically deny that there is any middle ground at all. As he writes,

> My claim was that once we give up on copying we can substitute "coping with reality" for "being responsible to reality." Without a superthing, how are we supposed to distinguish between a successful coping and fulfilled responsibility? Once we dispense with a superthing, what is there left to be responsible to save our fellow inquirers?[39]

Rorty goes on to suggest that since there can be no view that does not reflect our interests and values, we cannot even claim that Newtonian physics was objectively superior to Aristotelian physics. Here we see Rorty sliding into a pretty blatant relativism, like that of Bernard Williams', only applicable to science as well. All of Putnam's arguments against Williams could then be applied with equal force against Rorty. The main difference it seems goes back to the issue of naturalism: for Putnam, norms, while contingent and evolving, stand over the individual as principles that guide inquiry.

They determine the distinction between correct and incorrect uses of linguistic expressions, as when Bert stands to be corrected when he misuses "arthritis" to apply to his thigh. For Rorty, since the only fact of the matter is speech dispositions, norms emerge as just statistical indicators of what people in fact do—they have no real binding force. Hence they are optional and if we do not like a certain discourse we can always opt out of it and switch to another. Putnam's pluralism agrees with Rorty that certain discourses are optional, but he does not think that *every* discourse is optional. As a true pragmatist, he would maintain that the everyday discourse by which we get along with our peers is *not* optional. And once our ends-in-view are fixed, we find ourselves committed not only to the norms of a particular discourse, but to certain metanorms that govern all rational inquiry. No doubt Rorty would find Putnam's adherence to these norms of rationality a vestigial commitment to Kantianism, but to this Putnam can sensibly respond that he is preserving the best part of Kant's critical philosophy while throwing out its bad *a priori* elements.

It is interesting to see the reaction of Rorty to someone like Robert Brandom in this regard, since Rorty has called Brandom "the most important living American philosopher," and that while he and Putnam are just applying some insights of Dewey's, Brandom (and Davidson) are the real "original philosophers."[40] And yet for Brandom normativity is essential in the formulation of a sound semantics (and he even calls it "normative pragmatics"). We can understand why certain terms are essential in our linguistic practices (e.g., *de re* ascriptions) in terms of what a speaker is committed to when he uses them, and we can only understand semantic contents in light of the correctness of practical performances of judging and acting. I believe that Brandom's normative pragmatics can be made fairly consonant with Putnam's social externalism (though more needs to be said about this, since Brandom's view superficially resembles the conceptual role semantics that Putnam rightly criticizes). But Brandom rather unashamedly plays up the Kantian aspects of his view on language, and this would inevitably distance himself from Rorty's more naturalistic approach. Putnam's main criticism of Brandom is not directed to his positive views *per se*, but rather to his interpretation of the pragmatists, which Brandom reads in a very Rortyesque way as "a philosophical school of thought centered on evaluating beliefs by their tendency to promote success at the satisfaction of wants."[41] We have already seen how Putnam rejects Rorty's instrumentalist reading of the classical pragmatists, and his critique would equally apply to Brandom. So, to sum up the neo-pragmatist scorecard: Rorty and Brandom agree on their reading of the classical pragmatists as instrumentalists as opposed to Putnam's more realist interpretation, while Putnam and Brandom generally agree on normative pragmatics as opposed to Rorty's naturalism-cum-relativism. The jury is still out as to which viewpoint will define the neo-pragmatist movement, but I think that any such discussion ought to begin with a careful comparison and contrast of these three thinkers.

4.6. CONCLUSION

I hope that enough has been said about Putnam's drawings from the well of pragmatism to help motivate a new way of doing philosophy in the twenty-first century. It is one that has truly learned from the lessons of both traditional and more recent analytic philosophy. The old dualisms between language/world, mind/body, subject/object, fact/value are tired and can no longer be taken as providing the canonical problems for philosophers to focus on. At the same time, while absolute dichotomies are to be deconstructed or at least undermined by multivarious strategies (among them Putnam's brand of old-fashioned logical analysis), this by itself is not the end all and be all of philosophy. To think that would be to basically call for an "end of philosophy," and as Putnam once put it, philosophy always buries its undertakers. Rather, the pragmatic dimension to philosophy calls for making distinctions where they are useful in resolving real problems, and actively extending rational inquiry to all dimensions of life in the hopes that we can create a better world for ourselves and our brothers and sisters. Aristotle's goal of achieving human flourishing should be our goal as well, though we should pursue it well aware that teleological metaphysics is dead, and that all belief, whether philosophical or otherwise, is contingent but no less important for its contingency. Putnam's ultimate legacy to future generations of philosophers is the way he has approached the questions: humble enough to correct his views when they have faltered, but courageous enough to press them outside the boundaries of conventional wisdom. The quote from Rilke's *Letters to a Young Poet* that Putnam selected to preface his *Realism with a*

Human Face perhaps captures best the spirit of Putnam's legacy to philosophy: "Be patient toward all that is unsolved in your heart and try to love the *questions themselves* like locked rooms and like books that are written in a very foreign tongue. Live the questions now. Perhaps you will then gradually, without noticing it, live along some distant day into the answers."

NOTES

INTRODUCTION

1. Richard Rorty, *Review of Philosophical Papers: Volume 3*, London Review of Books (1983).
2. The only other full-length study of Putnam at the time of this publication is Christopher Norris's *Hilary Putnam: Realism, Reason, and the Limits of Uncertainty*, (2002), though Norris focuses mostly on Putnam's views on the realism debate and not on his philosophy as a whole.
3. John Passmore, *Recent Philosophers* (1983).
4. By "scientific naturalism" I mean reductive views that seek to explain commonsense discourse and intentional idioms in terms of a "higher-class" vocabulary of the natural sciences (or else eliminate those discourses). This is not Dewey's brand of naturalism, which was *not* reductive though it did try to inform (and transform) common experience through scientific method. This contrast will be clarified in the fourth chapter, but the reader should keep in mind that Putnam's targets are those like Quine, Fodor, the Churchlands, *not* Dewey.
5. Putnam says "not fully intelligible" rather than "unintelligible" since he doesn't want to simply dismiss all philosophical problems as pseudo-problems. See his discussion of "full intelligibility" which is influenced heavily by Stanley Cavell, in his Royce Lectures, reprinted in *The Threefold Cord: Mind, Body and World* (2002), pp. 82–83.
6. Wittgenstein, *Philosophical Investigations* (1984), §116. Although as we shall see in Chapter 4, a pragmatic perspective does not simply return us to our common experience but *transforms* this commonplace, which Dewey describes as often "stunted, aborted, slack, and heavy laden."
7. See *Post-Analytical Philosophy* (1985), ed. Cornell West and John Rajchman for a collection of articles on this new development among analytically trained philosophers.
8. *Words and Life* (1994), p. 552.
9. *Realism with a Human Face* (1990), p. xi. This reference to "the good" should also recall Aristotle's pluralistic critique of Plato's absolute conception of the good.
10. This contrasts sharply with Norris, who takes Putnam's early period to contain his most important and philosophically defensible work.

NOTES

CHAPTER 1: THE ROAD TO SEMANTIC EXTERNALISM

1. Putnam discusses the nuances of Reichenbach's views in "Reichenbach's Metaphysical Picture," "Reichenbach and the Myth of the Given," and "Reichenbach and the Limits of Vindication" in *Words and Life* (1994).
2. Nearly all the Positivists, Carnap included, eventually rejected phenomenalism for physicalism, and replaced behaviorism with some version of type identity theory (also known at the time as "central state materialism"). Putnam's functionalism can be seen as an outgrowth of a search for a position that would escape his own crippling objections to both behaviorism and identity theory. This discussion will be taken up in Section 3.1, "The Rise of Computational Functionalism."
3. Recent Putnam would, importantly, agree with the pragmatic attempt to repudiate traditional metaphysics and come to agreement on philosophical issues through rational inquiry, while rejecting the idea that rational inquiry should be simply equated with natural science or the project of "scientific unification." Early Putnam was often unknowingly caught between these two different philosophical orientations.
4. For a more detailed analysis of Carnap's views on analyticity, see Michael Friedman, *Reconsidering Logical Positivism*, chapter 7, "Analytic Truth in Carnap's *Logical Syntax of Language*" (1999).
5. In "Replies and Systematic Expositions," *The Philosophy of Rudolph Carnap* (1963), p. 932.
6. "Ontological Relativity" in *Ontological Relativity and Other Essays* (1969), p. 29.
7. This contrasts with terms like "phlogiston" which was abandoned once oxygen theory became well established.
8. "In Defense of a Dogma," *Philosophical Review* (1957).
9. This is a variation of an example originally posed by Edward Shirley in his "Putnam on Analyticity," *Philosophical Studies* (1972).
10. On this point Putnam is in agreement with Frege: a difference in reference entails a difference in meaning. It also attunes well to our actual practices of translation and interpretation.
11. This example shows that in Putnam's theory, a difference in extension alone is sufficient to entail a difference in meaning. However, we must keep in mind that meaning is vectored to both the stereotype and the extension: hence, if the stereotype changes, the meaning would also change. Thus Putnam writes that if a gas came into the environment and turned all lemons blue, then the meaning of "lemon" *would* change, since there was a change in the stereotype. This would not mean, however, that the yellow lemons that are still in my blender are no longer lemons. For "lemon" would still refer to the same natural kind, whose normal members had once been yellow but are now blue. There are cases, then, where a term can continue to refer to the same thing even though its meaning has changed.
12. In *Word and Object* (1960), p. 221.

NOTES

13. W. V. Quine, "On What There Is," reprinted in *From a Logical Point of View* (1980); Putnam, "What is Mathematical Truth," in *Mathematics Matter and Method: Philosophical Papers, Volume 1* (1979), pp. 60–78.
14. Putnam quotes the work of Charles Parsons and Geoffrey Hellman approvingly in this context (*Ethics without Ontology*, p. 82), though one may wonder what ontological gain there is by quantifying over modal objects (possible worlds) rather than set-theoretic objects.
15. In Putnam, H. "Is Logic Empirical?" *Boston Studies in the Philosophy of Science* (1968), pp. 216–241. Reprinted as "The Logic of Quantum Mechanics" in *Mathematics, Matter and Method* (1975), pp. 174–197. See his "Replies," *Reading Putnam* (1992) for a criticism of quantum logic.
16. *Psychosemantics* (1987), p. 110.
17. All parenthetical remarks are to this article, reprinted in *Mind, Language and Reality: Philosophical Papers, Volume 2* (1975a).
18. This point comes out clearer when we assess our ordinary attribution of beliefs: when we say "Putnam believes that elms are deciduous trees," we are crediting him with the concept *elm* despite his incomplete understanding—but this concept refers not to his private conception of elms but to the community concept (in this case determined by experts like botanists). Tyler Burge will make a very similar point, though notably he does not put it in terms of concept possession—see Section 1.5.1 for a comparison of Burge with Putnam.
19. See Gareth Evans, "The Causal Theory of Names" (1972) for the (by now) classical treatment of some of these problems for names, though these same criticisms have even more force when applied to natural-kind terms.
20. By "context of use" here I mean that it would change depending on which planet it was uttered on, *not* that it would change depending on each use on each planet.
21. See "Is Water Necessarily H_2O?" in *Realism with a Human Face* (1989).
22. This is a descriptive fact about linguistic practice, but this fact is itself guided by a norm: laypeople *ought* to defer to experts, insofar as they want to "get it right." Putnam clarifies this in a more recent article when he writes, "To ask what someone's, say Jones's words are about, how to interpret them, is a *normative* question. The question should not be confused with the question of what Jones would *say* his words are about, because very often speakers give terrible answers" (1994, p. 16). Nevertheless, I do think that if there were *no* willingness to defer to experts at all, these norms would be irrelevant to our everyday practices and thus would not figure into our meaning assignments. There is a reflective equilibrium here between norms and actual use which points to a more dynamic model than can be found in Putnam's theory. I will return to this point when talking about Putnam's pragmatic turn, in Section 4.2 "The Primacy of Practice."
23. Kim Sterelny in "Natural Kinds" (1983) observes that we can imagine other circumstances where the disjunctive interpretation would be clearly implausible: Consider a Twin Earth as before, except H_2O, if it were to exist on Twin Earth, would be foul-tasting to twin-earthlings.

NOTES

Similarly, if XYZ were found on Earth, it would be foul-tasting to us. In this case no one would argue that the extension of "water" was the same on both planets, XYZ or H_2O—and yet the psychological states of the twins would be identical.

24. See especially Akeel Bilgrami's "Realism without Internalism: A Critique of Searle on Intentionality," *Journal of Philosophy* (1989).
25. As found in *Renewing Philosophy* (1992) and his introduction to *The Twin Earth Chronicles* (1998).
26. See John McDowell, "Mind and Meaning" (1992) for defending and exploring the consequences of such a thesis.
27. This is at least the strategy Fodor adopts in works such as *Psychosemantics* (1987). Fodor's more recent view concedes much more to Putnam's externalism and is set out in his work *The Elm and the Expert* (1994). We will discuss his later viewpoint in Section 1.5.3.
28. In "The Meaning of 'Meaning'" Putnam writes of relational states such as "being jealous of y" as "psychological states in the wide sense, and we shall refer to the states that are permitted by methodological solipsism as 'psychological states in the narrow sense'" (p. 220). Since Putnam writes that one of the consequences of his argument is the rejection of methodological solipsism, he presumably intended to include as "wide psychological state" states like "believing that water is wet," but he never explicitly says so in the article. In fact he needs to assume that the twins share the same psychological states in order to derive his conclusion that "psychological state does not determine extension."
29. Another problem here is that if narrow contents are inexpressible, then speakers will not have cognitive access to them. But Fodor would not want to give up on the idea that we have privileged access to the contents of our own thoughts.
30. This notion of content will be argued for and defended in Section 3.4, "Pragmatic Realism and Intentionality."
31. It may be worth quoting Chomsky in full on this point: "Take Putnam's Twin Earth argument. We can have no intuitions as to whether the term water has the same 'reference' for Oscar and twin-Oscar: that is a matter of decision about the new technical term 'reference' . . . under some circumstances Putnam's proposals about the 'same liquid' a perhaps (unknown) notion of the natural sciences, seem very plausible; under other circumstances, notions of sameness or similarity, drawn from commonsense understanding seem more appropriate, yielding different judgments. It doesn't seem to me at all clear that there is anything general to be said about such matters, or that any general or useful sense can be given to technical notions such as 'wide content' (or any other notion fixing 'reference') in any of the externalist interpretations" (p. 27).
32. Putnam's diagnosis of this phenomenon of "recoil," which he sees rampant in analytic philosophy (and perhaps philosophy in general) will be taken up in the third chapter.
33. See Frank Jackson, "Reference and Description" (1998), and David Chalmers, "Two-Dimensional Semantics" (2006).

NOTES

34. The resulting position here is somewhere between Putnam's and Stephen Schwartz's in his "Putnam on Artifacts" (1978). Contra Schwartz, one can run a Twin Earth argument on artifact terms, even independently of the appeal to indexicality. But Schwartz is right to argue for a difference between nominal kinds, determined by form and function, and natural kinds, determined by internal structure.
35. In his "Individualism and the Mental" (1979), *Midwest Studies in Philosophy* 4, 73–122; and "Other Bodies" (1982), *Thought and Object: Essays on Intentionality*, 97–120. All parenthetical page references are to "Individualism and the Mental" unless otherwise noted.
36. For a prolonged argument of this kind against Burge, see Asa Maria Wikforss, "Social Externalism and Conceptual Errors," *The Philosophical Quarterly* (2001).
37. See his "Concepts, Definitions, and Meaning," *Metaphilosophy* 24 (1993), 309–327.
38. Note that this is different from what we would say about the meaning of "kinetic energy" through theory change, since in this case scientists *do* take themselves to be talking about the same quantity both before and after theory change. In that case, scientists would say that they were mistaken about what the term "kinetic energy" meant before theory change, whereas in Burge's thought experiment, it is assumed that both communities have correct knowledge about what "arthritis" applies to. This would *not* be a case of theory change but simply a case of different theories.
39. In *Knowledge and the Flow of Information* (1981).
40. This comes out pretty clearly in Putnam's *Representation and Reality* (1988), where Putnam uses these normative considerations to show that meaning cannot be captured by a scientific account—though here he focuses on conceptual role semantics rather than information-theoretic semantics.
41. First presented in "Knowing One's Own Mind" (1987).
42. This problem for causal theories is discussed at length by Sterelny and Devitt in *Language and Reality* (1993), pp. 63–65.
43. *Renewing Philosophy* (1992), pp. 36–49.

CHAPTER 2: EXTERNALISM, REALISM, AND SKEPTICISM

1. In *Realism and Truth* (1984).
2. Putnam famously adds that unless scientific theories were true of an independent reality, the success of science would be a *miracle*. As he writes, "Realism is the only philosophy that doesn't make the success of science a miracle" (1975b, p. 73).
3. "The Current State of Scientific Realism" (1984), pp. 41–42.
4. *Reason, Truth and History* (1982), p. 49.
5. Putnam calls this the "metainduction argument" and it has in and of itself given rise to a huge literature. See especially Laudan (1981).
6. Putnam's views here situate him closely with Jurgen Habermas and his Theory of Communicative Action: notably they both have taken aim

at various forms of anti-realism, and have endeavored to argue that skeptical arguments are in general self-refuting.
7. *Metaphysics* 1011b25. Combined with his theory of representation, Aristotle becomes the classical "copy theorist": statements are true to the extent to which their parts "mirror" or "replicate" an external reality. For Aristotle, this means that an image in the mind corresponds to an object; for modern copy theorists like early Wittgenstein and Russell, it means that the structure of a sentence corresponds to the structure of a fact or state of affairs.
8. In "The Semantic Conception of Truth" (1983), p. 36.
9. Field uses "physicalist" in basically the same sense as I have used "scientific naturalist" throughout this book.
10. *Meaning and the Moral Sciences* (1978), p. 32.
11. This example is taken from Anthony Brueckner's "Putnam's Model-Theoretic Argument" (1979).
12. See David Lewis (1983) and Michael Devitt (1997) also gives a version of this defense.
13. Alvin Plantinga (1982).
14. It is also ironic given that these philosophers take Putnam to be one of the architects of the causal theory of reference!
15. For more details as to the responses on both sides of the debate, see David Lee Anderson's "What is the Model Theoretic Argument?" in *Journal of Philosophy* (1993).
16. See especially Haim Gaifman, "Ontological Frameworks" (1981).
17. This is the strategy William Alston adopts in his *Realist Conception of Truth* (1984), chapter 5.
18. Wittgenstein's *Philosophical Investigations*, pp. 503–504. Obviously Putnam adopts the Cora Diamond-John McDowell view of later Wittgenstein as a realist rather than Dummett's anti-realist interpretation.
19. This follows from his account of radical interpretation, but it is also part and parcel of his critique of the "third dogma of empiricism," the scheme/content distinction, in his *The Very Idea of Conceptual Scheme* (1983).
20. "A Coherence Theory of Truth and Knowledge," *Truth and Interpretation* (1984), p. 125.
21. For a discussion on how bad this reading of Kant is, see Hickey, "Kant's Concept of the Transcendental Object," *Manuscrito* (2001).
22. Peirce, C. S. (1901), "Truth and Falsity and Error" (in part), pp. 718–720 in J. M. Baldwin (ed.), *Dictionary of Philosophy and Psychology, vol. 2*. Reprinted, CP 5.565–573.
23. In *Knowledge and Human Interests* (1973) Part III, p. 187.
24. See especially his introduction to *Realism with a Human Face* (1990) where he writes, "Many people have thought that my idealization was the same of Peirce's, that what the figure of a 'frictionless plane' corresponds to is a situation (finished science) in which the community would be able to justify every true statement (and to disconfirm every false one) . . . I do not by any means ever mean to use the notion

of 'ideal epistemic situation' in this fantastic (or Utopian) Peircian sense" (p. viii).
25. "Reply to Terry Horgan," *Erkenntnis* (1991), p. 421.
26. "Replies," *Philosophical Topics* (1992), p. 364. Against this, a realist might claim that negative statements are "simply true" because they correspond to "negative facts." This was in fact the position of Bertrand Russell in his *Philosophy of Logical Atomism*. On this point, Putnam would side with F. H. Bradley, who wrote in his *Principles of Logic* that "all negative judgments presuppose a positive ground."
27. For an excellent discussion of this, see Wolfgang Kunne's "From Alethic Anti-realism to Alethic Realism," in *Hilary Putnam: Pragmatism and Realism* (2002), pp. 144–165.
28. "Replies," *Philosophical Topics* (1992), p. 368.
29. "Reflections," on Hilary Putnam's *Reason, Truth and History* (1981), p. 569.
30. In *Skepticism and Naturalism* (1985), pp. 44–45.
31. As Stroud writes, "The thought that a thing cannot both be and not be yellow is precisely what forces the question of which of the things said from the two different standpoints [i.e., Science and everyday experience] is correct" (p. 185).
32. Putnam actually criticizes the formulation of N. L. Wilson's Principle of Charity in his "Language and Reality" (1975), though it is clear even here that there is a version of the principle of charity (what Putnam calls "The Principle of the Benefit of Doubt") that does apply to our translation practices.
33. In *Ethics without Ontology* (2004), pp. 49–51.
34. Jennifer Case, "The Heart of Putnam's pragmatic pluralism," *Revue Internationale de Philosophie*, p. 429. Putnam's Reply is found on pp. 437–438. See also *Ethics without Ontology* (2004), p. 43.
35. In yet another clarification, Putnam distinguishes between conceptual relativity proper, which concerns incompatible but true descriptions, and conceptual pluralism, which concerns compatible but different descriptions. Mereology would be an example of conceptual relativity, since we cannot say "there are 2 objects and 4 objects" while the argument countenancing the existence of both commonsense and scientific arguments would be an example of pluralism (there being no contradiction with saying, for example, there is a tree and there is a collection of particles over there). See *Ethics without Ontology* (2004), pp. 48–49.

CHAPTER 3: MIND, BODY, AND WORLD

1. For an assessment of the significance of Chomsky's work, see John Searle's "Chomsky's Revolution in Linguistics," *The New York Review of Books* (June, 1972).
2. Or at least, Turing proved this for a Turing machine that could simulate any other Turing machine, what he called a "Universal Turing Machine."

NOTES

3. Putnam makes this point more clearly in "Robots: Machines or Artificially Created Life?" (1964).
4. Although true enough, some forms of behaviorism do come dangerously close to saying that . . . Skinner's methodological behaviorism does not deny subjective experience but only says that we should not appeal to it from a scientific point of view; his ontological brand of behaviorism allows for subjective experience (or first-person mental reports) to provide "clues" to stimulus-response bonds. Ryle's logical behaviorism was concerned to combat the "official doctrine" of Cartesian dualism and to redescribe our psychological language which props up this official doctrine. Thus he would reject any talk of inner mental processes, but it isn't clear that he would reject all talk of conscious experience so long as this is not given a Cartesian interpretation.
5. "The Nature of Mental Events," (1967, 1975), p. 433.
6. This point was emphasized in Smart's version of the identity theory, in his "Sensations and Brain Processes" (1959).
7. For an argument of this kind, see Jerry Fodor and Ned Block, "What psychological states are not," *Philosophical Review* (1972) 81, 159–181.
8. David Lewis, Review of *Art, Mind and Religion*, *Journal of Philosophy* (1969). Jaegwon Kim (1992) also argues for a similar thesis: he agrees that multiple realizability shows that there is no general theory of the mind available to the identity theorist, but he argues for "local" scientific psychologies, each reducible to the theory of the underlying physical mechanisms of the structure type in question.
9. "Philosophy and Our Mental Life" (1975), p. 293.
10. See especially Zenon Pylyshyn's *Computation and Cognition: Toward a Foundation for Cognitive Science* (Cambridge: MIT Press, 1984).
11. Although notably philosophers like Jaegwon Kim (1982) have disputed the idea that (for functionalism and other nonreductive theories such as Davidson's) the mental causes the physical *qua* mental properties.
12. A notable debate over this issue was that between identity theorist Jack Smart and critic Jerome Schaffer; in his "Mental Events and the Brain," Schaffer (1963) argued that the only way to discriminate a mental state (of sensing an orange afterimage, for example) from a physical state was via some phenomenal property of the mental state, and that "topic neutral" approaches of the kind advocated by Smart could not resolve this difficulty.
13. Paul and Patricia Churchland, "Functionalism, Qualia, and Intentionality," *Philosophical Topics* (1981) 12, 121–132.
14. Putnam does say now that qualitative states cannot be reduced because they are interrelated to intentional states, and intentional states cannot be reduced because of the semantic objections.
15. Actually, since computational functionalism implicitly defines a mental state in terms of all other mental states, it follows that if any two organisms have different beliefs then they will not share *any* of the same beliefs. This motivates the search for a more sophisticated brand of functionalism, where an "equivalence relation" can be

NOTES

defined among different computational structures that makes them come out "the same" for purposes of psychological identification and explanation.
16. Fodor is well aware of this problem and has now opted for one notion of externalist content along information-theoretic lines. See Section 1.5 for Putnam's criticism of this position.
17. In "Does a Rock Implement Every Finite State Automaton?" *Synthese* (1996).
18. *The Elm and the Expert* (1994), p. 12.
19. "James' Theory of Perception," in *Realism with a Human Face* (1990), pp. 232–252.
20. In his *Empiricism and the Philosophy of Mind* (1997).
21. *The Threefold Cord: Mind, Body, and World* (1999), p. 177.
22. Kant's *Critique of Pure Reason* (B 75).
23. McDowell actually writes, "the aim here is not to answer skeptical questions, but to begin to see how it may be intellectually responsible to ignore them, to treat them as unreal, in the way that commonsense has always wanted to" (p. 113).
24. I think especially of Bertrand Russell's *Problems in Philosophy*, designed to perplex the beginning student into doubting the veridicality of perception.
25. To quote Putnam in full on this: "Winning through to natural realism is seeing the needlessness and the unintelligibility of a picture that imposes an interface between ourselves and the world. It is a way of completing the task of philosophy, the task that John Wisdom once called a 'journey from the familiar to the familiar'" (1999, p. 41). Contrast this with Bertrand Russell's remark in *Logic and Knowledge* (1956) that "the point of philosophy is to start with something so simple as not to seem worth stating, and to end with something so paradoxical that no one will believe it" (p. 193). It can be argued however that Putnam is going a bit too far in the other direction. Insofar as he wants to recapture the spirit of pragmatism, a pragmatist like Dewey was concerned not merely to inoculate common experience from philosophical criticism, but to effect a transformation of common experience by the application of intelligent inquiry in all domains of knowledge. We will return to this aspect of pragmatism in the next chapter.
26. "A Puzzle about Belief" (1979), p. 112.
27. In "A Modal Argument for Narrow Content," *Journal of Philosophy* (1991), p. 5.
28. Boghossian (1989) gives an extended argument of this kind, one appealing to various "twin-switching" hypotheticals. Suppose that, unbeknownst to her, Sandy is switched to Twin Earth in the middle of the night and she stays long enough on Twin Earth to acquire the twin-water concept. At some point, her utterances of "water is wet" would come to express different contents, even though she would be completely unaware of the change. She certainly would not be able to tell *by introspection* what she thinks or desires.

29. In "Individualism and Self-Knowledge," *Journal of Philosophy* (1988). Davidson (1986) gives his own reconciliation of externalism with self-knowledge, but for reasons Bilgrami (1992) and others have given, I do not believe it is telling against the following points.
30. In *Belief and Meaning* (1992) and "Can Externalism be Reconciled with Self-Knowledge?" *Philosophical Topics* (1992).
31. In "Response to Bilgrami," *Philosophical Topics* (1994), p. 390.

CHAPTER 4: NEO-PRAGMATISM AND THE REVITALIZATION OF PHILOSOPHY

1. Reprinted in *Words and Life* (1994), p. 152.
2. Peirce, C. S. 1992–1994. *The Essential Peirce*, ed. N. Houser and C. Kloesel (vol. 1) and the Peirce Edition Project (vol. 2), (Bloomington: Indiana University Press), p. 132.
3. James writes, "But so far as it (the Absolute) affords such comfort, it surely is not sterile; it has that amount of value; it performs a concrete function. As a good pragmatist, I myself ought to call the Absolute true 'in so far forth,' then; and I unhesitatingly do so now." "What Pragmatism Means" (1907, 2000), p. 37.
4. Except, he notes, for those who believes in the transubstantiation of the bread and wine into the body and blood of Christ.
5. One reason of course why Rorty (2003) says he has "no use" for works like Dewey's *Experience and Nature* or James' *Radical Empiricism*.
6. In "Putnam, Pragmatism, and Parmenides" (2003), p. 4.
7. One thinks of Chomsky's criticisms in this regard (see Section 1.3.3).
8. "The Philosopher-in-the-Making," *Contemporary American Philosophy*, II. (1930). Edited by George P. Adams and William P. Montague. New York: Macmillan Co.
9. A more detailed attempt to apply the scientific method to religious experience can be found in Ken Wilber's *The Marriage of Sense and Soul* (1998), though he never mentions the pragmatists. See especially "What is Science?" pp. 150–161.
10. I think especially of his "Wittgenstein on Religious Belief" in *Renewing Philosophy* (1992), pp. 141–152.
11. In the Dewey Lectures, most obviously, as when he writes that the goal of philosophy is simply to mark a "journey from the familiar to the familiar" (*Threefold Cold*, 1999, p. 41).
12. Thus Dewey writes, "What is averred to be implicit reliance upon what is given in common experience is likely to be merely an appeal to prejudice to gain support for some fanaticism or defense for some relic of conservative tradition which is beginning to be questioned" (1929, p. 33).
13. Alternatively, they may be hypotheses enlisted to explain some of the mystical experiences that James describes in his *The Varieties of Religious Experience*.
14. The *Harvard Review of Philosophy* (1991), p. 23.
15. See Gilbert Harman's *The Nature of Morality* (1984) for various arguments along these lines.

NOTES

16. Another tactic would be to say that ethical statements purport to refer to facts "out there," but that since there aren't any such facts, all ethical statements are false. This is Mackie's "error theory."
17. As argued in J. L. Mackie's *Ethics: Inventing Right and Wrong* (1981).
18. In *Ethics without Ontology* (2004), pp. 24–27.
19. Or even appeal to Dewey, though Putnam notes that for Dewey such general principles as would be derived (say, from a Rawlsian contract situation) would be too universalistic and abstract to apply to concrete problems in the ethical and political life.
20. *Realism with a Human Face* (1991), p. 138.
21. "Putnam on the Fact/Value Dichotomy," *Croatian Journal of Philosophy* (2002).
22. *Reason, Truth and History* (1982), p. 128.
23. In *Ethics and the Limits of Philosophy* (1985).
24. This should recall Putnam's analogous claim that while there is an analytic/synthetic distinction, there is no analytic/synthetic dichotomy.
25. *Ethics without Ontology* (2004), p. 129.
26. As quoted in Putnam (1994, p. 216), based on Dewey and Tufts' *Ethics* (Part III).
27. *The View from Nowhere* (1986), p. 73.
28. "A Coherence Theory of Truth and Knowledge" (1986), p. 309.
29. In "The Search for Logically Alien Thought: Descartes, Kant, Frege, and the *Tractatus*," *Philosophical Topics* (1991), pp. 158–159. Conant's essay is in part an elaboration on Putnam's "Rethinking Mathematical Necessity" in *Words and Life* (1994).
30. "The Will to Believe" in *The Will to Believe and Other Essays* (1979).
31. "Comments on Sleeper and Edel," Transactions of the C. S. Peirce Society (1985), p. 40.
32. "Response to Hartshorne," in *Rorty and Pragmatism: The Philosopher Responds to His Critics* (1995), p. 35.
33. *Articulating Reasons* (1999), p. 16.
34. In the *Dualist 2* (1995), pp. 56–71.
35. Although it should be noted that elsewhere Putnam writes that the average person is a realist but not necessarily a "metaphysical realist." Common ways of speaking suggest that objects and properties are independent of us, but this vague concept of independence does not yet imply any substantive view in the debate (certainly not one between, for example, idealists and realists) Putnam's argument here goes through so long as the majority of people do not believe that truth is simply a matter of being accepted by the majority of people.
36. *Realism with a Human Face* (1990), p. 24.
37. "A Comparison of Something with Something Else," *Words and Life* (1994), p. 344.
38. *The Threefold Cord: Mind, Body, and World* (1999), p. 3.
39. "Putnam, Pragmatism, and Parmenides" (2003), p. 11.
40. In *Philosophy Now* (2003).
41. "Pragmatics and Pragmatism," in *Hilary Putnam: Pragmatism and Realism* (2002), p. 40.

SELECT WRITINGS OF HILARY PUTNAM

Putnam, H. (1960) "Minds and Machines," in Sidney Hook (ed.) *Dimensions of Mind*. New York: State University of New York Press. Reprinted in Putnam (1975b).
— (1962a) "The Analytic and the Synthetic," in H. Fiegel and G. Maxwell (eds.) *Scientific Explanation, Space and Time, Minnesota Studies in the Philosophy of Science III*. Minneapolis: University of Minnesota Press. Reprinted in Putnam (1975b).
— (1962b) "It Ain't Necessarily So," *The Journal of Philosophy* 59, 658–671. Reprinted in Putnam (1975a).
— (1963) "Brains and Behavior," in R. J. Butler (ed.) *Analytical Philosophy, Second Series*. Oxford: Basil Blackwell. Reprinted in Putnam (1975b).
— (1964) "Robots: Machines or Artificially Created Life?" *Journal of Philosophy* 61, 668–691. Reprinted in Putnam (1975b).
— (1967a) "The Innateness Hypothesis and Explanatory Models in Linguistics," *Synthese* 17, 12–22. Reprinted in Putnam (1975b).
— (1967b) "Psychological Predicates," in W. H. Captain and D. D. Merrill (eds.) *Art, Mind, Religion*. Pittsburgh: University of Pittsburgh Press. Reprinted as 'The Nature of Mental Events' in Putnam (1975b).
— (1968) "Is Logic Empirical?" in Robert S. Cohen and M. W. Wartowski (eds.) *Boston Studies in the Philosophy of Science*, vol. 5. Dordrecht: D. Reidel.
— (1970) "Is Semantics Possible?" in *Metaphilosophy I*. Reprinted in Putnam (1975b).
— (1971) *Philosophy of Logic*. New York: Harper & Row.
— (1973) "Meaning and Reference," *Journal of Philosophy* 70, 699–711. Reprinted in Putnam (1975b).
— (1975a) *Mathematics, Matter and Method: Philosophical Papers Volume 1*. Cambridge: Cambridge University Press.
— (1975b) *Mind, Language and Reality: Philosophical Papers Volume 2*. Cambridge: Cambridge University Press.
— (1975c) "What is Realism?" Proceedings of the Aristotelian Society.
— (1977) "Realism and Reason," *Proceedings of the American Philosophical Association* 50, 483–498.
— (1978) *Meaning and the Moral Sciences*. London: Routledge & Kegan Paul.

SELECT WRITINGS OF HILARY PUTNAM

Putnam, H. (1981) *Reason, Truth and History*. Cambridge: Cambridge University Press.
— (1982) "Reply to Two Realists," *Journal of Philosophy* 79, 575–577.
— (1983) *Realism and Reason: Philosophical Papers Volume 3*. Cambridge: Cambridge University Press.
— (1987) *The Many Faces of Realism* (The Paul Carus Lectures, Washington 1985). La Salle: Open Court.
— (1988) *Representation and Reality*. Cambridge: MIT Press.
— (1990) *Realism with a Human Face*, ed. James Conant. Cambridge: Harvard University Press.
— (1991a) "Reply to Terry Horgan," *Erkenntnis* 43, 419–423.
— (1991b) "An Interview with Hilary Putnam," *Harvard Review of Philosophy* 2, 20–24.
— (1992a) *Renewing Philosophy* (The Gifford Lectures, St Andrews 1990). Cambridge: Harvard University Press.
— (1992b) "Replies," *Philosophical Topics* 20, Spring.
— (1994a) *Words and Life*, ed. James Conant. Cambridge: Harvard University Press.
— (1994b) "Replies," in Peter Clarke and Bob Hale (eds.) *Reading Putnam*. Oxford: Basil Blackwell.
— (1995) *Pragmatism: An Open Question*. Oxford: Basil Blackwell.
— (1996) "Irrealism and Deconstruction," in P. J. McCormick (ed.) *Starmaking: Realism, Anti-Realism and Irrealism*. New York: Columbia University Press.
— (1999) *The Threefold Cord: Mind, Body and the World*. New York: Columbia University Press.
— (2001) "Replies," *Revue Internationale de Philosophie* 55, 417–533.
— (2002) "Replies," in James Conant and Urszula M. Zeglen (eds.) *Hilary Putnam: Pragmatism and Realism*. London: Routledge.
— (2003) *Collapse of the Fact/Value Dichotomy*. Cambridge: Harvard University Press.
— (2004) *Ethics without Ontology*. Cambridge: Harvard University Press.

SELECT BIBLIOGRAPHY

Alston, William (1996) *A Realist Conception of Truth*. Illinois: La Salle.
Anderson, David (1992) "What is Realistic about Putnam's Internal Realism?" *Philosophical Topics* 20, Spring, 49–83.
— (1993) "What is the Model Theoretic Argument?" *Journal of Philosophy* 90, 311–322.
Bilgrami, Akeel (1989) "Realism without Internalism," *Journal of Philosophy* 86, 57–72.
— (1992a) *Belief and Meaning*. Cambridge: Basil Blackwell.
— (1992b) "Can Externalism be Reconciled with Self-Knowledge?" *Philosophical Topics* 20, Spring, 233–268.
Block, Ned (1982) "Troubles with Functionalism," in *Readings in the Philosophy of Psychology, Volumes 1 and 2*. Cambridge, MA: Harvard University Press.
— (1987) "Advertisement for a Semantics for Psychology," in P. French, T. Uething, and H. Wettstein (eds.) *Midwest Studies in Philosophy 10*. Minneapolis: University of Minnesota Press.
Block, Ned and Fodor, J. (1972) "What Psychological States are Not," *Philosophical Review* 81, 159–181.
Boghossian, Paul (1996) "What the Externalist Can Know *A Priori*," unpublished manuscript.
Boyd, Richard (1984) "The Current Status of Scientific Realism," in J. Leplin (ed.) *Scientific Realism*. Berkeley: University of California Press.
Brandom, Robert B. (1993) "Review of Hilary Putnam's *Renewing Philosophy*," *Journal of Philosophy* 91, 140–143.
— (1995) *Making it Explicit*. Cambridge: Harvard University Press.
— (2002) "Pragmatics and Pragmatisms," in J. Conant and U. M. Zeglen (eds.) *Hilary Putnam: Pragmatism and Realism*. London: Routledge.
Brueckner, Antony (1984) "Putnam's Model Theoretic Argument against Metaphysical Realism," *Analysis* 44, 134–141.
— (1986) "Brains in a Vat," *Journal of Philosophy* 83, 148–167.
— (1994) "Knowledge of Content and Knowledge of the World-" *Philosophical Review* 103, 327–343.
Burge, Tyler (1979) "Individualism and the Mental," *Midwest Studies in Philosophy* 4, 73–122.
— (1982) "Two Thought Experiments Revisited," *Notre Dame Journal of Formal Logic* 23, 284–293.

SELECT BIBLIOGRAPHY

Burge, Tyler (1988) "Individualism and Self-Knowledge," *Journal of Philosophy* 85, November, 649–663.
— (1989) "Wherein is Language Social?" in George, A (ed.) *Reflections on Chomsky*. Oxford: Blackwell.
— (1993) "Concepts, Definitions and Meanings," *Metaphilosophy* 24, 309–325.
Carnap, Rudolph (1967) "Empiricism, Semantics, and Ontology," in Richard Rorty (ed.) *The Linguistic Turn*. Chicago: Chicago University Press.
Case, Jennifer (2001) "The Heart of Putnam's Pragmatic Pluralism," *Revue Internationale de Philosophie* 55, 417–431.
Chalmers, David (1996) *The Conscious Mind*. Oxford: Oxford University Press.
— (2006) "Two Dimensional Semantics," unpublished manuscript.
Chomsky, Noam (1992) "Explaining Language Use," *Philosophical Topics* 20, Spring, 205–231.
Churchland, Paul and Patricia (1981) "Functionalism, Qualia, and Intentionality," *Philosophical Topics* 12, 121–132.
Conant, James (1991) "The Search for Logically Alien Thought: Descartes, Kant, Frege, and the Tractatus," *Philosophical Topics* 20, 1, 115–180.
Crane, Tim (1991) "All the Difference in the World," *Philosophical Quarterly*, January.
Davidson, Donald (1984) *Inquiries into Truth and Interpretation*. Oxford: Oxford University Press.
— (1986) "A Coherence Theory of Truth and Knowledge," in *Truth and Interpretation, Perspectives on the Philosophy of Donald Davidson*. Oxford: Basil Blackwell.
— (1987) "On Knowing One's Own Mind," *Proceedings of the American Philosophical Association* 61, 441–458. Reprinted in Goldberg and Pessin (1996).
Devitt, Michael (1984) *Realism and Truth*. Oxford: Basil Blackwell.
— (1990) "Meanings Just Ain't in the Head," in *Essays in Honor of Hilary Putnam*. Oxford: Basil Blackwell, pp. 79–103.
Devitt, Michael and Sterelny, Kim (1990) *Language and Reality*. Cambridge: Basil Blackwell.
Dewey, John (1929, 1960) *The Quest for Certainty*. New York: G. P. Putnam & Sons.
— (1930, 1958) *Experience and Nature*. New York: Dover.
Donnellan, Keith (1966) "Reference and Definite Descriptions," in *Philosophical Review* 75, 281–304.
Dreben, Burton (1992) "Putnam, Quine- and the Facts," *Philosophical Topics* 20, Spring, 293–315.
Dretske, Fred (1981) *Knowledge and the Flow of Information*. Cambridge: MIT Press.
Dummett, Michael (1974a) *Frege: Philosophy of Language*. Cambridge: Harvard University Press.
— (1974b) *Truth and Other Enigmas*. Cambridge: Harvard University Press.
— (1992a) *The Logical Basis of Metaphysics*. Cambridge; Harvard University Press.

— (1992b) *The Origins of Analytic Philosophy.* Cambridge: Cambridge University Press.
Ebbs, Gary (1992) "Realism and Rational Inquiry," *Philosophical Topics* 20, Spring 1–34.
— (1997) *Realism and Rule Following.* Cambridge: Harvard University Press.
Evans, Gareth (1982) *The Varieties of Reference.* Oxford: Oxford University Press.
— (1994) "The Causal Theory of Names," in A. W. Moore (ed.) *Meaning and Reference.* Oxford: Basil Blackwell.
Falvey, K. and Owens, J. (1994) "Externalism, Self-Knowledge, and Skepticism," in *Philosophical Review* 103, 107–137.
Field, Hartry (1972) "Tarski's Theory of Truth," in *Journal of Philosophy* 69, 347–375.
— (1982) "Realism and Relativism," review of Hilary Putnam's Reason, Truth and History, in *Journal of Philosophy* 79, 553–567.
Fine, Arthur (1984) "The Natural Ontological Attitude," in J. Leplin (ed.) *Scientific Realism.* Berkeley: University of California Press.
Fodor, Jerry (1987) *Psychosemantics.* Cambridge: MIT Press.
— (1991a) "A Modal Argument for Narrow Content" *Journal of Philosophy* 88, 5–26.
— (1991b) *A Theory of Content.* Cambridge: MIT Press.
— (1994) *The Elm and the Expert.* Cambridge: MIT Press.
— (1998) *Concepts: Where Cognitive Science Went Wrong.* Cambridge: MIT Press.
Fodor, Jerry and Lepore, Ernest (1992) *Holism: A Shopper's Guide.* Cambridge: MIT Press.
Forbes, Graeme (1995) "Brains in a Vat Revisited," *Journal of Philosophy* 92, 205–222.
Friedman, Michael (1999) *Reconsidering Logical Positivism.* Cambridge: Cambridge University Press.
Gaifman, Haim (1975) "Ontological and Conceptual Frameworks," *Erkenntnis* 9, 329–351.
— (1994) "Metaphysical Realism and Vats in a Brain," unpublished manuscript.
Goldberg, Sanford and Pessin, Andrew (eds.) (1996) *The Twin Earth Chronicles.* New York: M. E. Sharpe.
Harman, Gilbert (1982) "Metaphysical Realism and Moral Relativism," review of Hilary Putnam's *Reason, Truth and History*, *Journal of Philosophy* 79, 568–575.
— (1988) *The Nature of Morality.* Princeton: Princeton University Press.
Hickey, Lance (2001) "Kant's Concept of the Transcendental Object," *Manuscrito* 24, 103–139.
Horwich, Paul (1990) *Truth.* Oxford: Basil Blackwell.
Jackson, F. (1998) "Reference and Description Revisited," *Philosophical Perspectives* 12, 201–218.
Jackson, F. and Pettite, P. (1988) "Functionalism and Broad Content," *Mind* 97, 382–400.

SELECT BIBLIOGRAPHY

James, William (2000) *Pragmatism and Other Writings*. Ed. Giles Gunn. New York: Penguin.

Kant, Immanuel (1980) *The Critique of Pure Reason*. Ed. Norman Kemp-Smith. New York: St. Martin's Press.

Katz, Jerold (1984) *The Metaphysics of Meaning*. Cambridge: MIT Press.

Kim, Jaegwon (1992). "Multiple Realization and the Metaphysics of Reduction," *Philosophy and Phenomenological Research* 52, 1–26.

Koethe, John (1979) "Putnam's Argument against Realism," *The Philosophical Review* 88, 92–99.

Kripke, Saul (1979) "A Puzzle About Belief," in Margalit A. (ed.) *Meaning and Use*. Dordrecht: Reidel, pp. 239M.

— (1980) *Naming and Necessity*. Cambridge: Harvard University Press.

— (1982) *Wittgenstein: Rules and Private Languages*. Cambridge: Harvard University Press.

Kunne, Wolfgang (2002) "From Alethic Anti-realism to Alethic Realism," in J. Conant and U. M. Zeglen (ed.) *Hilary Putnam: Pragmatism and Realism*. London: Routledge.

Loar, Brian (1988) "Social Content and Psychological Content," in Grimm and Merrill (eds.) *Contents of Thought*. Tucson: University of Arizona Press. Reprinted in Goldberg, Sanford and Pessin, Andrew (eds.) 1996. *The Twin Earth Chronicles*. New York: M. E. Sharpe.

McCullogh, Gregory (1991) "Externalism and Skepticism," *Analysis*.

McDowell, John (1984) "Intentionality De Re Senses," *Philosophical Quarterly* 34, 283–294.

— (1986) "Singular Thoughts and the Extent of Inner Space," in Subject, Object and Content. Oxford: Oxford University Press.

— (1992) "Putnam on Mind and Meaning," *Philosophical Topics* 20, Spring, 35–48.

— (1993) "Wittgenstein on Following a Rule," in A. W. Moore (ed.) *Meaning and Reference*. Oxford: Oxford University Press.

— (1994) *Mind and World*. Cambridge: Harvard University Press.

McGinn, Colin (1977) "Charity, Interpretation, and Belief," *Journal of Philosophy* 74, 521–535.

— (1989) *Mental Content*. Oxford: Basil Blackwell.

McKinsey, Michael (1991) "Anti-Individualism and Privileged Access," *Analysis* 51, 9–16.

McMullin, Eman (1984) "A Case for Scientific Realism," in J. Leplin (ed.) *Scientific Realism*. Berkeley: University of California Press.

Mellor, D. H. (1977) "Natural Kinds," *British Journal for the Philosophy of Science* 28, 299–312. Reprinted in Goldberg, Sanford and Pessin, Andrew (eds.) 1996. *The Twin Earth Chronicles*. New York: M. E. Sharpe.

Miller, Richard (1991) "Realism without Positivism," *Philosophical Topics* 20, Spring, 85–114.

Nagel, Thomas (1986) *The View from Nowhere*. Oxford: Oxford University Press.

Norris, Christopher (2002) *Hilary Putnam: Realism, Reason and the Uses of Uncertainty*. Manchester: Manchester University Press.

Passmore, John (1985) *Recent Philosophers*. La Salle: Open Court.

SELECT BIBLIOGRAPHY

Perry, John (1977) "Frege on Demonstratives," *Philosophical Review* 86, 474–497.
Peirce, C. S. (1901), "Truth and Falsity and Error" (in part), pp. 718–720 in J. M. Baldwin (ed.) *Dictionary of Philosophy and Psychology, vol. 2*. Reprinted, CP 5.565–573.
— (1992–1994) *The Essential Peirce*. Ed. N. Houser and C. Kloesel (vol. 1) and the Peirce Edition Project (vol. 2), Bloomington: Indiana University Press.
Quine, W. V. O. (1953) *From a Logical Point of View*. Cambridge: Harvard University Press.
— (1960) *Word and Object*. Cambridge: MIT Press.
— (1969) *Ontological Relativity and Other Essays*. Cambridge: MIT Press.
— (1973) *The Roots of Reference*. La Salle: Open Court Press.
— (1990) *Pursuit of Truth*. Cambridge: Harvard University Press.
Reichenbach, Hans (1938) *Experience and Prediction*. Chicago: University of Chicago Press.
Ricketts, Thomas (1994) "Carnap's Principle of Tolerance, Empiricism and Conventionalism," in Clark and Hale (ed.) *Reading Putnam*. Basil Blackwell.
Rorty, Richard (1979) *Philosophy and the Mirror of Nature*. Princeton: Princeton University Press.
— (1982) *Consequences of Pragmatism*. Minneapolis: University of Minnesota Press.
— (1989) *Contingency, Irony, and Solidarity*. Cambridge: Cambridge University Press.
— (1995) "Bald Naturalism and McDowell's Hylomorphism," lecture given at Columbia University, August 3, 1995.
— (2003) "Putnam, Parmenides and Pragmatism," unpublished manuscript.
Schiffer, Stephen (1992) 'Belief Ascription," *Journal of Philosophy* 89, 499–521.
Schlipp, Arthur, ed. (1963) *The Philosophy of Rudolph Carnap*. La Salle: Open Court.
Schwartz, Stephen (1978) "Putnam on Artifact Terms," *Philosophical Review*, 566–574. Reprinted in Goldberg, Sanford and Pessin, Andrew (eds.) (1996) *The Twin Earth Chronicles*. New York: M. E. Sharpe.
Searle, John (1983) *Intentionality*. Cambridge: Cambridge University Press.
Shagrir, Oron (2005) "The Rise and Fall of Computational Functionalism," in Ben-Menahem (ed.) *Hilary Putnam (Contemporary Philosophy in Focus)*. Cambridge: Cambridge University Press.
Shirley, Edward (1972) "Putnam on Analyticity," *Philosophical Studies* 24, 268–270.
Smart, JJC (1959) "Sensations and Brain Processes," *Philosophical Review* 68, 141–156.
Soames, Scott (1984) "What is a Theory of Truth?" *Journal of Philosophy* 81, 411–429.
Stalnaker, Robert (1989) "On What's in the Head," in J. Tomberlin (ed.) *Philosophical Perspectives*. Atascadero: Blackwell. Goldberg, Sanford

SELECT BIBLIOGRAPHY

and Pessin, Andrew (eds.) (1996) *The Twin Earth Chronicles*. New York: M. E. Sharpe.

Sterelny, Kim (1983), "Natural Kinds Terms," *Pacific Philosophical Quarterly* 64, 110–125. Reprinted in Goldberg, Sanford and Pessin, Andrew (eds.) (1996) *The Twin Earth Chronicles*. New York: M. E. Sharpe.

Strawson, P. F. (1985) *Skepticism and Naturalism*. New York: Columbia University Press.

Strawson, P. F. and Grice, P. (1957) "In Defense of a Dogma," *Philosophical Review* 65, 141–158.

Stroud, Barry (2002) *The Quest for Reality*. Oxford: Oxford University Press.

Tarski, Alfred (1983) "The Semantic Conception of Truth," in John Martinich (ed.) *Philosophy of Language*. Oxford: Oxford University Press.

Warfield, Ted (1995) "Knowing the World and Knowing our Minds," *Philosophy and Phenomenological Research* 55, 3, 525–545.

Wiggins, David (1994) "Putnam's Doctrine of Natural Kind Terms and Frege's Doctrines of Sense, Reference and Extension: Can They Cohere?" in *Meaning and Reference*.

Wikforss, Asa (2001) "Social Externalism and Conceptual Errors," *The Philosophical Quarterly* 51, 217–231.

Wilber, Ken (1998) *The Marriage of Sense and Soul*. New York: Random House.

Wittgenstein, Ludwig (1953) *Philosophical Investigations*. Oxford: Oxford University Press.

Wright, Crispin (1994a) "On Putnam's Proof That We are Not Brains in a Vat," in *Reading Putnam*.

— (1994b) *Truth and Objectivity*. Oxford. Oxford University Press.

Zemach, Edward (1977) "Putnam's Theory on the Reference of Substance Terms," *Journal of Philosophy* 73, 116–127. Reprinted in Goldberg, Sanford and Pessin, Andrew (eds.) (1996) *The Twin Earth Chronicles*. New York: M. E. Sharpe.

Ziff, Paul (1960) *Semantic Analysis*. Ithaca: Cornell University Press.

INDEX

Alston, William 124
analyticity 2, 10–12, 40–1
antipsychologism 19
Aristotle 54
Austin, J. L. 118

behaviorism 7, 97, 101, 105–7
Bergstrom, Lars 149
Berkeley, George 73
Bilgrami, Akeel 129–31, 172n, 178n
bivalence 67
Block, Ned 111, 114
Bohr, Niels 11
Boyd, Richard 51
Brains in a Vat 3, 50, 79–90
Brandom, Robert 136, 160–3
Brueckner, Antony 84, 174n
Bruner, Jerome 97
Burge, Tyler 37, 39–42, 128–30

Carnap, Rudolph 7–11, 19
Case, Jennifer 94
causal constraint 80–1
causal-historical theory of names/
 kinds 23–4
Chalmers, David 35, 108, 116
Chomsky, Noam 32–5, 97–8
Churchland, Paul & Patricia 109
Conant, James 157
conceptual relativity 90–4

Davidson, Donald 43, 56, 66, 68, 69,
 72, 81, 83, 93, 133, 136, 156, 159
Deacon, Terrance 33

deflationism 56, 124
Dennett, Daniel 90
Descartes, Rene 79, 98, 117, 128
descriptivism 35–7
Devitt, Michael 49
Dewey, John 125, 139–45, 153–4,
 164–5
Diamond, Cora 124
disjunction objection 27–8
division of linguistic labor 15,
 21–2, 25
Duhem-Quine thesis 16
Dummett, Michael 2, 4, 55, 57,
 66–9

essence 12, 15, 24
Evans, Gareth 171n
externalism, metaphysical 22, 26
externalism, objections to 27–39
externalism, psychological 30–2,
 125–9
externalism, semantic 3, 8, 18, 20–7,
 61, 80, 111
externalism, social 22, 25–7, 39,
 46, 142

fact-value dichotomy 146
fallibilism 154–5
Field, Hartrey 49, 55–60, 64
finite-state automaton 115
Fodor, Jerry 18, 30–2, 42–6, 111–12,
 116, 126–8
Frege, Gottlieb 8, 9, 19
functionalism 3, 8, 18, 98–105

Index

functionalism, global 112–13
functionalism, objections to 106–16

Gaifman, Haim 174n
Godel's Incompleteness Theorem 9
God's Eye perspective 50
Goodman, Nelson 72
Grice, Paul 11

Habermas, Jurgen 75, 173n
Harman, Gilbert 90
Heisenberg's Principle of Uncertainty 17

indexicality (Natural Kind terms) 22, 37–8
information semantics 42–6
Innateness Hypothesis 32
internal realism 2, 49–54, 70–8
inverted spectrum 107–8

Jackson, Frank 35–7
James, William 4, 118–21, 139, 156, 157

Kant, Immanuel 8, 50, 55, 62, 64, 70–4, 95, 121, 136, 148, 165
Kaplan, David 35–7
Katz, Jerold 11
Kierkegaard, Soren 158
Kripke, Saul 14, 23–5, 126, 137
Kuhn, Thomas 149
Kunne, Wolfgang 175n

Lewis, David 137
logical positivism 7, 8

McDowell, John 4, 120–4
Mackie, John 148
Marr, David 110
Master Realist Argument 77–8
mathematical realism 16–17
meaning holism 110–11

metaphysical realism 3, 15, 49–54, 61–6, 76–9, 141–2
methodological solipsism 19, 117
Modal Logic 18
Model-Theoretic argument 3, 49, 60–2
Moore, G. E. 147
moral realism 17, 147
multiple realizability 97, 101–4

Nagel, Thomas 53, 85, 156
narrow content 31
natural kinds 12–15, 20–2
naturalism, scientific 15–18, 30–5, 42, 64–5, 169
normativity 25, 26, 42, 68, 133–6, 163–5, 171
Norris, Chris 169

Parsons, Charles 17
Passmore, John 1
Peirce, C. S. 75, 138–42
Popper, Karl 150
pragmatic maxim 138
pragmatic realism 2, 3, 78
Principle of Tolerance 9
psychological explanation 4, 30–2, 126
Putnam-Quine Indispensability Argument 16

quantum logic 17
Quine, W. V. O. 2, 4, 7, 9, 10, 16, 40, 56, 62, 113, 137, 159, 163

Reichenbach, Hans 7, 10
Relativity, Theory of 10, 17
rigid designation 23
Rorty, Richard 1, 4, 5, 49, 136, 137, 140, 158, 159–66
Russell, Bertrand 8, 177n

scientific realism 2, 3, 7, 8, 50–4
Searle, John 28–30

Index

Sellars, Wilfred 120
skepticism 154–6
Sterelny, Kim 171 n
Strawson, P. F. 11, 92
Stroud, Barry 92

Tarski's Theory of Truth 54–61
token physicalism 100
Turing machines 18, 98–101
Twin Earth thought
 experiment 20–39, 89, 129, 141–2
Two-Dimensional semantics 35–7

type identity theory 97, 101–4

vector theory of meaning 13–14
verificationism 7, 8, 66–8

Warfield, Ted 88
Weiss, Paul 87
Wikforss 173 n
Williams, Bernard 151–4, 156, 164
Wittgenstein, Ludwig 3, 4, 8, 9, 62,
 69, 124, 136, 157
Wright, Crispin 86, 90

www.ingramcontent.com/pod-product-compliance
Lightning Source LLC
Chambersburg PA
CBHW061833300426
44115CB00013B/2361